ALEX

THE MAN BEHIND THE LEGEND

DAVID LYONS

❀ Created with Vellum

ALEX

REDBARN

ABOUT THE AUTHOR

David Lyons is a Dublin-born international bestselling author. He worked on the sports desk of the *Irish Daily Star* for almost twelve years as as well as the sports desks of *Star on Sunday* and *Irish Daily Mail*. He produced football articles for *Sunday World*, for *Irish Independent* and for a host of football websites under a number of different pseudonyms, including David O'Beirne and Ben Adam. He was editor of the world's fastest-growing football website in 2013 before being offered his first publishing deal. He went on to have number one selling books in Ireland, Canada, Australia and the UK. He currently lives in Birmingham, UK, with his wife Kerry, and their daughter Lola.

CONTENTS

For
Adam & Ben

ALEX*

*It's pronounced Alec, not Alecs

2018

IT WAS A SATURDAY MORNING, JUST BEFORE EIGHT A.M. AND whereas he'd spent decades at this particular time of the day on this particular day of the week attempting to second guess what his opposite number had planned for their touchline battle later that afternoon, on this specific Saturday morning he was sitting up in bed doing nothing. Which was highly unusual for Alex, even in his retirement, for he finds it nigh on impossible to *do nothing*.

That's not to say he isn't capable of sitting still. He is. But he only sits still to observe. For a few hours a week Alex likes to watch quiz shows on TV—the harder the better. His specialist subject? No, not football. American Politics. Or the American Civil War to be more precise. Another reason he sits still is to read. He has a library in his Manchester home. Most of the shelves are filled with hardbacks. And a lot of those hardbacks are about his favourite subject: American Politics. A lot of them detail the American Civil War, or the life and times of John F. Kennedy—another fascination of his. If a book on his shelves isn't about either of those two specific subjects, then it is almost certainly about history in some guise. Modern history. Or "young history" as Alex himself labels his favourite pastime. He's pretty much a student of any major event that occurred over the course of the twentieth century. The Irish fight for independence, for example. Alex has, genuinely, in the past cited Irish rebel Michael Collins as a hero of his—an intriguing thing to admit for a man raised as a Protestant on the banks of the River Clyde in west Glasgow. Anyway, the point is that on this specific Saturday he was sitting up in his bed *doing nothing*. Not watching a TV Quiz Show. And not reading about twentieth century history. He actually can't quite recall what he was thinking while he was sat up, though it is quite likely that Doncaster Rovers' game against Wigan Athletic, due to be played later that day, was on his mind. Wigan — once run by his old friend Dave Whelan, and a club Alex had huge influence on (Whelan used to genuinely seek Alex's opinion on his managerial appointments, even when Wigan were a rival club of Manchester United's in the Premier League) were just one win away from being promoted back into the Championship having slid down the divisions in seasons prior. And while Alex would have loved to have seen Wigan promoted, he didn't want that victory to come at the expense of his son. Darren Ferguson was at this point manager of Doncaster Rovers. And so Alex was torn—even if he would never have admitted that to his own offspring. Doncaster Rovers were going to finish mid-table either way that season, so the result didn't matter as much to his son. Whereas it meant everything to Wigan.

The main reason Alex was sat up doing nothing was because he hadn't been feeling great. He wasn't feeling bad. Just "not great". He had had a "fuzzy head" since the Thursday in the way one's head can feel fuzzy just before they come down with a common cold. It was actually the first time since his retirement exactly five years prior that he had felt under the weather; certainly under the weather enough to not want to get out of bed. He was loving retirement; had been revelling in it and was basking in the freedom it afforded him and his devoted wife, Cathy. Since retiring, he had written two books both exceeding

100,000 words (the second of his autobiographies simply entitled *My Autobiography* at the tail end of 2013, which was followed by a book titled *Leading* written with his close associate Michael Moritz in 2015); read countless books and manuscripts and listened to audio tapes on American history; holidayed with friends and family multiple times; been a special guest at Harvard Business School in Boston; been a guest at the Oscars; been to Wimbledon centre court for finals weekend; to the Masters at Augusta and the Kentucky Derby, and helped coach the European Ryder Cup team in Gleneagles. He also attended Old Trafford for almost all home Manchester United games as well as a number of aways—though only after originally holding off for three months to give his successor David Moyes some space. He had attended at least forty funerals. And hung out with extended family members having made a conscious decision that's what he wanted to spend time doing during his retirement: making up for lost time and particularly revelling in the company of the newest members of his family—his grandchildren. All eleven of them. He also spent time continuing to learn new languages, though friends have been hesitant to compliment his studies in that regard. Patrice Evra, when asked about Alex's French, cackled a long laugh and when he composed himself, shook his head and replied, "No comment." Alex had actually been learning French and Spanish in his final years as a manager, so taken aback was he by his former assistant manager Carlos Queiroz. As soon as he laid eyes on Queiroz, Alex was besotted.

'He looks like a movie star,' he once said of the Portuguese tactician. 'He's got these eyes that look like they're piercing through you. And he speaks five languages, y'know? Five languages! Jeez.'

Queiroz's multi-lingual skills were the reason he won the job of assisting Alex in 2002 because Alex's squad was by now so diverse that it was impossible for him to get his team briefings across without at least four translators present. By this stage he had players such as Cristiano Ronaldo (Portuguese), Patrice Evra

(French), Ji Sung Park (Korean), Gerard Pique (Spanish), Eric Djemba-Djemba (Cameroonian), and Kleberson (Brazilian) in his dressing-room. So, in 2005, and inspired by his second in command, Alex decided he was going to take Spanish and French lessons. He continued the studying into his retirement, but only when he could find the time, and when he was in the mood. Except, on this specific Saturday he wasn't even in the mood for getting out of bed, let alone practising his French verbs. But he did try to get out of bed, only because he was bored by sitting still and doing nothing. He remembers peeling back the duvet, his feet touching the carpet and his attempt to stand upright. But from there he has no memory. He would collapse, very fortunately, into a shoe rack. It was the tumbling noise of the shoe rack that alerted Cathy who had been pottering about downstairs. If she hadn't heard the crashing, it is very likely Alex would have lost his life that Saturday morning. When Cathy raced herself upstairs to see her husband laying amongst loose shoes and broken shelves, she already feared he was gone. His chest wasn't moving.

It was just gone nine a.m. when the ambulance pulled up at the front entrance of Macclesfield District Hospital. While Alex was being examined by doctors, Cathy spent the time gripping her mobile phone to her ear, (a device she had, until this particular day, considered more of an inconvenience than anything) talking to two of her sons; Mark and younger brother Darren—who at the time of receiving the phone call from his mother was sitting on his own couch at home, planning — as manager of Doncaster Rovers — for his touchline battle against Wigan Athletic later that afternoon. Her other son, Darren's twin Jason, was already by her side. She had rung him first, her voice filled with panic, with the news of his father's collapse. Within minutes, Jason was at their house in Wilmslow and, having checked on his father who had by this point come somewhat around and was sitting up against the wardrobe in his bedroom, decided to ring their family doctor. Upon hearing of Alex's circumstances, the doctor immediately feared a bleed on the brain and insisted Jason ring for an ambulance.

An hour after that phone call, while Mark and Darren were driving towards Macclesfield hospital, Cathy would ring them again, telling them their father was being transferred to a specialist brain ward as a matter of urgency at Salford Royal Hospital. Here, they would eventually embrace their shaking mother just an hour before their father was induced into a coma in preparation for emergency brain surgery.

It had been a roller-coaster of a morning for Cathy. She had been humming to herself in the kitchen before she heard the crash from the floor above. When she witnessed Alex lying there, she was convinced she'd seen the last of him. Then moments later, he was sitting up and talking to her albeit doe-eyed and stuttering, until an ambulance raced him to hospital. Inside that hospital, Alex seemed fine and was sitting up and talking yet again, until he was informed his issues were brain-related. At that moment he began to panic. He was petrified; not of dying— the thought didn't actually pass his mind. What he was fright- ened of most of all was losing his memory. He prided himself on his memory; could reel off starting elevens of matches he watched as a teenager back in the 1950s and had a remarkable knack of recalling the dates of all that had occurred within the library of "young history" books he had read back at his home. Yet despite sitting up and talking, Alex was in grave danger.

'We can't guarantee anything,' a doctor informed Cathy and her sons.

After Alex was wheeled away for his make-or-break surgery, Cathy, Mark, Jason and Darren would spend the next three hours sat around an uncomfortably tiny round table in the hospital canteen, desperately trying to not contemplate the worst.

Just before midday, a press release from Doncaster Rovers, informing fans that their manager wouldn't be attending their big game later that afternoon "due to family reasons" piqued the interest of every sports journalist in the country. "The family reasons", it was being suggested around Manchester, had something to do with Alex. And so, a multitude of phone calls were made from the desk of every sports desk in the country to all family members of the Fergusons; to Manchester United sources; to Doncaster Rovers sources; to work associates of Mark's, and colleagues of Jason's—all in search of the story. The problem the reporters faced was that none of the sources they contacted knew a thing. Not until Cathy and her three sons gave permission for Manchester United to release a statement on their behalf; a statement that went out half an hour after Alex's complex surgery had been completed and while he was being wheeled unconscious into an intensive care unit in the Hope Building of the Salford Royal Hospital. It was a press release that, while quite abrupt, would not only shock the footballing world, but also, oddly, do the unthinkable, and unite it.

"Sir Alex Ferguson has undergone emergency surgery today for a brain haemorrhage. The procedure has gone very well but he needs a period of intensive care to optimise his recovery. His family request privacy in this matter."

The news united the football world in so much that Manchester City fans would run onto their team's pitch the following day after a dour scoreless draw against Huddersfield Town to spread a banner wide in front of TV cameras that read: "Football aside, get well soon Fergie". And Liverpool Football Club released a statement without hesitation when they first heard of Alex's plight. "The thoughts of everyone at Liverpool Football Club are with Sir Alex Ferguson and his family following the news that the former Manchester United manager is ill in hospital. A great rival but also a great friend who supported this club during its most difficult time."

As the football world was uniting, Alex's brain was swelling, and his chances of ever waking up from the coma he had been induce in to were decreasing. Despite his family's pleas for answers, doctors couldn't console them with any degree of certainty. Every single brain injury is like a fingerprint in that it is uniquely individual. At this stage, the family understood that Alex may be one of the few lucky ones who makes a full recovery and be back to normal in the space of a few months. Alternatively, there was a high risk of a major stroke anytime within the next 48 hours, which likely would have rendered him permanently disabled. The other alternative was unthinkable for Cathy. The notion that Alex may never wake up.

At one point, as they were pacing the corridors of the hospital, Darren read online that the most likely scenario was that his father would never be the same man again, and may never be able to talk or communicate as he used to. Though he never informed his mother of this damning research, deciding instead to keep her spirits as high as he could while they waited. There was an air of serendipity in the fact that they were all pacing the corridors of the ICU in the Hope Building, for it was Alex who had officially opened that specialist unit six years prior.

'This new hospital development will noo doubt enhance the great work the team at Salford Royal already deliver tae patients in Greater Manchester,' he had said in his thick Glaswegian accent just before he cut the ribbon. 'These much-improved facilities will be of great benefit to the people of this region.'

They certainly brought great benefit to him. He was under the care of a team of five practitioners led by renowned surgeon Joshi George who specialises not only in spine surgeries and cancer surgeries, but also invasive neurosurgery of the brain and skull.

It was impossible for Mr. George to know exactly how or even who the patient would be when he would eventually wake from his coma. Alex's entire memory could be wiped out. He may not even know who he is himself when he comes around, if he comes around at all. Memory loss is a strong possibility for brain haemorrhage victims, especially so if the patient experiences even the most minor of strokes during the surgical procedure or in the proceeding days.

It was two days later when the Ferguson family were invited into his room, informed that Alex had stirred and was now awake. It was time for their moment of truth.

They had discussed that, no matter what man they were met with in that ward when they walked in, they wouldn't rush him with questions; that they'd give him some breathing space, some time to readjust to his new reality.

He stared up through squinted eyes — though he rarely stared any other way — as the blurred figures of his nearest and dearest ominously entered his ward. Then he blinked repeatedly and gave a light cough before lifting his head from the pillow.

'What was the score in the Doncaster game?' he asked.

1941-1964

'AHCUMFIGOVAN' SCREAMED THE BATTERED METAL SIGN THAT HUNG, for decades, from two rusty nails on the back wall of his office in Carrington—Manchester United's training headquarters.

Govan was his home town—a town that mirrored the man in so many ways. But whereas the man had grey hair and was often dressed in an all grey suit, at least he had some colour to his face, Govan had no colour at all. It looked grey no matter what street you turned onto.

In middle-age, in the throes of his successes at Manchester United, Alex recalled reading an article about himself some years prior.

'It said, "Alex Ferguson has done really well in his life despite coming from Govan."' He scoffed. 'It's because I come from Govan that I have achieved what I've achieved in ma life.'

He is adamant that the skills he learned, that helped him become such an inspiring leader, were instilled within him when, as a young-ster, he would roam those grey streets of Govan.

Football is a sport sprayed by a shower of both intriguing and nonsensical statistics. But few are more eye-opening than this little tid-bit: The four greatest managers throughout British footballing history were practically all neighbours—all raised in the same maze of grey streets that web away from the banks of the River Clyde in Glasgow. Sir Alex Ferguson himself, Sir Matt Busby, Jock Stein and Bill Shankly were all brought up within a radius of thirty miles of each other, although, of course, in different years through the first half of the twentieth century.

Govan was a shipbuilding town—and had been for one hundred and one years before its most celebrated son was born. Lizzie Ferguson (nee Hardie) was nigh on a decade younger than her husband Alex Ferguson Snr but her intellect (she was well read and naturally worldly wise) made up for the gulf in their age gap. In fact, she was often regarded as the more mature of the pair. She was certainly the most inquisitive. Though that's not to say Alex Snr was lacking in intellect. It could be argued, however, that he was partial to stretching the odd truth. Alex Snr had told both his sons (Alex and Martin) when they were growing up that he had played football at a professional level for Glentoran in Northern Ireland. If he did, Glentoran know nothing of it. But play football, he did. And live in Belfast, he did. So there may have been some grain of truth to his claim to fame. What's likely is that he trialled for Glentoran, and as part of that trial played in a friendly match or two. But a player by the name of Alex Ferguson has never been registered in Glentoran FC's history books. What he was mainly doing in Belfast was working for Harland and Wolff—the famous shipyard in which was built the *Titanic*. His parents had moved to Belfast for that reason — seeking work in the shipyard — and most family members, from brothers to cousins and uncles, grafted alongside Alex Snr. But when he was offered the opportunity of a cosier work environment — in a warm office in sunny Birmingham — he jumped at the opportunity and moved to the Midlands a week after his twenty-sixth birthday. It would become apparent, however, that warm offices weren't quite his thing. He hadn't even turned twenty-seven by the time he decided to move on. This time he moved north to Glasgow to find work, once again, in the shipyard business. He would settle in Govan, where he would later bump into the strikingly mature and ever-so-inquisitive Lizzie Hardie.

Their love story is typical of its time. They met, fell in love, married and had two sons, all within a span of twenty-four months. Their first son, Alex, was a mistake. A surprise. Unplanned. Humanity wasn't supposed to be awarded the presence of Alex Ferguson. Alex Snr and Lizzie were only courting at the time but, caught up in the midst of their whirlwind romance, Lizzie fell pregnant. And although it was thought of as sinful, both Alex Snr and Lizzie were secretly delighted they were expecting, as it meant they *had* to marry—something they had been talking about since they had first met but felt too insecure to follow through with given that their parents would likely object to things happening so fast. They wed in a small ceremony on June 10th, 1941, with Lizzie showing a minor bump. On the last day of that same year, Alex was born. Martin, his brother, would come along on December 21st the following year. Having birthdays so close to Christmas meant only one big present a year for the Ferguson boys, but they were as content as any of their peers growing up on those grey streets of Govan. The Fergusons weren't well-off by any stretch. But their boys never went hungry. Lizzie's attention to detail in running the family home saw to that. Alex Snr would bring home his well-earned coins from the shipyards each and every Friday and from there Lizzie would see to how they were spent. Alex once recalled that, as a young boy, he came across his father's weekly wage slip, though he can't quite remember which year it was. But what has never escaped his mind was the gross figure underlined at the bottom of that pay slip. The equivalent of £7 Alex Snr had been paid for that week—and in that week, Alex remembers, his father had worked an additional twenty hours of overtime on top of his regular forty-hours. He literally earned less than 12p per hour worked.

'People tell me mine was a poor upbringing,' Alex would say five decades later. 'I don't know what they mean by that. It was tough, but it wasn't bloody poor. We mabee didnae have a TV. We didnae have a car. We didnae have a telephone. But I thought I had everything I needed, because I had friends and family. And I had a football.'

Although their setting was grey, Alex remembers his upbringing as colourful and joyous. The Second World War had just ended and he, Martin and all of their friends were being raised by folk who were filled with relief as well as a hope of a brighter future. Govan was a typical post-War Britain town. At six p.m. every weekday, a whistle would signal the end of a dockyard shift and, without hyperbole, up to three thousand men would flood the streets of Govan, all eager to get home to the hot meal their better halves would have spent much of the day preparing for them. Every night, not just at weekends, each of the hundreds of pubs in Govan (that's not hyperbole either. It has actually been confirmed that in the 1940s, there were fifty pubs on a one mile stretch of road in Govan alone) would be bursting at the seams with each patron swinging their beer mugs from side-to-side as they sang — or roared — along to the choruses of pub ballad after pub ballad.

The Fergusons actually lived in a first-floor flat above one of those noisy pubs on Shieldhall Road, which was in the shadows of the stands of the famous Ibrox Stadium. Their living room also acted as a bathroom—with a zinc bath tucked in between the brick wall and the oversized armchair Alex Snr would rest in after his long shifts at the shipyard.

Alex and Martin both attended, firstly, Broomloan Primary School and then — when they were eleven years of age — Govan High School. There are no records of their results from either school, but both Ferguson boys were said to have excelled in academia, though Alex was considered far from the perfect student even if he was well liked by his teachers.

'The old saying of, "he could start an argument in an empty room", comes to mind,' his former teacher Elizabeth Thomson would say many years later. It'll tell you the man Alex is that he would continue to host "Missus Thomson" to his home in Cheshire for meals five decades on, until she passed away just as his career as a manager, aged seventy-one, was coming to an end. Alex adored Missus Thomson so much, despite her regularly punishing him with six wraps on the knuckles with an old black, leather belt she used to keep in her desk drawer. In fact, he adored her so much that when she would marry, Alex would order his best friends from school to turn up at the church on the wedding day to see her off. Alex and his classmates beamed from the back of the church, scruffy in their torn hand-me down clothes, as Missus Thomson scowled down the aisle at them.

'I remember feeling that we *had* to be there that day,' Alex recalled five decades later. 'We loved her.'

Alex and Martin quite often got themselves into scrapes at school, and as a result regularly felt the sting of Missus Thomson's belt across their knuckles. But Martin is, still to this day, insistent that his part in the mischief was all driven by his elder brother.

'The truth is, Alex was a bit of a terror,' Martin would admit. 'He'd half the school frightened of him because it *had* to be Fergie's way.'

A lot of the Ferguson brothers' mischief centred around the love they formed for the team they had chosen to support in Glasgow. Alex used to bunt his younger brother over the wall at Ibrox Stadium before scaling it himself so they could get to see Rangers in action without having to pay for tickets. On the odd occasion, and because they were getting cocky with their breaking and entering skills, the Ferguson boys would steal thick mugs from the Ibrox canteen because they knew they could sell them on for a few pennies to a trader down by the banks of the River Clyde. On at least two occasions they were caught red-handed and were grabbed by their collars by policemen and dragged all the way home.

On another occasion during their mischief-making days, Alex was led to a narrow street of Govan by some older lads who he assumed wanted to befriend him. When they produced a bottle of wine for him to take a swig from, he took it, tipped it into his mouth and only realised that he was drinking urine after it had hit the back of his throat. He spat, smashed the bottle on the ground and ran for home to wash his mouth out. He would later, to school mates, claim he exacted revenge on those boys by tracking them down one-by-one and "giving it to them". His peers believed Alex to be a brute capable of fighting older boys, but they also knew him to be a storyteller.

Although Alex the teenager was impressive with his fists, what made him really stand out was that fact that he could converse like an adult. He had a way with words, and could instantly gather a crowd by reeling off anecdotes. Alex loves to tell stories, always has done.

His stature as a boy-cum-man at the school was rubber-stamped by the fact that he was really good at football. Being the best footballer meant all of the other students looked up to him. In fact, it wasn't just Alex. Both Ferguson boys were considered the best two players at their school, though it must be said that the dreams they had of becoming the Rangers No.9 were far from unique to them. Every teenage boy in Glasgow wanted to either be the Rangers No.9, or the Celtic No.9—depending on which side of the tracks you came from.

The Fergusons…. well, they criss-crossed those tracks several times. It's complicated, but this is how it went down. Alex's grandfather and grandmother (on his father's side) were an unorthodox couple in that they were a Protestant (his grandmother) marrying a Catholic (his grandfather). Their son, Alex Snr, would be raised Protestant, however, because in those days there was a higher chance of finding employment if you were educated at a Protestant school. But he had such hatred for the sectarian divide that he chose, out of spite, to be a Celtic fan—and would often wear, to much controversy, the green and white hoops of the Catholic club under his dockyard apron when he went out to work. When he met and fell in love with Lizzie Hardie, he realised history was repeating itself. The Fergusons were once again the talk of the neighbourhood. Another mixed marriage. Lizzie came from the other side of the tracks having been raised in a strict Catholic household. Despite that, it was she who decided, when Alex and Martin were born, that they would be raised Protestant (again, because it would make finding employment easier) but it would be left up to them to support whichever team in Glasgow they felt they wanted to. Alex and Martin weren't as morally balanced as their father. They opted for the blue team, not only to match their Protestant upbringing, but mostly because that was the team their friends supported. When they used to break into Ibrox to watch the Gers in action, Alex would stare at the No. 9 (who in those days was Willie Findlay) and daydream that it was him out there instead. That daydream took one step closer to reality when Alex, while playing for his school team, caught the eye of a scout from Drumchapel Amateurs—a lauded footballing academy in Glasgow that had a fine reputation for hosting the chief scouts of both Rangers and Celtic on a regular basis. There, Alex would be trained by local hero Douglas Smith as well as a young up-and-coming coach who went by the name of David Moyes—the father of the man Alex would appoint as his successor at Manchester United some fifty-five years later.

However, despite giving every training session and every game for Drumchapel his all, a scout from Rangers would never tap Alex on the shoulder to offer him an opportunity to live out his dream.

He did impress one scout in particular, however—a scout from Queens Park who was so taken by the lanky teenager that he demanded Alex meet him the following week. In that second meeting, Alex was offered a contract, though the contract didn't take much reading. And it certainly didn't read of any numbers. Alex would be getting zero in remuneration for playing for Queens Park—only the thrill of turning out at Hampden Park for every home game even if the famous old stadium's stands would echo with emptiness.

Alex had just turned sixteen and was feeling rather deflated that no other offers were coming his way. And so, despite palming Queens Park off for a few weeks in anticipation of an offer from a bigger club, Alex reluctantly signed the contract that didn't read of any numbers. In doing so, he knew he would have to find employment. He might have just signed for a well-known club who play in a very well-known stadium, but he wasn't quite a professional footballer just yet.

He would take a job at a tool-making factory called Remington Rand where he would earn £30 a week to begin with. But although he was a tough worker and never had a problem getting his hands dirty, Alex proved to be somewhat of a headache to his bosses after he took it upon himself to get involved in the Workers Union, bringing arguments to them regularly such as insisting on more health and safety provisions within the workplace or, on occasion, badgering them for pay-rises on behalf of other workers.

Arguing genuinely seemed like a natural instinct for Alex from a young age. Not only do his teachers remember him as argumenta-tive, but his moaning was incessant at Remington Rand. On top of that he would argue with his coaches at Queen's Park, too—largely irritated by the fact that he was often overlooked for matches come Saturday. The truth is, Alex was largely hit and miss at Queen's Park during his time there—sometimes offered the No.9 jersey, some-times left out completely (in those days there were no substitutes). Yet he did still manage to score fifteen goals in the 31 appearances he made for the club over a two-and-a-half year period.

He was frustrated with all aspects of his life by the time he was turning nineteen with the dream he had confidently envisioned for himself far from playing out as his reality. He was beginning to believe he would never wear the No.9 jersey for Rangers—and that he'd end up working as a union representative in the tool-making trade for the rest of his life. In fact, he was genuinely contemplating packing in football altogether, and giving the union work more of his time, when, out of the blue, he was approached by Willie Neil—a scout for St Johnstone. The Js were a club whose history didn't quite live up to that of Queen's Park, but they did, in those days, look like they were likely to have a brighter future. They had just been promoted to the First Division and Neil told Alex that he was the exact type of striker St Johnstone needed to lead them into a new dawn. The contract put to Alex was a pay as you play deal; very common back then for players who worked part-time and played football part-time. But Alex worked out that if he made the striker's position his own at St Johnstone — which is what Neil pretty much told him was a foregone conclusion — and got paid every week, then he'd finally be a full-time footballer. A proper professional.

However, it turned out he was naive to believe Neil because it became apparent that Alex wasn't the perfect type of striker St Johnstone were looking for at all. Manager Bobby Brown liked Alex and thought his determination to win at all costs mightily impressive. But he wasn't a huge fan of Alex's abilities on the ball and as a result, Alex struggled to break into the first team. With no games, came no pay and his time at St Johnstone wasn't helped by the fact that Remington Rand had moved factories, meaning he had to travel to Hillington—on the opposite side of Glasgow to where St Johnstone trained on weekday evenings after his long shifts. The commute wasn't only time consuming. It was expensive. Alex was finding himself poorer for having opted to move to St Johnstone.

Despite his heavy load, Alex managed to impress Brown in training enough to ensure that anytime experienced striker Jimmy Gauld was either injured or suspended, the Govanman himself would be given a first-team opportunity. But only thirty-seven of those opportunities came in the three seasons that Alex played for St Johnstone (during which he managed to score nineteen goals) and he had to once again question whether or not he should give up chasing a professional football contract. He didn't despise being a union representative at Remington Rand though, even if he was constantly tired. There was a girl working there who was easy on the eye, and that proved enough for him to continue his pain-staking commutes to and from training in the evenings. Though that tiring commute was soon to come to an end.

He was sitting on Alex Snr's armchair, taking a rare moment to himself one Sunday afternoon, when the brand-new house phone trilled, startling him.

'Hellu,' Alex said, answering.

'Hellu,' an equally thick Glaswegian accent replied. 'Cannae speak to Alex Junior, please?'

'Aye, It's Alex Junior speaking… who's this?'

'Ma name's Jock Stein,' the caller said. 'I've seen you play, son. And I'd like you to sign for Dunfermline. We wannae offer you a full-time contract.'

ALEX THE FOOTBALLER

Duncan Ferguson. Or Peter Crouch.

They're the two most recent footballers from with whom you could draw an accurate comparison of Alex Ferguson in terms of playing style. Duncan because of the fire with which he played. Crouchie for his languid and awkward presence.

Alex, himself, would scoff at those comparisons without hesitation. He feels he was a much more gifted footballer than the average attendee at East End Park or Ibrox in the swinging sixties will ever tell you he was.

In his own mind, Alex had a sublime first touch and an awareness about him that gave him a razor-sharp edge on defenders. Mirrors of the player Alex felt he played like can actually be found stapled through the teams he would later produce as a manager. At Manchester United, for example, he went from signing Mark Hughes, to Eric Cantona, to Teddy Sheringham, to Dwight Yorke, and then on to Dimitar Berbatov and Robin van Persie—a constant roll call of strikers who played with a puffed out chest, who constantly had their back to goal, who could spin from that position on a dime, who had such a silky first touch — be it with their head, their chest, their knee or their foot — that could cushion the ball to the exact blade of grass that benefitted them the most—all the while making the art of football look rather effortless. The striker who played with a puffed out chest and with his back to goal was Alex's favourite type of player; the type he built all of his teams around. And he thought, genuinely, that he, himself, was that type of player. To this day he remembers, his playing career in a different light to those who played with or against him.

'I was top scorer in every team I ever played in,' Alex gloats.

That's kinda true. But also kinda not true. Alex wasn't top scorer at either Queen's Park or St Johnstone when he was a part-time pro. But he *was* the leading scorer at all of the clubs he played for as a full professional. However, gloat he is entitled to, for Alex Ferguson made 337 appearances in professional football and scored 182 goals. That's a goal every 160-minutes which is an impressive ratio for any striker from any era in football's history. And, it must be said, he managed that impressive one goal for less than two games played consistently over a span of seventeen full seasons, at every club he was at. It's just that a large percentage of those 182 goals weren't quite as silky or as smooth as the Govanman himself remembers them to be. Simply put: Alex was an effective footballer—for every team he played in. But he was no Cantona. He was no Berbatov. He wasn't the touch and spin type of striker his rose-tinted spectacles convince him he had been.

Alex, although only five foot, ten and three-quarter inches (he always ensures the three-quarters are counted and he would never say he was just five foot, ten, or five foot, eleven, simply because he is truly insistent on attention to detail) was a lanky, wiry and awkward player. His height doesn't read too tall from the page, but in the flesh Alex's stature, still to this day, seems to contradict this official measurement. He really does appear much taller in person. In his playing days, his limbs were gangly and bony and he used every edge of those bones to his advantage. In fact, it's nigh on impossible to enter a conversation with any of Alex's contemporaries without the word 'elbows' being mentioned within a matter of seconds. It's quite telling that when the subject of Alex the footballer comes up 'elbows' sure does get mentioned more times than 'feet'.

'He had the sharpest elbows you'd ever see,' ex-pro Alex Totten once told the great journalist Michael Crick.

'We used to say that he sharpened his elbows before he went onto the pitch,' his Dunfermline teammate Bert Paton recalls.

'He was a very difficult opponent,' says John Greig, the ex-Rangers captain, 'not because of his ability, but because of the way he played. He always had his elbows out. We used to say he could wear his boots on his elbows.'

Alex did, like the future Manchester United stars named above, play with his chest puffed out, but that was mainly because he was creating wings for himself with his arms. His default posture on the pitch was chest out, elbows protruding and wide at a ninety-degree angle with his forearm muscles clenched and his fingers gripping the cuffs of his sleeves (he's on record as saying he adopted that particular style from his hero at the time, Denis Law).

With that posture ever present, complete with a constantly sunken brow, Alex the footballer was strong, physical, in your face, and up for every fight imaginable. It was rare he went two minutes on the pitch without raising his voice at somebody, whether it be a member of the opposition, a teammate, or any one of the three match officials.

It wasn't just his elbows, though. Alex was bony and sharp all over. His knees were as much an asset to him as his feet, and Alex was even known to score a goal with his hip on more than one occasion.

Having long, wiry limbs is the sole reason Alex accumulated such a hefty goals tally throughout his playing career—they are also the reason he was sent off eight times during his seventeen years as a player. So many of Alex's goals arrived from crosses, with him getting a toe, or a knee, or a hip, or a head — or even his nose — on the ball to poke it over the line ahead of defenders.

There was a debate to be had during his playing days whether Alex was just a lucky striker, or whether he happened to score so many of those types of goals because he was a superb reader of the game. His management career would go on to end that debate. Very few, if any, have ever been able to read the beautiful game as well as Alex Ferguson.

Though it must be said that the debate about whether Alex was more a Duncan Ferguson/Peter Crouch than an Eric Cantona/Dimitar Berbatov-type in terms of style becomes somewhat redundant when you consider he played at a lower level than all of those players.

The entirety of Alex's career was spent in Scotland. In the Scottish First Division (now the Scottish Premiership) mainly, bar one season in which he played for Falkirk in the second division.

After playing as a semi-pro at both Queen's Park and then St Johnstone before his big move to Dunfermline, Alex would go on to get his dream move to Rangers from where he would later sign for Falkirk, which is where he would stay for four years before a swansong season at Ayr United.

He'd score fifteen goals in thirty-one appearances for QP, nineteen in thirty-seven for the Js, sixty-six in eighty-nine games for Dunfermline, twenty-five goals in forty-four games for his boyhood club Rangers, thirty-seven in ninety-five appearances over four years for Falkirk and nine goals in his final season in which he played twenty-four games for Ayr United.

Alex would also score ten goals while representing Scotland at international level on just nine occasions, though there is a debate to be had over the validity of those international claims.

Despite proving himself to be a handful of an attacker in the top Scottish division, Alex found breaking into the Scottish national team an almost impenetrable wall.

His hero, Denis Law, was the most obvious brick in that wall, but behind Denis was a long and ridiculously talented queue of Scottish strikers. Alan Gilzean, Jim Forest, Willie Johnstone and Ian St John, for example, were all considered ahead of Alex in the pecking order for the national team at different spells during his career.

But Alex did manage to nab himself some caps, though the term 'caps' is to be mentioned with caution—even if Alex himself considers them 'caps'. He was picked to represent the Scottish League against an England League select on two occasions in 1967. And later that year he was named as part of the Scotland squad that would travel the world, taking in Canada, Australia, New Zealand, Hong Kong and Israel. On this tour, Alex would score ten goals in seven appearances, though it must be said that the opposition could hardly be considered world class. Aside from that, most of the best Scottish players, such as those who played for Celtic and Rangers or for top teams in England like Manchester United or Leeds United, had withdrawn their players from the lengthy tour. The validity of the caps handed out for that tour has been debated for decades. What is most fair to say is that tours such as the one Alex embarked on with Scotland in the summer of 1967 would certainly award full caps today. Half a century ago, though, international caps were a more complex matter. There were different variations of how you could represent your country in days gone by.

What's most interesting about Alex the footballer is that he was naturally right-footed yet played predominantly with his left foot. He took set-pieces with his left-foot, scored most of his goals with his left foot and made key passes with his left foot. That was because Alex Snr, who was very passive-aggressive when coaching both Alex and Martin as youngsters, would insist — repeatedly — that they practise with their weaker foot.

'You need to be two footed if you wanna make it, son,' he would remind them on tap.

Alex would practise so much with his left foot under these orders from his old man that by the time he made it as a pro, his left foot was stronger than his right.

Aside from being a nuisance to opposition defenders, Alex was also a nuisance to his teammates, certainly a nuisance to his manager and those who operated at board level for the clubs he played for. His mouth was rarely shut in the dressing-room, much like the barking union representative he had once been, though he considered his 'team talks' as motivational. Most of his teammates appreciated Alex's passion, and certainly his determination to win at all costs, but his managers, it's fair to say, were less keen on his incessant input. What's most unfortunate to Alex, when he looks back on his playing career, is that none of those managers ever happened to be Jock Stein.

Three weeks after personally ringing Alex to ask him to sign for Dunfermline, Stein left the club with the lure of Hibernian proving too strong for him to turn down. Alex was heartbroken at the time, assuming his promise of a professional football career had died before it was given life. He was twenty two at the time. However, Stein's scouting report on Alex was so in-depth and glowing that his successor, Willie Cunningham (a stern Northern Irishman with whom Alex would form a love-hate relationship), would still opt to green light the transfer. So, on the twentieth of June, in 1964, Alex signed his first professional contract. Dunfermline had swapped attacker Dan McLindon in exchange for his services. No further fee required.

Alex was a little deflated by the contract he was signing though. It was worth only £27 a week—less than he was getting at Remington Rand at the time, with whom he had just handed in his notice. There were bonuses tied up in his contract that made it complex, but Alex figured that if he earned a number of his bonuses (such as scoring a goal each week—something he had full faith he could do), he would be able to bridge the gap in wage.

He made an immediate impact on his teammates at Dunfermline, though more so because of his mouth, than his feet. While everyone could see, instantly, the natural instinct he had to get on the end of moves and finish them off, it was his attitude that really left the players' jaws ajar. He demanded professionalism from everyone he worked with—a trait carried over from his time working at Remington Rand as a union representative and later, as shop steward. He moaned. A lot. He hated losing. Even in training matches.

'He was a born winner and a bad loser,' Harry Melrose, the then Dunfermline right winger recalls. 'It didn't matter what he was doing… playing golf or whatever…he had to win. If there was a game to be had, whether you be friend or foe, he would have to win it. By fair means or foul. If he lost, he'd be in the bath afterwards with a big scowl on his face.'

Alex's motormouth wasn't just on full mode in the dressing-room. Even in the evenings if he and a few of the players were out socialising, he would find it nigh on impossible to shut up about the game; rattling on and on about statistics as if he were a proper football nerd and not just a footballer, or — his favourite topic — discussing the different tactics manager Willie Cunningham could and *should* be adopting.

Alex would hold court around a pub table, and snatch at the condiments. Then he'd use the saltshaker, the pepper shaker, the ketchup bottle and even loose tea bags to help form the lines of his favoured formations.

His then manager, Cunningham, remembers Alex constantly coming to him with ideas.

'As time went by, Fergie started getting into it more and more and he started bringing all sorts of information and statistics to me. He got into things a lot deeper than some of us.'

Alex's nerdiness for statistics is born from his fascination with "young history" coupled with his eidetic memory. Even today, he can still melodically reel off the starting XI of teams he played with sixty years ago as well as the scoreline of certain games and even the times of the goals scored.

His Dunfermline career got off to a steady start. He'd score nine goals in his first sixteen matches before being hampered by a ligament injury. It would rule him out for a month, but he recovered just in time to complete a long-held ambition of playing in Europe.

He was back in the team to face Gothenburg away in a second leg of the Fairs Cup (now the Europa League), with whom they would draw 0-0 to win on aggregate in what Alex would describe as his toughest game ever.

'Aye, I really cudda slept straight after that one,' he admits.

Dunfermline then went on to beat Stuttgart 1-0 over two legs before bowing out to Atletico Madrid. Alex loved playing in Europe. He felt the cultures each of the cities he played in made his life experience all the richer.

Driven by Alex's goals, Dunfermline would go on to compete for the title that year — all the way up to the final game of the season — as well as get themselves to the Scottish Cup Final. They should have won the title, really. They were in a three-way race with, no, not Celtic and Rangers, but Kilmarnock and Hearts. The Old Firm were taking a year off it seemed. Well, in truth, Celtic had taken many a year off by this stage, whereas Rangers had won six of the previous nine championships. All of that was about to change for Celtic, however, as when Jock Stein would take over as their manager the following year, he would lead the Parkhead club to an unprecedented nine league titles in a row, as well as a famous European Cup win. Alex lauds Stein's achievements at Celtic as not only monumental, but inspirational in terms of shaping his own football philosophy, even though he was forced to play his whole football career in the shadow of Stein's and Celtic's rip-roaring success.

Before that though, Alex had a chance of a title in his first season with Dunfermline. All they needed to do was beat St Johnstone in their final game after coming off the back of beating Celtic 5-1 and Rangers 3-1 over the previous two weekends to go into the final week as favourites. But they only managed a 1-1 draw against the Js, and Alex missed a series of chances to put the game — and indeed the title — to bed. Alex took it bad, but in truth Dunfermline wouldn't have been contending for the title in the final weekend of the campaign had it not been for Alex's goalscoring that season. Besides, he and his teammates had the

Cup Final to look forward to the following week—a tonic to help cure the hangover.

Only Alex's hangover was about to get a lot worse. Despite being nervy on the off-chance of him being dropped due to his poor performance the week prior, Alex had assumed he would be playing when he hadn't heard otherwise by manager Willie Cunningham up to an hour before kick-off. But when Cunningham came to the dressing room to read out his team, he was flanked by two members of the Dunfermline board of directors and Alex immediately knew something was up. He squinted around the dressing room upon hearing Harry Melrose and John McLaughlin's names mentioned as the two strikers. There were no more names to be read—substitutions would not be permitted in the sport until the following season.

'You bastard!' Alex roared from his corner of the dressing room before launching to his feet to confront his manager. Cunningham was too nervous to inform the bullish Govanman to his face in the build-up to the final that he wouldn't be playing, and so had to have two board members stand by his side for protection to stem the inevitable reaction Alex would machine-gun around the dressing room once told the news.

Thirty-five years later, when he was writing his first autobiography, *Managing My Life*, in 1999, Alex was still riled by this snub.

He would write, "Looking back, I make no apology for the way I reacted. My view is that when a manager is not prepared to give a dropped player his place by telling him the bad news in advance, then there can be no complaining if, when the axe falls without warning just before kick-off, there is an emotional response. This was a Cup final; every player's dream. I always let players know their position (if they're dropped) before I announce the team in front of the entire squad."

Alex would let his players know well in advance, as — as a manager — he used to look at a full football season in separate sections. He would eye fixtures five and six games at a time and figure out which players he needed for certain positions to tackle a particular section. He'd shuffle his squad for games accordingly and let players know in advance what games they would be playing in. For example, in order to let a player down, who wouldn't be playing for the next two games, Alex would give them a reason much like, 'It's because I want you fit to play Spurs and then Everton back-to-back at the beginning of October. I need you fit and at your best for those two fixtures.' That way, the dropped player would have a responsibility and a mission to look forward to. A dropped player rarely left Alex's office feeling as if they'd just been dropped. That leadership approach (which you can read about in detail later) was most certainly influenced by the heartbreak he suffered an hour before the 1965 Scottish FA Cup Final.

Managing a player's mental state was as important to Alex as coaching their feet. He knew his players had a natural gift for the sport, otherwise they wouldn't be playing at such an elite level. What he needed to do, in order to turn them into winners, was to alter their mental wellbeing. Alex understood that all of the greatest winners who win again and again and again throughout all of sports history hold one true trait in common: they were all mentally stronger than their opposition, whether that be the great Chicago Bulls team that paralleled Alex's great Manchester United side through the 1990s, or Tiger Woods who took the sport of golf to another level around the turn of the century; or tennis greats Roger Federer or Serena Williams, or especially so the All Black teams through rugby union's history. A team of great players is a good advantage. A team filled with a winner's mentality is a total scales-tipper towards success. While Alex felt that his Dunfermline manager Willie Cunningham was a good coach, in that he improved players' abilities on the ball, he didn't really do much for the most important trait required in winners—evolving their mental state. Alex would take note of such a flaw and determine that he would never fail in that regard when he eventually became a manager.

After his thunderous row in the dressing-room of ahead of

that Scottish Cup Final, Alex put in a transfer request. But it was to be turned down. Though rather than moan (and boy could he moan), he resolved to make his next season with Dunfermline the best he would ever have. Which is what it turned out to be. He scored forty five goals in fifty one matches after healing his rift somewhat with Cunningham. But the Pars would be left empty-handed yet again come the end of the season. Despite Alex's goalscoring form, they would recede in the league table—finishing fourth, and thirteen points adrift of a rejuvenated Celtic under Stein, who would hold off their bitterest rivals Rangers to win their first title in twelve years.

At the end of this season, Alex repeated himself. He handed in a written transfer request; not because he had fallen out with his manager this time, but simply and arrogantly because he felt he wasn't going to win any medals with the Js. Newspapers had been linking him with more glamorous clubs. Rangers were reported to be interested, so too were Newcastle United down south. However, his request was, once again, turned down and in truth, neither Rangers, nor Newcastle, made an official approach to sign him. In that summer, while he was waiting for an offer to come in, he took his coaching badges. He was only twenty-five, but was already thinking beyond his football career, not just because he had a nose for leadership, but because he had heard way too many horror stories of former footballers slumping into a bad mental state following their retirement. So, in the same summer that England were winning the World Cup, Alex Ferguson was taking his coaching badges.

Alex's move away from Dunfermline wouldn't come for another year. Though at one point he was getting worried nothing would transpire despite, again, repeated reports in the papers. He was constantly linked with Rangers but had heard nothing official. And there was also a persistent rumour that Nottingham Forest would make a bid that July. But while Alex waited and waited for news to come in he began to grow frustrated when it looked like he may have to stay at Dunfermline. It was getting close to the time players were due back for pre-season training when Alex answered the door to a handsome young man he hadn't met before.

'Ma da wants you to come see 'im. But you can't be seen.'

The visitor handed Alex a piece of paper with an address scribbled on it and then left, looking left and right to make sure nobody had spotted him.

Alex called to the address later that day. It was Scot Symon's house—the then Rangers manager. Within forty-eight hours his boyhood dream would finally become a reality. He was finally a Rangers player with £4,000 extra in his bank account (the most money that bank account had ever held up until that point), which he personally negotiated with Symon as a signing on fee, and an agreement of on-going wages of at least £80 per week—twice what he was earning at Dunfermline.

The dream of being the Rangers No.9 would turn into a night-mare, however. Not on the pitch, though. On the pitch Alex was the club's top scorer in both seasons he would play for his boyhood club, even if Rangers were by then playing in the shadow of their great neighbours. But once inside, once a Ger, he began to fall out of love with the club he chose to adore when he was just eight years of age. For starters, the dressing-room was a much more experienced dressing-room than Alex had played in before. He was now teammates with some major names in the sport and his voice was somewhat diluted in such company. Around players like Davie Provan, Jimmy Millar and Ronnie McKinnon, Alex felt slightly inferior, and so he wasn't the usual loud-mouthed leader he had been in all of his previous dressing-rooms. Though, in truth, his stature within the squad was the least of his worries. What was truly troubling for him was the bigotry that seemed rife around the corridors of Ibrox Stadium.

'What religion is yar wife?' club director Ian McLaren asked Alex, literally moments after he had signed his contract.

Alex answered, 'Catholic.'

'Where d'yer get married?'

'At a registry office.'

'Aye, well that's alright, then.'

McLaren was deadly serious. Alex was astonished. Though he'd go on to learn that that was how they talked around here.

Although work was being done in Glaswegian communities to rid football terraces of religious bigotry, it seemed one club's corridors in particular required a scrubbing, too. Alex recalls the club physio once being ordered to remove his tie having turned up for a meeting, because the tartan in the design had green in it. Celtic had evolved quicker than Rangers with regards the religious divide, and had, at the time Alex was playing for the Gers, a Protestant managing the team in the shape of Jock Stein. Whereas at Rangers, the notion of a Catholic being manager of their club was so outrageous that it could hardly even be considered a notion. It's quite telling that Rangers didn't sign their first Catholic player until some twenty-two years later, in July, of 1989 —when Maurice Johnson would move to Ibrox from Nantes. Even then, that signing was met with a great deal of scepticism by not only a number of Rangers supporters, but those at the board level of the club.

Alex could never make sense of the bigotry. But then, his and his brother's upbringing in Glasgow had been quite unique. They had stemmed from two generations of mixed-religious families. Hating somebody because of their religious status was a foreign concept to the Fergusons. The bigotry might have been heard near their doorstep, but it would certainly never be heard beyond that doorstep. It initially occurred to Alex during his first summer at the club that Rangers were perhaps bitter due to Celtics' high achievement of having just won the European Cup. But he would soon learn that bitterness and bigotry had been a fixture at the club for decades. And would continue to be for decades more.

Willie Allison's role at the club was undefined, but the well-known journalist certainly sat in on many of chairman John Lawrence's meetings and acted as chief advisor and spokesperson for him, whether he had an official title or not. Lawrence was an elderly man, well into his eighties, and it seemed Allison was the one he relied on to run the club's press relations. Which was a shame. For Allison's bigotry ran deep. Allison was "a religious bigot of the deepest dye… as dangerous as he was despicable" Alex would write in his autobiography, *Managing My Life*.

Alex sure did like manager Scot Symon, though. But their relationship wouldn't last long. Frustrated by Celtic's successes both home and abroad, Symon was sacked three months into Alex's spell at Ibrox. He would be replaced by Davie White, who would go on to run Rangers close to the title in Alex's first season, though Celtic would manage to pip them on the final day when the Gers were beaten at home by Aberdeen. The Rangers dressing-room was attacked by an angry mob of supporters that day, and Alex received a kick to the knee from one of them.

The discomfort Alex felt on his first day of signing for the Gers, when he was probed about his wife's religious beliefs, would never recede. The bigotry was rife, and so, despite having a boyhood dream of playing as the Rangers No.9, Alex put in a transfer request as soon as his first season ended. This would be denied. An act Alex went through on no fewer than eight out of his seventeen years as a professional footballer. Some ex-players speculate Alex put in a transfer request every summer just to negotiate himself a little pay rise. Such speculation has never been denied.

So, Alex played another season with Rangers, where he would, again, just miss out on major honours. Celtic would beat Rangers to the title, clearing them by five points this time and then the Catholic club of Glasgow would beat the Protestant club of Glasgow again to the secondary piece of silverware in Scotland, the Scottish Cup—thrashing them 4-0 in a one-sided affair. Alex would play in that final, but his involvement in the first team had been come-and-go for the second part of that campaign, given the fractured relationships Alex had formed at the club. It wasn't his teammates Alex had a problem with. His disdain was for those running the club. On top of that, he had a constantly strained relationship with manager, Davie White.

Alex remembers watching Jock Stein celebrate with his players after that Cup Final in 1969 and being in awe of the camaraderie he witnessed. It seemed as if being a Celtic player meant winning in every way imaginable. The team was a rock-solid unit. And Alex was hugely jealous.

Rangers would sell him as soon as that season was over, after — yet again — he had handed in another transfer request. It seemed as if he was finally on his way to Nottingham Forest having flirted with them summers prior, but a late bid by Falkirk would produce a U-turn, mainly because Cathy didn't fancy much moving down south. And so he would remain in the Scottish top flight, saying goodbye to the last chance he would ever have of becoming a player in the more advanced top division of England.

Alex rarely went long without an argument, but his time at Falkirk can certainly be considered his most calmed period as a footballer. That's not to say his four years at Falkirk were plain sailing—they weren't. He would get into a lot of scraps with teammates and scrapes with club officials, but he felt a sense of harmony — and, more importantly to him — a sense of respect in the Falkirk dressing-room. That was partly down to his now-settled relationship with manager Willie Cunningham who had signed Alex not just because of his goalscoring nous, but because he knew he could be an influence in the dressing-room. By this stage, Alex was an experienced pro and so his heated, passionate approach in the dressing-room was finally befitting his stature. By this chapter in his career, lunch meetings with his teammates around canteen tables to watch Alex play with the salt and pepper shakers were plentiful and well-attended. And Cunningham was chuffed that Alex was boosting team morale.

Yet despite having the sixties version of Duncan Ferguson/Peter Crouch as their star forward, as well as his fire in the dressing-room, Falkirk never really reached any great heights. They finished mid-table, mostly, during Alex's four years at the club, though they were always more concerned with the relegation trap door behind them throughout a season than they were the Old Firm at the top.

After four years of no progression, the board of directors called time on Cunningham's reign and with his own contract running out, Alex, too, would opt for a new venture. Though he knew it to be his last one. At thirty-three years of age, and with his legs, and elbows, running wary, Alex was offered a sizeable, but undefined, contract with Ayr United. Falkirk would certainly miss Alex and Cunningham's presence after they'd departed. They would finish rock bottom of the division the following season and be relegated, while the Govanman's dressing-room leadership, if not so much his feet (he was in and out of the team for his last season, scoring nine goals from twenty-four appearances), would help Ayr United to the dizzying heights of seventh. Alex would end his football playing career without having won a major trophy.

It was a void he was determined to fill as a manager.

1964-1974

THE GIRL IN REMINGTON RAND ALEX THOUGHT WAS EASY ON THE EYE? Her name was Cathy Holding. Not only was she pretty, but she had a firecracker of a personality—complemented with the driest of deliveries that would constantly have Alex tittering. Cathy, although no man wants to admit this of their other half, reminded Alex so much of his mother. And just like Lizzie Hardie, Cathy Holding was not backward in coming forward. Although, even at that, no woman — not even the confident Cathy Holding — made the first move in those days. It was all down to the man. Alex made that move under the dim lights of the Locarno Dance Hall—a well-known haunt on Sauchiehall Street in the heart of Glasgow that, in those days, bounced to a score of Beatlemania every Sunday night. Alex and his friends had been regular attendees to Locarno and, one night, out of the blue, the pretty girl from work showed up. He knew, as shop steward, that it was best he attempt to court Cathy outside of the factory, for asking her out in work, even in the early sixties, may have been frowned upon. So, cheered on by his friends, Alex stoked up the courage to stride across the dance floor.

'Wannae dance?'

They danced the night away, and by the time the DJ played the final song of the night — *Smoke Gets in Your Eyes* (Sunday nights *always* ended with the same slow ballad in those days) — Cathy was resting her cheek on Alex's shoulder. Alex had fancied Cathy ever since he first laid eyes on her. She, however, took some convincing because the first time she saw him he looked like trouble.

'He had just broken his nose,' Cathy recalls. 'He had two black eyes as well. I didnae know what to make of 'im. I thought he was a right baddun. Ma pal said, "Maybe he's a boxer".'

Alex was a handsome chap. His height helped, as did his smile as, unusually for a man of his upbringing, he maintained two perfectly neat rows of teeth. He was fashionable too, though you'd be hard pushed to find somebody in Britain in the early sixties who wasn't at least *trying* to be fashionable. Alex's efforts were consistent in that regard: a Crombie jacket, pointed creased trousers and Winklepicker shoes would complement his Perry Como-inspired hair-do (which was basically a side-parting from left to right that Alex would retain as his hair style for the rest of his life). Cathy's pretty features were framed by a highly-fashionable beehive do, though unlike her husband, she would go on to evolve her look as time passed.

Alex's brother Martin, funnily enough, remembers thinking their relationship simply wouldn't last, only because Alex had become, by his early twenties, something of a ladies' man.

'Well, to me at the time, when Cathy came on the scene, I thought she was just another girlfriend. Because he had had a few before her. I genuinely thought 'I wonder how long she'll last?''

However, Alex's good friend, John Donachie, thought otherwise from the get-go.

'I remember thinking 'This is it'. That was Alex done. It was game, set and match. He had found the girl of his dreams. They were getting married.'

It was late in 1964 when Alex and Cathy started dating, half-way through Alex's final season as a part-time player. He would sign his first professional contract some nine months later and although he wasn't flush, he knew he had to make another commitment that, for once, had nothing to do with a ball. He purchased a ring and popped a question Cathy had somewhat expected him to ask. Their discussions hadn't been about when they'd get married, but more so *how* they'd get married. With Alex a Protestant, and Cathy a Catholic (following his father's and his grandfather's footsteps), their choices were pretty limited, especially so as Cathy's parents were traditionalists in this regard.

They'd eventually marry at Martha Street registry office on the morning of Saturday, the twelfth of March in 1966, with the ceremony ending in time for Alex to hop into his brother and best man's car and be driven to East End Park where he would play a somewhat passenger role in Dunfermline's 1-0 win over Hamilton. There'd be no honeymoon, either. This particular year Dunfermline were doing well in Europe and Alex was playing games in midweek as well as on Saturdays. And then, when there was a summer break in the domestic season, he was called up for the Scotland team that would spend the summer of '66 travelling the globe, winning international caps or not winning international caps, depending on which side of that argument you fall on.

There was time, however, and money, to buy a lovely home just after they wed—a three bedroomed, semi-detached, contemporary build in Simshill on the south side of Glasgow that cleaned out Alex's savings of £3,005 exactly. It would be the home Cathy would live in while Alex's career took him from city to city, as both a player and then, initially, as a manager over the next dozen years.

Alex was high on life during the summer of '66, despite England being crowned world champions. Not only was his playing career progressing at a rapid rate, and his coaching badges bagged, his personal life was as healthy as it possibly could have been: new wife, new home, new club, new life. However, neither he — nor nobody who knew him then — could have predicted that just two years later he would be battling bouts of depression. Certainly not when in the midst of his happiness he would be offered something he had been dreaming about since he was a wee boy. The No.9 jersey for Rangers.

Bizarrely, as soon as he began to wear that jersey, the grin which in the mid-60s was a permanent fixture on Alex's face, would begin to fade.

It wasn't just the bigotry at boardroom level that stole the sting from his excitement of being a Ger, the dressing-room bothered him too. Though it wasn't necessarily the players. He got on with all of them just fine. It was the manager, David White. Alex grew to quickly resent him, simply because White proved to be stubborn and ignorant to any of Alex's input. At every other club Alex had been at, from his young days at Drumchaple Amateurs, he had always had an influence in the dressing-room. He liked his voice to be heard. But he was silenced at Rangers.

After two years of coming around to the fact that his dream was in fact turning into a nightmare (despite scoring regularly for the first team with that No.9 on his back), Alex's mood began to dip. He stopped singing around the house. And he wasn't as jovial with his friends when they would socialise.

Cathy wanted him to move away from the Gers, but Alex's stubbornness wouldn't allow it. This had been a life-long dream. Cathy didn't care which jersey he was wearing. She just wanted her husband back. She'd noticed he was drinking more. Not much. Just more. He had never been a big drinker, Alex, even during those Sunday nights at Locarno Dance Hall. But during his time at Rangers, the one beer Alex would normally have on a night out had turned into three of four.

Former Rangers centre back John Greig remembers one particular low point during the Gers' early summer tour of Denmark in 1969 — which was just after the Govanman had been immersed in a blazing row with David White, and as a result, was banished to train with the junior team at Rangers.

'I walked into the hotel and there was Alex. And he was drunk. Now, that was unusual. He was shouting and bawling at the top of his voice in the hotel foyer. And he was wearing these bright red pyjamas. Everyone in the place was staring at him. I had to talk to him.'

The truth is, Alex's heart was broken by unrequited love. The club he had looked up to had looked down on him from literally the minute he had signed his contract with them. It drove Alex to depression. Thankfully for him it would be the only period in his life that he would suffer from this mental illness. The worst of it lasted for about five months, from February in 1969 to late June that year, when he was finally released from his Rangers hell thanks to his old football manager, Willie Cunningham.

Cunningham convinced Alex to sign for Falkirk, over Nottingham Forest, with the promise of a lucrative contract. And as soon as Alex signed on the dotted line, his smile would return. Suddenly, Cathy could hear him singing around the house again, and his friends were getting the jovial Alex when he'd turn up for social events.

There had been talk in the Ferguson household of him leaving the sport altogether after Rangers, such was his depression. But his determination to prove those who had rendered him into this state wrong overrode his low moods. Cathy helped, too. She didn't want him moping around the house.

'I didnae want him at home,' she said. 'No. I wanted him outta the road, y'know. He'd get in the way. I know a lot of wives felt like that. Y'know, the dockyard workers when they used to break up for summer holidays and they'd be home, the wives would be screaming. No… I didnae want him home all the time, that's for sure.'

She certainly didn't want Alex moping around the house at that stage of their lives because by the time his strife at Rangers was coming to an end, Mark had been born. And money was tight. If Alex hadn't signed for Falkirk, it may well have been a struggle, financially, for Alex and Cathy to raise their wee family in their Simshill home.

Two years into his time at Falkirk, Cathy would fall pregnant again.

'Twins,' she would say to her husband with a concerned look on her face after returning from a visit to the hospital.

They were both ecstatic in one sense — as they had often talked about a big family — but Cathy's concerned look upon revealing the news to Alex was justified. Alex may have been flying high for Falkirk and earning more money than he ever had, but things were still tight. His footballer's salary was considered middle-of-the-road and so Alex and Cathy's worries weren't immediate. But they were constantly aware that a footballer's career doesn't last too long, and with Alex almost thirty years of age when the twins (Darren and Jason) arrived, there were already questions over just how long he had left in the game.

To prepare for his retirement from football, and just before he signed his last contract with Ayr United, Alex decided to invest all his savings in his family's future. Although he had done all his coaching badges and was determined to stay in the game as a manager once he hung up his boots, he knew there were no guarantees of success down that path. So, he bought a pub. Well... he bought a few pubs.

But the first one he purchased, originally called Burns Cottage, but which he would rename Fergie's, was a real challenge. Burns Cottage had once been a rip-roaring success of a bar situated just off the Govan Road, having launched the careers of many bands. But by the time Alex took over as landlord, the live stage was as historic as the pub's reputation, and it was now operating just like any one of the many regular pubs the dockyard workers would frequent after a long day's work. But in much the same way as he would have success in any field he would enter, Fergie's became a massive hit under Alex's ownership. In the afternoons, after football training, Alex could be found scrubbing the floors of the pub, or down the cellar clearing out battered old kegs, or — more often than anything else — polishing the stage equipment of the downstairs lounge he had just refurbished. He liked a singsong, did Alex, even though his friends would rib him for being tone deaf. Still, that didn't deter him from murdering a Neil Sedaka song every free chance he would get. Proving he didn't take the criticism aimed at him as a player to heart, Alex would ironically call the new lounge The Elbow Room.

Life at Fergie's was never dull, not when a lot of its patrons were tangled up in organised crime. It's fair to say that there were more than a few elbows thrown in The Elbow Room. Alex recalls once coming out of Ayr United's training ground to be met by a man running towards him shouting, 'There's somebody in Fergie's with a shot gun.'

'I loved being a publican,' Alex would later say. 'I'd never come across so many wonderful characters. There were historians, poets, psychiatrists, bums, fighters, lovers… the lot.'

Having turned Fergie's around from being a sleeping giant (much like he would do to Manchester United in coming years), Alex invested in more pubs. He purchased Shaws, a well-known haunt in the Bridgeton area of Glasgow and began to put in place the same refurbishment job he had done at Fergie's. It was only a few weeks after buying this new pub, along with his friend Sam Falconer, that Alex realised he didn't hold the same passion for this bar as he did for Fergie's. The clientele were different. This pub was located in the Protestant heartland of Bridgeton, and songs filled with bigoted views struck up readily, much to Alex's frustration. The theme of these songs — regardless of whether they came from Protestants or Catholics — were Alex's genuine pet peeve. They made his skin crawl, mainly because his father had raised him and Martin to stay mute any time one of those songs was being sung in their presence. Even on the terraces of Ibrox, Alex and Martin would keep schtum when bigoted chants were being screamed at players.

But while Alex was managing pubs to reclaim their glory days, he was mostly day-dreaming about managing football players, not bar men. And not long after he hung up his boots for the last time as an Ayr United player, and aged only thirty-two, Alex let Scottish football clubs know that he was looking for a job. He knew he had a reputation in the game for being a studious tactician, as well as an obsessive leader. Besides, it was a no-brainer. Nobody who had been aware of Alex's football career would have thought of him as a pub landlord. He was primed for football management and had been studying the game and practising leadership skills his entire adult life. Many of his peers couldn't wait to see what he would achieve as a manager. He no doubt talked a good game, and he sure did sound impressive when detailing what the pepper shaker should do during different phases of the ninety minutes as he pushed it around the table.

'Alex would talk tactics all day if you'd let him,' his friend John Donachie would say about their playing days together.

It was finally time for the Govanman to prove that his walk could match his talk.

ALEX AND HIS TACTICS

'I WANNAE DO IT THE MANCHESTER UNITED WAY,' ALEX INSTRUCTED his players in the lead up to the 2011 Champions League Final. It would be Alex's sixth European final to manage in (a joint record. He would win four of those trophies—also a joint record), yet this final would be his biggest disappointment out of those six. In fact, it would be his biggest disappointment in all his years as Manchester United manager.

In the lead up to the game, the players weren't impressed with their manager's approach, which was highly unusual. Experienced pros such as Wayne Rooney and Rio Ferdinand were certain their legendary manager was making the wrong call. He was. Alex got it drastically wrong by trying to remain truthful to the DNA he had instilled within the football club since he had taken over some twenty-five years earlier. He was about take on arguably the greatest club side that has ever existed, and Barcelona would prove as much by going on to dominate United in that 2011 final with the scoreline of Barcelona 3-1 Manchester United flattering the Red Devils.

Barcelona, led by manager Pep Guardiola, partnered Xavi and Iniesta as a midfield two to play ten yards ahead of Sergio Busquets—the deep-lying and deeply under-appreciated central sweeper. This triangle gave Michael Carrick and Ryan Giggs (the only two midfielders Alex opted to play with) the run around. That evening, Carrick and Giggs (two stalwarts of Alex's success with United over many, many years) looked like two kids playing against three adults. They barely got a sniff of the ball. Wayne Rooney would label Alex's tactical approach to that Champions League Final as "suicidal".

'I remember Alex Ferguson saying, "We're Man United and we're going to attack, it's in the culture of this football club", and I was thinking "*I'm not too sure about this*,"' Rooney would say years later. 'All the players knew, deep down, it was the wrong approach, and sure enough we got outplayed.'

Alex would only admit that United were simply beaten by the better side.

"Barcelona were the best team any of my sides ever lined up against. Easily the best,' he would write in his 2013 post-retirement autobiography, simply entitled *My Autobiography*.

But he stopped short of suggesting that if he could go back in time he would approach that final any differently.

"We might have (reached a different result) by playing more defensively, but by then I had reached the stage with Manchester United where it was no good us trying to win that way. If we had retreated to our box and kept the defending tight, we might have achieved a different result. But I don't blame myself. I just wish our positive approach could have yielded a better outcome."

It's more than unfair to begin a chapter about Alex's approach to tactics with a strong negative. But it just goes to show that no matter how much of a genius you might appear with salt and pepper shakers during lunch, on rare occasions those condiments can be left standing on the wrong side of the table. Though leaving them standing on the wrong side of the table for a Champions League Final is as fatal as it gets. Deep down, Alex knows he called that game totally wrong, even if he hasn't admitted as much publicly. Though it must be said, Alex calling it wrong occurred on very few occasions over his two thousand games in management.

When Alex used to mess around with the condiments on a breakfast table during his playing days, he always set those condiments out in a 4-4-1-1 formation. More so than innovative, this shape was a slight variation on the mainstay shape almost every club in Britain were adopting at the time.

Where Alex did prove to be particularly innovative though was when it came to obsessing about the opposition's shape as much as he would obsess about his own. He took immense joy in being pragmatic in that sense. And while it sounds rather alien to label Alex a 'pragmatic manager' in that it is clear even to the novice eye that his teams were mostly a joy to behold, certainly in how they transitioned into fast-paced counter attacks, the truth is that labelling his teams 'pragmatic' is a factual way to describe Alex's tactical approach. He was obsessive in his studying of other teams and thrived on picking out their weaknesses while at the same time noting their strengths. Then he would set up his team to negate those strengths and thereafter take quick advantage of the weaknesses he had spotted. Alex's first mission, tactically, as a manager, was to suffocate the opposition. Key to winning any match, Alex always felt, was in the nullifying of the most creative players of the opponent, and then, in-doing so, counter-punching. Alex Ferguson was a pragmatist, tactically. A disguised pragmatist. He wasn't the all-out attacking philosopher some of his teams, particularly in the early days of his management, fooled us into thinking he was.

The basic 4-4-1-1 that Alex held preference for over most of his career consisted of a straight back line of four defenders; a right full back, a left full back and two centre halves. In order for Alex's approach to come to fruition, the full backs needed to be among the fittest players in the team as they had responsibility to not only hold that back line of four as best they could when their team was not in possession of the ball, but to assist the winger ahead of them in forward forays whenever their team was in possession. This sounds like basic instruction in the modern age, but the manner in which Alex utilised his full backs was innovative in the mid-seventies when he started managing. The two centre-backs didn't have to be the best centre-backs in the world — individuality in football didn't count for too much to Alex — but they *had* to complement each other. One of them would have to be a great reader of the game, while the other had to be a tough tackler. One had to be good on the ball, the other not necessarily. Two of the same wouldn't do. Each of them had to adopt different approaches to the art of defending. Yet those approaches *had* to complement each other.

Ahead of the two central defenders would sit two central midfielders, who, like the partnership behind them, would need to complement each other's attributes. In earlier days, when Alex managed in Scotland and including his first seasons as manager of Manchester United — particularly when he had Bryan Robson to call upon — Alex held preference for playing with two box-to-box midfielders who would need to cover as much ground as the full backs. But that set-up would later evolve into a more balanced approach where one of the central midfielders would be expected to sit and cover little ground while the other would take more responsibility in transitional attacks. Flanking those two midfielders would be the poster boys of an Alex Ferguson team —the two wingers. Fast and skilful, these players had to cover as much ground as the full-backs and would often be tasked with playing along the line of wherever the ball was at any point in the game. These wingers were key for Alex's pragmatic approach to work, whereby his team would allow the opposition to do what they normally did before stalling their approach by nullifying their best player's involvement in that attack and, in turn, transferring possession over to United who would aim to be on the edge of the opposition's penalty area within a matter of seconds using these two wide players to carry possession. To the average attendee at Love Street or Pittodrie or Old Trafford, this looked like quick, slick all-out attacking football. But the starting point for so many of the goals Alex's teams scored over the decades was cemented in innovative pragmatism. He purposely lured the opposition in, conned them into thinking they were free to play as they usually did. Then they would suffocate them and take advantage. Ahead of the midfielders were two lone lines of strikers, always ready to pounce. They were trained to be set for action when the opposition had the ball, knowing a quick transition may occur at any moment. The single lines of lone strikers consisted of a No.10, if you will, who would play ten yards shy of the opposition's defensive line, and a No.9 whose job was to play *on* the line of the opposition's defensive line. The No.10 housed Alex's favourite player: the 'intelligent' striker—the one who he thought mirrored himself; chest puffed out, back to goal. The subtlety in which this player would assist in the transition of these counter attacks would prove as key an attribute in the make-up of an attack as the pace of the wingers either side of him.

The pragmatic, counterattacking 4-4-1-1 approach worked an absolute treat for Alex in Scotland, though it has often been argued — and argued well, especially by those who have played under him — that while Alex's tactics benefited his teams marvellously, it was more his man-management that led them to success over any great nous. The teams, after all, that he led to trophies in Scotland were so much more than the sum of their parts, that tactics alone couldn't have been responsible for them toppling the Old Firm, let alone the cream of Europe. The Old Firm, after all, had, by far, the best players in every position in the country in their ranks. It could only have been Alex's ability to shift the mindset of his players that helped his teams to huge success up north. It's an argument that can only hold true. Alex's man-management (which has its own dedicated chapter later in this biography) was more innovative than his tactics. But it was his tactics that helped him beat Celtic and Rangers in particular when his teams would come up against them, simply because he would stifle their most creative players and then counter punch them. Celtic and Rangers players hated playing against Alex's teams. They never had an easy time of it, simply because of Alex's pragmatic ways. Unlike modern managers such as Jurgen Klopp or Pep Guardiola, Alex Ferguson was happy for the opposition to have the ball. He felt that if you had the ball, then you were more susceptible into making an error. His team's pragmatic approach to football focused on patience, until they could force these errors before turning possession over so that when United had the ball, they had it with only one purpose in mind—getting to the edge of the opposition's box as quickly as possible. That's why Alex's teams are fondly thought of as exciting to watch. They attacked with great pace. But in truth, for most of the ninety minutes of a football match, an Alex Ferguson team was content with being patient.

The 4-4-1-1 wasn't an overly rigid system. The shape would interchange during games, with players drilled on the possible adjustments they would have to transition into when Alex would inevitably bark from the touchline. If, for example, Alex's team were a goal up with minutes to play and he opted to see the game out at that result, the tactics and formation would shift defensively. Upon hearing a bark, the full-backs would no longer be required in an attacking sense, tasked now with continually holding the defensive line in which one extra player had now joined — normally one of the two central midfielders — to form a back line of five. Then the No.10 would drop into midfield to form a line of four, alongside the wingers who would sit ten yards further forward than the full backs. Ahead of them stood a lone striker, who would more often than not be the quickest player in the eleven, so that if an opposition attack did break down at either the line of four deep-lying midfielders or at the line of five defenders, this attacker could sprint away with possession and attempt to run the clock down. In contrast to that, if Alex's teams were chasing a goal in the final minutes of games, the 4-4-1-1 would become a 2-3-5. Sometimes, the five at the top would be made up of actual attackers, not defenders tasked with charging forward in desperate search of an equaliser. Alex had preference for sitting two strikers on the bench beside him, just in case they were a goal down with time running out. It wasn't just the starting eleven that Alex would pre-empt as he would plan for games. His options from the bench were just as vital. Quite often, the substitutions he made in games weren't the result of what had gone on on the pitch that day, but pre-planned. He liked to change one of his forward players in the 78th minute, assuming the game would run about three minutes into injury-time, meaning the opposition's defence would be up against fresh legs for the final fifteen minutes of any game. If anyone was geeky enough to take a look through Alex's game-by-game line-ups over the years, they would find the number seventy-eight asterisked beside a striker's name more often than not. The substitute striker would be sent on to the pitch with one instruction, 'Yiv got fifteen minutes to score a goal.'

On top of his tactical approach, Alex trained his players to be consistently aggressive, dominant and resilient through games. He instilled in them a 'never say die' attitude that they would adopt for any game situation, whether they be 3-0 up, one goal up, or one goal down.

A most impressive statistic that highlights this influence on his players is that United won 183 points from turning deficits into wins within the final ten minutes of games in the Premier League alone under Alex's watch. While this says a lot about fitness, and mentality, it may say more about Alex's willingness to take a tactical gamble in the final minutes of games.

'The gamble didn't always work,' Alex would say, 'but when it did, it was worth more than three points. That dressing-room after the game… can ya imagine? And the fans walking oot of the stadium, bouncing… they bounce when ya score a last-minute goal. I think last minute goals encapsulate ma time at Manchester United.'

After huge success in Scotland, Alex would utilise his 4-4-1-1 counter attacking approach for nigh on twenty years at Old

Trafford until a certain Portmigueser, who christened himself the Special One, came rolling into town, gifting Alex the toughest test of all his years in management and, as a result, causing him to reassess his most trusted tactical approach. It wasn't so much that Jose Mourinho saw Alex's pragmatic approach to management and raised him times ten, it was more because a new society of non-football playing managers was forming, all equipped with so much video analysis that it rendered Alex's 'I'll study the opposition with ma own eyes to spot their strengths and weaknesses' almost redundant, or certainly dated, at the very least. Realising that the new breed of manager was trumping him in pragmatism, Alex was forced to evolve. It pained him to readjust though, not only because he knew it would take at least two season for the adjustments to bear fruit, but more so because he understood his teams would now need to take control over central areas of the pitch and in order to do so, he would have to sacrifice his fondness for two wide players.

Prior to Mourinho's introduction to the Premier League, all of United's closest rivals for titles over the seasons — be it Kenny Dalglish's Blackburn, Kevin Keegan's Newcastle or, the more successful Arsene Wenger's Arsenal — played a fluid 4-4-2 system. Alex knew how to combat that. He knew how to be pragmatic against it. He knew how to win against it. More often than not, he *did* win against it. But the game was on the cusp of a tactical evolution.

Mourinho changed the landscape of English football, tactically. There's little argument against that. What was debated at the time, though, was whether Alex could adapt. Skeptics shouldn't have been too quick to judge however, as the Govanman was about to change where the salt and pepper shakers would sit on his breakfast table and go on to have the best and most successful run of his career right up until his retirement in 2013. Though, as he had feared, it would take time for the adjustment to bear fruit; what with Mourinho's Chelsea winning back-to-back titles in 2005 and 2006 while the salt and pepper shakers got used to their newest surroundings.

Alex actually sat in his office with newly appointed assistant manager Carlos Quiroz (who he had appointed not just because the United dressing-room was by now filled with a multitude of foreign players and Carlos could speak five different languages, but also because he was tactically astute and Alex felt that he needed fresh ideas) where they both played around with salt and pepper shakers, or their equivalent, which was by now orange and blue magnets on a huge tin white board. They were seeking to work out how Manchester United would evolve tactically in the era of the new-age super pragmatic managers.

They came up with a shape of 4-3-3, which was certainly not innovative in that it mirrored Jose Mourinho's formation, but a shape they felt they could get the most out of, given the squad they currently had and the transfers they envisioned for the future. This change of formation would gain United more control in the centre of the park than they were used to, but for this change to bear the juiciest of fruits, they would have to sign the one player they both agreed they had to sign. If anybody had been made privy to Alex Ferguson and Queiroz's plan in early 2005 to replace Roy Keane with Michael Carrick, they'd have thought them insane. Keane, by this stage, was arguably the best and most influential midfielder in England, while Carrick was a different kettle of fish altogether: quiet, calm, composed. But he was a student and, therefore, a reader of the game, and that was the exact attribute Alex and Carlos were looking for. Carrick was disciplined in the extreme; a player who would simply do every-thing asked of him every game—no losing possession of the ball, no finding himself out of position, no unforced errors. He was the epitome, to Alex, of the perfect new-age No.6. They both knew, however, that prising him away from Tottenham Hotspur would prove no easy feat. A fee of £16m would help, and so, months after letting Keane go midway through the 2005-2006 season (which you can read about in fine detail later), Carrick would become the main midfielder at Manchester United, leading the club to their most successful period in their entire history. Over the next seven seasons, up until Alex retired in May of 2013, Manchester United — with their new 4-3-3 formation in which Carrick played the most pivotal role —would go on to win five Premier League titles (losing out on one on goal difference, and the other with literally the last kick of the season) and appear in three Champions League Finals. The club had only ever appeared in two Champions League Finals in their entire history up until that point.

The 4-3-3 would allow for a trident of attacking players, though Alex had to sacrifice the out and out wingers that he and the fans not only adored but had become accustomed to. Of course, he always ensured the central player in that trio of attackers played with their back to goal, with their chest puffed out. Alex would raid Tottenham Hotspur again for the services of Dimitar Berbatov to play that role after losing patience with Ruud van Nistelrooy (more on that later, too) and then, when the Bulgarian's legs had gone, would raid Spurs' fiercest rivals Arsenal to nab Robin van Persie for that role in what would prove to be Alex's swansong season. The two in midfield who would flank the disciplined role of the No.6 played mostly by Carrick, required a lot of running, both in and out of possession. These two players needed to be super fit athletes. And so, in losing his wingers, Alex turned to Ryan Giggs to play a key role in the centre of the pitch and would then shift between runners such as Ji Sung Park, Darren Fletcher or Shinji Kagawa to play on the opposite side of Carrick. The 4-3-3 disciplined approach appeared laboured, certainly in comparison to that of the quick counterattacking 4-4-1-1, and it played out more continently which dampened, somewhat, the fiery atmosphere inside Old Trafford as the familiar roar of supporters rising from their seats as a counter attack ignited effectively died out. But the new approach did, to its credit, manage to collate trophies much more readily.

Regardless of the shape Alex's eleven players would adopt over the years, each of them was always armed with the knowledge of what was expected of them individually when they stepped foot on to any pitch. Alex's most insistent tactical approach was that every player understood the tactical approach. They had to understand what their role entailed when their team was in possession of the ball, and they had to understand what their role entailed when their team didn't have possession of the ball. They were also armed with an insight, having been shown video analysis, into the player they would be up against; that opposition player's strengths, his weaknesses and how he was likely to go about his individual battle that day. Discipline in carrying out the tactics laid down by Alex was the one key attribute he looked for in any player he scouted. If a player couldn't carry out what was expected of him in a pragmatic sense, no matter how good his natural ability, there was no room for him in the dressing-room. This philosophy was why, in 1995, Alex turned down the opportunity to sign Zinedine Zidane. It wasn't that he couldn't see what the rest of the world could see: Zidane was simply one of the most naturally gifted stars in the game with the ball at his feet. But Alex knew the Frenchman wasn't an ideal fit for any of the roles he had in his midfield. Alex could have signed Zidane in '95, but instead chose to promote, to the first team, a spotty nosed and freckled-faced academy graduate named Nicky Butt. He knew Butt filled two of those roles perfectly, and that he would undoubtedly carry out any order laid down by his manager.

'Butt would do any job set out for him,' Alex would say of the player he considers the most underrated of the Class of 92. 'Give him a job to do on a great player — any great player — he would see to it.'

Butt would go on to man-mark Juventus's Zidane out of the Champions League semi-final second-leg in 1999, keeping the Frenchman quiet and seeing to it, without seemingly any fuss on his behalf whatsoever, that United made it to the final. That was

Alex's favoured way of beating opponents, especially top-level opponents. He would nullify their main threat, and more often than not use an array of underrated work horses in his team to carry out such tasks. Having pointed out, at the outset of this chapter, a flaw Alex once made on the big stage, it's only fair that a number of his victories are highlighted too, seeing as there were, after all, a lot more victories than there were defeats. The underrated players Alex used in this specific regard over his years at Old Trafford included Mike Phelan (who would later become his assistant coach), Phil Neville, Ronnie Johnsen, Darren Fletcher, Ji Sung Park, John O'Shea and Phil Jones among others. All were, like Butt, totally inferior footballers in comparison to the likes of Zidane. But Alex would never have had it any other way. Discipline over ability wins every time. For example, Phil Neville was often called into the United eleven in the md-to-late 90s, despite not being a regular first teamer, any time Arsenal's name rolled around in the fixture list. Alex understood more than anyone how much Patrick Vieira dictated the tempo of the Gunners' play and by simply taking him out of the equation by having Neville constantly nip at his heels, the Frenchman was often rendered redundant in these top-of-the-table clashes. Ji Sung Park was called on to carry out the same job against the same opponent years later. The Korean would also be an influential figure as United began to assert themselves in Europe during the late-noughties. Park man-marked the great Andre Pirlo out of the entire 180 minutes of a two-legged affair in 2010, causing the Italian legend to write in his autobiography: "Ferguson unleashed Park Ji-Sung to shadow me. He rushed about at the speed of an electron. He'd fling himself at me, his hands all over my back, trying to intimidate me. He'd look at the ball and not know what it was for. They'd programmed him to stop me. His devotion to the task was almost touching."

Pirlo called it spot on. Alex had instructed Park that the ball during those 180 minutes was of little use to him.

'Your job today is not aboot touching the ball, it's not aboot making passes, your job is Pirlo. That's all. Pirlo!' Alex would yell that instruction numerous times though Park's interpreter in the week leading up to those games. United would advance to the semi-finals having swept the Italian giants aside 7-2 on aggregate, with Pirlo looking like a passenger in both legs.

The adaptable pragmatic approach was the preferred philosophy of the Govanman mainly because it was a totally adaptable philosophy which would allow him to cycle through team after team over the long-term. Whereas he always felt a definitive tactical philosophy wasn't cyclical, being tactically adaptable meant it was easy to evolve the team and that in turn meant Alex could collate many trophies over multiple years. The idea of winning one title never interested him. His football philosophy (which you can read about in detail later) was always about competing for multiple trophies over multiple years.

For this long-term success to come to fruition, Alex had to adapt tactically as any manager in history. Not only did he begin his career managing players on £30 a week before evolving to his players earning ten-thousand times as much, Alex also went from bettering part-time managers such as Stan Anderson and John Hagart in the mid-seventies, to bettering the likes of tactical innovators such as Arsene Wenger and Jose Mourinho. Without his team's ability to adapt tactically, decades of success simply wouldn't have been possible. He would have had to have adopted his tactical approach at one club, then move on to another club in order to have achieved the long-term successes he did. But staying at one club and getting the best out of a group of players before moving on never interested him. He felt a rigid and definitive tactical philosophy could take teams to great heights, but it would only take them to these heights in the short-term. A rigid and definitive tactical philosophy is not cyclable. That is why he always felt his tactics should be pragmatic and adaptable.

When posed with a question about his tactical approach during a Harvard Business lecture he gave at the lauded Boston-based university in 2014, Alex said: 'I realise that the system within a football team doesn't have the complexity of what is required to design a nuclear submarine, build 50 million mobile phones or organise clinical trials for a new drug. But like every organisation, a football team needs to be well run and has to be sure that the system is deeply ingrained. Our product just happened to be a football team rather than a car or a washing machine, and our whole reason for being was to make sure all the pieces of our team — all the different players — fitted together.'

Alex never felt as if it was the lines of a 4-4-1-1 or a 4-3-3 that specifically helped the teams he managed to unprecedented success, but more so the fact that the players playing in any of those positions, whatever the formation be over the years, understood *exactly* what was required of them when they were on that pitch.

For Alex, the discipline required to carry out the tactics totally outweighed the ingenuity of the tactics themselves.

To compound all that had been written above, Alex would write in *Managing My Life*: "I am always amused by (pundits') eagerness to concentrate almost exclusively on technical and tactical comparisons. Frequently they discuss football in abstract terms, overlooking the reality that it is played by creatures of flesh and blood and feeling. Tactics are important. But they don't win football matches. Men win football matches. The best teams stand out because they *are* teams, because the individual members have been so truly integrated that the team functions with one single spirit."

For the Govanman, man-management trumped tactical nous every single time.

1974-1978

DESPITE HIS REPUTATION IN SCOTLAND AS AN UP-AND-COMING MANAGERIAL prodigy, Alex had to start at the bottom. In fact, it was almost literally the bottom. The club that would give him his first break into management had just sacked their manager Bob Shaw after they'd finished sixteenth in Division 2—the fourth worst position in Scottish professional football. That might sound like a bleak starting point. But that's not how Alex saw it. He felt the only way was up. What *was* bleak, however, was the fact that he'd turn up for his first training session at East Stirlingshire in early July in 1974 to find out he had inherited a squad of only eight players. And none of them were goalkeepers.

Alex would write in his 1999 autobiography, *Managing My Life*: "When I met with chairman Willie Muirhead, the honesty in his face and the ease in which I felt in his company persuaded me to take that job. But once the reality of the playing resources was unveiled, the decision began to look suicidal."

After he had blown the whistle on his first training session with his eight outfield players, Alex would call to Muirhead's office for a meeting.

'You do knoo ya need eleven players to field a football team, plus two subs, right?'

Muirhead was apologetic for overselling the project to Alex during his initial interview, and when the Govanman demanded a transfer kitty to at least meet the Scottish FA's quota for competition, the owner exhaled a thick cloud of smoke from one of the thirty cigarettes he would light every day, and said, 'I'll see what I can do.'

An hour later, he rang Alex at home.

'Two thousand pounds. It's all I've got.'

Muirhead had emptied his savings account, having felt not only bad about overselling the project to Alex, but because he was genuinely buoyed by the Govanman's enthusiasm.

Two grand was a small number with regards football even in the mid-70s, and Alex knew it wouldn't run so far when the squad needed so much surgery. So, he began to study the free transfer market—trying to find young and hungry players who had been let go by clubs at the end of the previous season. It's hardly the best place to start — signing others' cast-offs — but Alex didn't sign any player for the sake of it. He did a full check on any prospect's background, speaking not only to previous coaches of theirs, but to folk who knew them personally. The question he always wanted an answer to was this: 'Will the player do as I ask him to?' As mentioned before, and will be mentioned again, discipline would be *the* key attribute Alex looked for in a player. Discipline would prove to be a much stronger attribute for him than ability. He would sign five players that summer, three who arrived on free transfers, and two of whom he would splash — to the penny — all two thousand of the pounds Muirhead had given him.

The standard of ability was so low in Alex's first training sessions that he felt a need to transform the training routine. He introduced programmes that would enhance the players' technical ability on the ball, so poor were the first touches, and the short passes. The programme he founded that day is a programme he was still coaching Manchester United's first team in his final years as manager some thirty-nine years later. Another philosophy Alex gave birth to in his opening weeks as a manager that he still held dear until his final season at Manchester United in 2013 was his insistence that young players would form part of his squad. He travelled around to see underage teams play on Sunday mornings and would invite the most promising teenagers to train with the East Stirlingshire first team. He did this for two reasons. Firstly, he knew that if he caught players young, gave them their first break and could instil his football philosophy within them then they would prove loyal and disciplined to him over the long-term. And secondly, because he knew that nothing lit a fire under the arse of an experienced professional footballer than the threat of a seventeen-year-old coming up behind him who played in his position. This constant threat that Alex strived for, added to his new training regime, propelled the East Stirlingshire players. They began to work their socks off in training and they entered the new campaign feeling, for the first time in a number of years, as if they weren't amongst the worst professional teams in the country. After six weeks of pre-season training, Alex had achieved what he set out to achieve. He had totally changed the mentality of the entire dressing-room.

His methods saw to it that by the end of November, East Stirlingshire were third in the division and feeling dizzy—not just from the heights of their lofty position, but because of the whirlwind presence Alex had proven to be at the club. He'd had had run-ins with players and run-ins with board members, yet everybody was excited for his revolution. He was transforming the club beyond anything they could have envisaged when they hired him. East Stirlingshire were planning for a bright future with Alex at the helm when, only five months in, the Govanman would receive a phone call from his former love-him-hate-him manager Willie Cunningham, who was by this stage the boss of St Mirren.

'I'm gonnae step down,' Willie told Alex, 'and eh… I've recommended you to the board.'

Alex scoffed at the notion. Not only was he just in the door at East Stirlingshire and producing miracles, but St Mirren were one of the teams East Stirlingshire had ridden roughshod over in the Second Division. East Stirlingshire were third. St Mirren were third from bottom. Although Alex dismissed Cunningham's attempts to lure him away from the Shire, a niggling thought remained in his head up to two weeks after that phone call. So much so, that he felt compelled to seek the advice of the one manager he held above them all. He got hold of Jock Stein's number and gave the Celtic manager — who had just celebrated his ninth title in a row with Celtic — a call.

'Listen Alex, do yasel' a wee favour,' Stein told him. 'Go sit in the stand at Fir Park (East Stirlingshire's echoey and unfinished home ground) and take a good look around. Then go do the same at Love Street (St Mirren's glorious four-standed home ground).'

When Alex told the players at The Shire that he was leaving, they were, to a man, devastated. They felt they'd come a long way under their new manager. Although he'd only been there for five months, it seemed much longer in so many respects. Alex felt terrible, but not as terrible as he would feel when he would observe the new squad he had inherited in training.

St Mirren was a club that held great status, but that was all in the past. The squad Alex took charge of was ageing, unfocused and lacking the passion and determination he demanded in his players. It was no wonder they had sunk to near bottom of Scotland's professional game.

Though with a bigger budget and wider staff numbers than he had at East Stirlingshire, Alex began to put in place a football philosophy that would not only bear fruit at Love Street, but at Aberdeen and then at Manchester United over the next four decades.

He sent his scouts (the best of which, Alex would admit, was a local taxi driver, and proper character, who went by the name of 'Baldy' Lindsay) on a mission to find the best teen talent around the outskirts of Glasgow, teens he would use to light a fire under the arses of his ageing first-teamers. He knew Celtic and Rangers would hold all of the pulling power for kids inside of Glasgow's boarders, so he purposely stretched the search further afield.

'Get to their mothers,' Alex would tell 'Baldy'.

'Huh?'

'The mothers will make the best and most rational decisions for their boys. If we win the mother, we win the boy.'

This was another tactic Alex would continue to use for decades. He literally swooned Lynne Giggs — mother of Ryan — when, in 1987, he would repeatedly call to their family home to have cups of tea with her. After weeks of call-ins, Alex turned up on Ryan's four-teenth birthday with a present: a professional contract at Manchester United. Giggs, who had been training with Manchester City's academy, and who went by the surname Wilson (his father's name) in those days, would now be switching allegiances. Simply because his mother was, by now, certain that Alex would take good care of her boy. Giggs would go on to become the most decorated footballer in British footballing history at Manchester United, as well as the club's longest-serving player.

Alex was planning for the long-haul at St Mirren and drafted in his old Rangers teammate Davie Provan to be his assistant. Their main objective in that first season was, despite being second from bottom, to finish inside the top six. It was a tough ask, but Alex felt that the introduction of newly recruited young players to train with the first team, coupled with his modern coaching and pragmatic tactics, would lead them to that much-coveted spot. It was a pivotal year in Scottish football. The Scottish FA were restructuring the Leagues the following season. Instead of two divisions of eighteen clubs, from the 1975-76 season there would be three divisions of twelve clubs. The new Premier Division would be formed by the top twelve finishers in the First Division in 1974-75, and the bottom six, along with the top six of the Second Division, would enter a brand new First Division. The bottom six of the Second Division would then form a newly branded Second Division with six new clubs from the amateur leagues. Alex's mission was pretty much a relegation battle. Or a promotion battle, depending on which way one looks at it.

Either way, they made it — just about — by winning their last game of the season to seal sixth spot, securing their place in the First Division, just one promotion away from where Alex really wanted to manage—the top tier of Scottish football where he could pit his wits against Jock Stein's great Celtic side and his old favourites, with whom he was still holding bitter regard, Rangers.

He would have to wait, however. St Mirren's objective for their first season in the newly branded First Division was to not get relegated, simply because they wouldn't be able to compete with bigger spending clubs; clubs who were well ahead of them in their development and half of whom had just come from the top flight. Alex was fine with biding his time to manage in the Premier Division, as he was aware of what he was building at Love Street. The young players Alex had assembled were beginning to show real promise under his tutelage and began pushing the senior pros out of the first team. The kids played a massive part in the overachievement of The Saints that year, finishing fifth and, by and large, shrugging off any threat of relegation before the season had even reached the Christmas period.

Buoyed by the rebirth at the club, what with fans returning to Love Street in their thousands for the first time in years, Alex felt he owed the club a debt of dedication himself. So he sold his two pubs he had purchased, and knuckled down for a real shot at Premier Division management with a squad so promising and young that one local newspaper would nickname them "Fergie's Fledglings".

At this time, heading into the 1976-77 season with his hungry squad, mostly filled with late teens, Alex's personal life was mirroring his professional life—as it tended to do. The family home is Simshill felt more comfortable, not just because there was now a family of five filling it, but because Alex's contract was so secure and, for once in his life, lucrative, that the fear of having no food to feed his children had now all but receded. It in fact it had totally receded by the time St Mirren would sack him some twenty months later. But before that axe would shockingly come out of left field, from the mouth of the club's chairman Willy Todd (likened, in many regards and in hindsight, to Decca Records' refusal to sign The Beatles), there was the mission of getting the Saints promoted to the top flight so Alex could pit his wits against Glasgow's Old Firm.

St Mirren were top of the First Division by February and, by far, playing the best football of any side in the country. The speed in which the youngsters would counter-attack and leave their opponents in their wake stunned Scottish football, and Alex Ferguson became the number one mentioned named when the subject of most promising young managers arose.

In the midst of that season, with the Saints five points clear at the top, Alex would find out, from one of the many moles he had situated around the outskirts of Glasgow, that former Liverpool and Celtic striker, now Alex's 'back to goal with chest puffed out' No.10 at the Saints, Frank McGarvey, had been spotted drinking the night before a game. Alex was livid. He called over to Frank's house, told him in no uncertain terms, with his arms flailing and his face purple, that he was finished at the club and that his bags at the training ground would be packed for him the next morning. This wasn't just an act. He was deadly serious. He couldn't have his most senior pros proving to be bad examples for the youngsters. Alex had laid down his rules about alcohol in no uncertain terms at every club he would manage. It shouldn't be touched. Not if you wanted to play at the most elite level. Despite pleas from close-knit teammates, all of whom adored McGarvey, Alex was not for turning. Not until two weeks later when McGarvey would approach him while he was out with Cathy heading to an awards do. In fact, he didn't approach them. He more jumped out from behind a pillar, because he knew Alex was due at the ceremony and had been standing around waiting for him.

'I'm so sorry, boss,' McGarvey would cry. He would then go on to shower Alex with so many promises and declarations, in such an emotional manner, that it left Cathy no choice but to intervene.

'Ah c'mon, Alex,' she said. 'How many more times does he ha' tae say sorry.'

Alex didn't relent. Not there and then. Not until Cathy had annoyed him so much at the awards do later that night, that he would throw his hands up in the air and resist, 'Right, Cathy! I'll give the lad one more chance.'

McGarvey would go on to be such a pivotal player for the Saints over the second half of that campaign that St Mirren ran away with the title—gifting the former great club a new dawn in the top division, as well as Alex a first crack at the Old Firm as a manager.

It would be a tougher task than he had imagined, and although his brief of not getting relegated was met in his first season, Alex would not fulfil his own goals that season of finishing in the top half. It would be the first time his goals hadn't been met over a season as a manager. Although he would, using his pragmatic approach, give the Old Firm a good run for their money in each of the occasions the Saints played them that year, they would inevitably be drawn into a relegation battle; only staving off the threat with four games to go by the end of the 1977-78 campaign. Alex wasn't angered by any of his players' performances. His young side were simply no match for the country's greatest players week in, week out. They had, in earnest, done themselves proud by staying in the top flight, though it became apparent to them by the end of the campaign that their boss wouldn't be staying in situ.

Billy McNeil had just left Aberdeen for Celtic after the Glasgow club rather messily and unforgivably had asked Jock Stein to step aside, and there was only one manager Aberdeen had in mind to replace McNeil.

Alex had met with Aberdeen chairman, Dick Donald, behind St Mirren's back and was adamant he was going to take on the new challenge. But he was wary that he may not be able to negotiate his way out of the water-tight contract he had with the Saints. He did hope, however, that no matter how successful he had been at St Mirren that he had had so many run-ins with Willie Todd that the chairman might actually be glad to get rid of him.

As it happens, and before Alex could tell his board that he was set for pastures new, he would be called to a meeting with Todd in which the chairman would read him the riot act by detailing thirteen rule regulations Alex had broken (such as smashing cups in the dressing-room and handing off-the-cuff bonuses to players without the board's consent, as well as off-the-cuff player fines) and told him there and then in a heated exchange that the Govanman was sacked.

Alex reacted by laughing, then snarling, 'Y'only s'posed to sack someone if they're not good at their job.' He walked out, shocked, but buoyed in the knowledge that his next move had already been put in place. He, of course, couldn't tell Todd what was on the horizon during their final meeting, as that would have revealed the poaching that had gone on. But he so desperately wanted to.

The Saints fans would be furious with the board for the sacking and all Scottish sports reporters went in search of the reasoning behind the decision. Indeed, Alex's sacking has remained somewhat a mystery four decades on, mainly due to the fact that both side's public versions of the story were always poles a part. Alex claimed Todd and he clashed, not just in personality, but in work ethic, and would tell journalists that the chairman didn't like how much control he was generating at the club. Todd would claim, to journalists, that Alex's handling of fining players, be it for lateness or not wearing the proper attire set out by the manager, was unethical and not endorsed by the club. The truth, however, while it was diluted somewhat by both of those propaganda-infused reasons, was that Todd had actually become privy to Alex's talks with Aberdeen, and so fired the Govanman before he could resign. That's the answer to the mystery. Tit for tat. It is, admittedly, a disappointing conclusion to the four decades-long mystery, mostly because it renders comparisons to the The Beatles and Decca Records legend rather redundant. Willie Todd didn't sack Alex Ferguson because he couldn't see the genius in him. He sacked him because he knew he was off to Aberdeen anyway and wanted to stick his dagger in first.

Six weeks later, Alex would turn up for his first training session at Aberdeen in mid-July of 1978 and, standing in the middle of a square dressing-room, told the sitting and intrigued squad he had just inherited that they were about to become the best team in Scotland. Not one of them believed him.

ALEX IN THE DRESSING-ROOM

His face was purple, his finger was pointing, and his mouth was spewing with rage. The Arsenal players could be heard celebrating in the away dressing-room, which certainly wasn't helping.

'Fuckin' disgrace,' he spat around the dressing-room. He was disgusted by his team's performance in which they were dumped out of the FA Cup by their fiercest rivals at the time right in front of the Old Trafford faithful. The scoreline was 0-2. The first goal had been unfortunate; a free kick that deflected off the side of David Beckham's head — who was stood in the wall — before flatfooting goalkeeper Fabian Barthez. But the second goal — the one that truly dumped United from the cup — could and perhaps should have been stopped. Edu, the Arsenal playmaker, was somehow allowed to turn in midfield from where he had a free run towards the edge of the United box. He would slip a through ball to Sylvain Wiltord to fire a low shot beyond Barthez to make it 0-2, ending the game as a contest.

'Fuckin' disgraceful performance,' Alex continued to spit. 'And you!' he said, pointing at his star winger. 'You let your teammates down!'

Beckham was shocked that he was the one being singled out.

He hadn't had a great game, certainly by his standards, but nobody wearing red that day could hold their head high.

'I couldn't have done anything about that second goal. He was away from me before he turned.'

'You're a fuckin' disgrace.' Alex's purple face was glowing, his finger still pointing, his mouth still spitting. 'You let your teammates down. You let all those fans down. You've let me down.'

'There's no way that was my fucking fault. He was away from me. I couldn't have caught him.'

Alex took a step towards a row of boots lined up in the middle of the dressing-room. He was about ten feet from Beckham who was sat on the bench answering back—still arguing that there was nothing he could have done to prevent that second goal.

As Alex began to roar back he let fly with his foot, and a number of witnesses inside the dressing-room that day agree that the boot he kicked seemed to swivel in slow motion, making a swoosh-swoosh sound, before it slapped the right-winger an inch above his left eye. The slap was loud. Then there was a split second of silence… before Beckham rose to his feet and strode towards his manager for a physical confrontation, with blood streaming towards his eye. Six United players got up, too—to bear hug their teammate in an attempt to hold him back from the Govanman.

'Sit t'fuck down,' Alex snarled at him. 'You've let everybody here down.'

Alex remained bullish, his face still purple, his finger still pointing and his mouth still spitting as he continued to lecture his players. But in the same moment that physio Rob Swire was trying to stem the bleeding of Beckham's brow, Alex was feeling pretty terrible about what had just happened.

'If I'da tried that kick a hundred times, it'd never have hit him,' he recalled years later. 'The boots were just lyin' there and I just swiped at one… honestly, if I'd have meant to hit him, I couldnae have.'

It wasn't the first time a player had stood up to confront Alex during one of his dressing-room rollockings, and it wasn't the first time players had to intervene by holding a teammate back from gunning for the Govanman. But this incident, which took place on the fifteenth of February, 2003, was the first time such a confrontation had happened in quite some time.

'I'd mellowed, aye,' Alex admits of his dressing-room behaviour. 'In my later years I definitely mellowed, no doubt aboot that. I had tae. Football changed. Players changed. So I had tae change.'

Beckham wouldn't agree that his manager had mellowed by the turn of the century. The tiny scar the megastar still has today, on the arch of his left eyebrow, would be a forever a reminder of his final season as a Manchester United player (which you can read all about in a later chapter).

Despite the Beckham incident — which made headlines on the front pages of every national newspaper — Alex isn't lying about his dressing-room evolution by suggesting he mellowed over time. The dressing-room atmosphere at Manchester United by the turn of the century was in stark contrast to the dressing-rooms he took charge of at the beginning of this managerial career, especially in the seventies and eighties. There is evidence through anecdotes from players who played under the Govanman over the years that suggest he underwent three eras of different dressing-room behaviour. The seventies and eighties —when he managed players not too dissimilar to himself who he felt he could rollock in order to motivate. The nineties—where money was being introduced into the game and Alex had to curtail his 'hairdryer' treatment as he began to manage more sensitive men. And then from the turn of the century until his retirement in 2013—where his dressing-rooms were mostly filled with continental players, men who grew up under different circumstances and in different cultures whom he realised the hairdryer could never work on.

It was Mark Hughes who coined the phrase 'hairdryer' to describe Alex's furious dressing-room rollockings. Alex would, over the years, downplay the metaphor. But it is Hughes who is closer to the truth. In Alex's earliest days of management, at East Stirling, at St Mirren, at Aberdeen and for the first five years, at least, at Manchester United, the Govanman was akin to a bull in a china shop inside his dressing-rooms. 'China shop' is another accurate metaphor to use, as Alex very often took his frustrations out on the teacups that could, in those early days, be found on tables in the middle of a dressing-room. The smashing and shattering and crashing and clattering of china was often the background score to an Alex Ferguson full-time rant, no matter how much he has tried to downplay his bullying behaviour.

'There is a lot of myth about this hairdryer nonsense,' Alex once said. 'It happened mabee half a dozen times in twenty-seven years at Manchester United, and the players will tell you that.'

Beckham will tell you different. So too will Giggs who was a member of Alex's dressing-rooms from 1990, until 2013—all the way through two of those dressing-room evolutions. Giggs thinks he has seen it all. But he hasn't, really. The Alex Ferguson dressing-room behaviour that preceded the Welshman's presence was a different animal entirely. Giggs may have been in the dressing-room when cups of tea were being swiped off the table by his manager. But he wasn't in those Scottish dressing-rooms through the seventies and eighties where Alex would crunch his shoes across the broken china before stooping down to go nose-to-nose with players and yelling at them from the back of his throat. He would almost goad them on, as if he was inviting them for a fist fight.

In a 2012 interview with Claire Balding for the BBC, Alex would brush upon his evolution in the dressing-room. He would tell the broadcaster: 'I've definitely mellowed... no doubt aboot that. From ma early days of dealin' with British-born players to dealin' with the players of today who come from many different cultures… They are more fragile today, no doubt aboot that.'

Alex changed his man-management as the men he managed changed. But in each way he evolved his dressing-room approach, the bottom line was always the same. Every way he acted and every word he spoke inside the confines of the dressing-room all centred around control. Alex *had* to have control of his dressing-room. There simply was no other way. His belief was that as soon as a manager cedes control of his dressing-room, he is dust. And while Roy Keane has scoffed at Alex in the years following his controversial exit from Manchester United (which you can read about in detail later), the Govanman is always quick to point out that there is a distinct difference between control and power.

Keane has said in the past: 'Everything is about control with him. He strives for it.'

But Alex makes no apology for seeking control. A football team is made up of many variables; sometimes up to thirty players and five first-team coaches. If one man doesn't have complete control, then a team simply can't function as one unit.

Alex would write in *Leading*: "A leader who seeks control is very different from one who craves power. There's a big difference between control and power. The leader of any group usually has considerable power, but it's something that can easily be abused. One of the side-effects of the abuse of power is when someone leads by fear of intimidation. As time went by I learned to control my temper. Some of this was just the passage of the years. But, more importantly, I realised that a display of temper is more effective if used sparingly. I just don't believe that you can get the most out of people if they are perpetually afraid of you."

Alex never believed the likes of Willie Miller, Alex McLeish, Gordon Strachan, Kevin Moran and Steve Bruce — the types of players through the years that he would scold face-to-face — were ever afraid of him. Each of those named could have probably taken him out, save for wee Strachan. But they needed screaming at because that is how Alex felt he could control their performance levels. In the nineties, players such as Denis Irwin, Paul Scholes, Eric Cantona or Andy Cole couldn't be handled in the same manner. A face-to-face rollicking simply wouldn't get the best out of those personalities. Then, by the time his dressing-room was filled with players such as Cristiano Ronaldo, Nani, Anderson or even reserved British stars such as Owen Hargreaves and Michael Carrick, the hairdryer well and truly had to be hung up.

Alex would justify his evolution in terms of dressing-room approach by writing: "The press made it appear as if I was in perpetual bad temper. If you look at my teams, it is evident that they enjoyed playing and they tended to express themselves in an uninhibited fashion. People do not do that if they are quaking in their boots or if their boss has made them afraid of their own shadows. If that had been the case at United, people would have seen a team that concentrated on avoiding defeat rather than winning."

It's difficult to argue against his dressing-room approaches no matter the era of his managerial career given that he was consistently successful. But it's worthwhile delving into a couple of the rollockings through the years, nonetheless.

There is one such occasion when his Aberdeen players were all smiles and high-fives as they re-entered the dressing-room following a neat 1-0 win over Partick Thistle at Pittodrie. They had no idea of the eruption that was forthcoming. Alex had been made aware, just before the match, that a number of his players had been spotted by one of his spies in a pub called the Waterloo two nights prior to the game. And they were certainly drinking more than the one beer a week their manager told them they could have.

He didn't say anything pre-match, for fear of dropping points, and following the full-time whistle, the players were expecting a congratulatory after-match review when they got back to the dressing-room. Instead, their manager let fly.

'Fuckin' unprofessional wee bastards,' he yelled.

The players didn't know what was going on.

He berated them, pointing at them one by one and insisting they were not professional enough to play for Aberdeen. When he got back to the centre of the dressing-room, he picked up a large glass bottle of Lucozade and threw it over the players' heads. Nobody ducked. Nobody moved. Alex's roars had shocked them stiff. Instead, some of them sat there as sticky orange fizz and shards of glass dropped to the shoulders of their jerseys and on to their hair.

'You wee fuckers go near the Waterloo one more time and yer oot o' this club!'

The rant had been filled with such fury that when Alex left the dressing-room to calm himself down, the players all looked at each other as if to say, 'What the fuck was that all about?'

They were so confused that skipper Jackie Copland had to call to Alex's office about half an hour later before the players left for home to find out exactly what had riled him so much.

Copland would return to the dressing-room with a letter from Alex ten minutes later, detailing that if any player was caught in the Waterloo again they would be turfed out of the club. All players were under orders from their manager to sign it. All of them did.

In the nineties, dressing-room outbursts were less common, but they still may have involved a drinks bottle in some guise as Ryan Giggs can attest.

'Honestly, sometimes, y'know, he would have fights with the players, or nearly have fights with them. He would be screaming at you. I remember against Juventus (Giggs is referring to the 1-0 defeat United suffered in Turin in 1996), I spent a whole half dribbling and yeah, Conte was taking it off me. At half-time, the manager just went for me straight away. "Stop dribbling in midfield!" This argument just started up and I had these blackcurrant drinks that we used to take at half-time and I just threw it at his feet.'

The blackcurrant would spray Alex's shoes and he would erupt at the winger. His face was as purple as the stain left on the dressing-room floor. Giggs wouldn't return for the second half.

In the noughties, no dressing-room anecdote can top the one time he swiped his foot at a row of boots in the middle of the Old Trafford dressing-room before one arrowed its way towards David Beckham's left eyebrow. But the most honest portrait of Alex in the dressing-room is far removed from the control-freak who was capable of turning purple while rollicking players after matches, which in fairness to him was a rare occurrence given that his teams — wherever he managed — had a habit of winning. Most of the time he spent inside a dressing-room was pre-match, not post-match or at half-time. And in pre-match, Alex had to be steady. He had to be confident. And he had to be concise. It was imperative he got his message across. Communication was key. And it was for these minutes of his entire working week that Alex felt he truly earned his salary.

He would often lie in bed at night in the mid-point between consciousness and unconsciousness thinking about themes. He always felt his team talks should have a specific message, rather than come across as a random lecture.

'I used to lie in bed thinking about themes where I could address the players that would make an impact on them,' he told his son Jason while making the documentary *Never Give In*. 'I would talk about miners, shipyard workers, welders, toolmakers. You know, people who've come from poor backgrounds. I used to ask them: "What did your grandfather do? What did your father do?" I have to get the feeling inside them that what their grandfathers worked for, their grandmothers, is part of them.'

Alex used his great man-management skills (which you can read all about in a later chapter) of drilling into his players' backgrounds to help motivate them on an on-going basis. Delving right into a player's gut by being personable was always a key ingredient in his team talks.

'I remember,' Patrice Evra recalls, 'the 2008 Champions League Final like it was yesterday... being on the pitch, yes. But mostly I remember the team talk. The boss came in, and looked at us all, "I have already won," he said. We all looked, thinking... what?'

Alex actually pointed at Evra first.

'Take Patrice here,' he said. 'Patrice grew up on the outskirts of Paris with twenty-three brothers and sisters. Imagine the stresses and strains his mother had to make to put food on the table each day for all of them? Just so they could survive, and have some sort of life for themselves. And look at where you are now, Patrice.'

Alex then turned to Wayne Rooney.

'Waz grew up in the poorest of all neighbourhoods in Liverpool where working class people have to work big hours for small wages. It was street living for Waz and his family. Street living. Your grandfather had to fight to survive and I know your parents had to fight to survive. They had to fight to even pay for your football boots when you were young. And look at where you are now, son.'

Park Ji-sung was sitting next to Rooney.

'And Ji, you grew up just outside Seoul where money was so tight that you didn't know if you could afford pencils to go to school. You told me that once. No money to buy a pencil. Imagine that? And look where you are now, Ji.'

Alex would go around the dressing-room, painting a picture for each player's working-class, and sometimes even less than that, upbringing. Then he would revert back to the present day and say, 'and look at where you are now. Look at this room. Men from all corners of the world coming together to achieve what you have achieved. Look at where you've come from. And look at where you are today. Minutes from playing in a Champions League Final. I know I've already won. Bringing you all together and having you here with me… I've already won. I know I've won. Now it's time for you to win. Win for your grandparents who fought and worked so hard to raise your parents. Win for your parents who fought and worked so hard to raise you. And look at what they raised? A warrior. A champion. Go out there and be a champion. Not for me. I've already won, because I manage you. I've brought you all together. That's my victory. But you can be a champion for everybody who came before you. For everybody who helped you reach this moment of your life.'

'I had hairs on the back of my neck,' recalls Evra. 'We all did. We all got goosebumps. Then we went out and won the Champions League.'

Alex also tugged at the heartstrings of his players in the same competition's showpiece in 1999. At half-time, United found themselves a goal down and certainly looking second best in the contest after a gruelling schedule in which they'd just claimed the Premier League on the last day of the season eleven days prior and the FA Cup at Wembley just four days before.

'This is the European Cup Final,' he said at half-time. 'The European Cup! We all watched European Cup Finals when we were kids. Right now there are kids at home watching this one. It'll be history for them soon; history they can talk aboot forever. Where is your name going to be mentioned in their history, huh? Look,' he said, 'The European Cup is going to be presented tonight. What you all gonnae do? Walk by it, just look at it? Y'knoo if you don't win this game, then you don't get to touch that trophy, don't you? Whatcha gonna do? Just walk by the European Cup knowing you cannae touch it? Imagine walking by the European Cup and not being able to touch it? Imagine?'

United would lift the cup by scoring two injury-time goals.

Of course, the team talks centred around United's two European Cup wins under the Govanman have been tales told by players due to the historic value of them. But in truth, dressing-room shenanigans and teamtalks are rarely spoken about in football. There is an unwritten rule in the professional game that no matter what level you play at, be it in the Premier League or in non-league, what goes on in the dressing-room stays in that dressing-room. Players, staff and managers, to their credit throughout the game, stay loyal to that rule. But there are a small number of anecdotes of Alex's motivational team talks that have squeezed through the barriers of the rule, given their context.

One day, ahead of a Premier League game against Arsenal, twenty-five players were sat in an arc on pentathlon bikes around the mass training hall at Carrington when the front door opened and in walked twenty-nine strange faces.

'Y'knoo who these men are?' Alex asked his players.

The players squinted, thinking one or two faces might be familiar, but not quite placing them.

'These guys spent two months trapped underground in a Chilean mine.'

Some players gasped. All of them stopped pedalling.

'Imagine that. Imagine having to hold on to every pocket of air to continue living. Imagine not knowing how much air there is left for you to breathe. Theirs is a story of bravery, courage, and teamwork. It is a story of triumph over adversity. Imagine what they've bin through. Can you put yourself in their position? Two months. Trapped. Now…' he said, turning to his players, 'they've spent two months trapped in a cave. All I'm asking you to do is beat fucking Arsenal over ninety minutes tomorrow.'

The following day, ahead of the big clash, Alex barely spoke up in the dressing-room. When he did, just ten minutes before the players left for the pitch, he simply said. 'I gave ye yer team talk yesterday. If that didn't motivate you, you don't deserve to be here.'

And that was that. United won the tight and fiery clash 1-0.

It had been Bobby Charlton who had extended the invitation to the Chilean miners to attend the Arsenal game. Alex went one further by inviting them to the training ground the day before, just so he could deliver a team talk he had thought about while in the mid-point between consciousness and unconsciousness one night.

Alex often liked to use the fans inside Old Trafford for motivational purposes, too. He would discuss their working week, telling players that local fans were likely to have put a tough fifty hours of labour in this week just so they could afford their ticket into this ground to watch them play.

'Now you fuckin' go and make their week worth it, y'hear me?' he often said.

When United were pipped to the league title in 2012, thanks to Manchester City's outrageous victory in the dying seconds of the title race, the Sunderland fans who United had just played in front of, opted to mock the United players.

'You see them,' Alex said, pointing back out to the stadium once United were back in the confines of their dressing-room. 'Let's remember their cheery fuckin' faces all next season when we fuckin' whitewash this league.'

United would win the next title, in Alex's last season, by a landslide, with the Govanman often reminding his players of the Sunderland fan celebrations as the campaign unfolded.

When United were trashed 4-1 by Liverpool in Old Trafford in 2009, a game in which Steven Gerard famously scored and then kissed the camera, the home fans cheered the losers off by shouting 'United, United, United.' Some of the players couldn't believe the amount of support they were receiving given their awful performance on the day. Alex laid into his players for their abject display, then pointed out to the fans who were still chanting. 'Ye hear them? Ye hear them singing for us right now? We have tae win the league for them. We *need* to win this league for them.'

United would pick themselves up from that embarrassing defeat to win the league title within the next five weeks. Each of the players kissed the Premier League trophy into the same touchline camera lens Gerard had puckered up to the month prior.

The Chilean miners story is somewhat apt given that Alex had often referenced miners in his team talks down the years, even as far back as his days as East Stirlingshire manager.

'I'd talk about shipyard workers, tool makers, steelworkers, miners all the time; reminding the players where they came from, or how the men who came to watch them play often had a hard week's work just to afford their ticket; that their performance in these next ninety minutes was all these people had to look forward to all week. Aye, I often used the working class to get many points across. Every player could relate in some way. They had a mother or father or grandparents who worked in these places... they knew... they always knew. And it touched them.'

Preaching about the working class was a go-to theme for a lot of Alex's team talks. So too, was his anecdote about geese.

'I liked to change up ma team talks and really think about them as much as possible, but I'm sure there are players like Giggs or Scholes who musta heard me talking about geese a dozen times.'

Alex is referring to the fact that this breed of bird flew up to five thousand miles in two V-shaped formations with the second group in the slipstream of the first. When one bird gets tired, two come down to look after him until he recovers, then they all catch up and the cycle continues until they eventually reach their destination.

'Now, these geese are flying thousands of miles just to catch up with the sun. All I'm asking you to do is play ninety minutes of fuckin' football as a team.'

Bizarrely, Alex would use that same team talk when invited to be an unofficial coach for the European Team at the 2014 Ryder Cup (which you can read about in a later chapter). The anecdote impressed the European players so much that they often reminded each other of geese before teeing up each morning as the competition played out. Upon lifting the Ryder Cup, having bettered the Americans by five clear points, two V-shaped formations of geese would fly over the golfer's heads. They couldn't believe the serendipity of it all.

There are occasions when Alex didn't feel need to reel off an anecdote about the working class or geese. Sometimes he felt the less said, the bigger the impact.

When Manchester United found themselves 3-0 down to Tottenham Hotspur by half-time at White Hart Lane in 2001, Alex let the players sit in the dressing-room wallowing in silence. The only noises that could be heard were the slurping and sipping of their drinks. The boss didn't say a word. Not until the bell rang to signal they must return to the pitch…

'Next goal wins this game,' he said.

United would score the next goal through Andy Cole before going on to claim a 3-5 victory.

'I listened to his team talks for twenty years,' Gary Neville recalls. 'There wasn't one single team talk he delivered where he didn't talk about the need to get up every single day and make it a choice about whether you worked hard or not. As football players, we should be proud to say we work as hard as we possibly can for ourselves, our families and for each other. People always ask how did we keep that up and win and win and win again, and it was because of that: we had it ingrained in us by the manager that it was our duty to come in and work as hard as we possibly could.'

Of course, the sanctuary of the dressing-room wasn't built solely for pre-match motivational team talks, nor post-match rollockings. Most of the talk inside the confines of the dressing-room was to ratify the training sessions that had led up to this moment: the final debrief before the motivational team talks about geese, or miners, or grandparents, had even begun.

Two days before any game, Alex and his coaches would sit the players in a TV room where they would watch video analysis of their opponents. This is when Alex would show himself to be the pragmatic tactician he was. He would, for example, show footage of Tottenham full-back Kyle Walker and detail to Ryan

Giggs exactly what Walker's weaknesses were, detailing how he could best the defender over the ninety minutes. The videos would be short and concise because the Govanman felt that players bored if they watched too much footage.

In these analysis meetings, Alex admitted: 'I would always dwell on our opponents' weaknesses—partly to exploit them and partly to impart in my players a sense of what was possible.'

The following days on the training ground, the first team would work on how best to exploit their opponents' weakness by taking part in shadow matches. In the dressing-room on the day of the game itself, Alex would ratify to the players all they had learned over the past 48 hours and would constantly use the line, 'This is how we beat this lot.' Then he would let his players know who was in the starting eleven. In truth, those who weren't picked had already been told, and those who were starting already had a strong inkling they were in the team because they hadn't been called to the manager's office to be told the reason they weren't playing.

Inside the dressing-room Alex normally stood beside a huge white board with magnetic markings that he would set out in the shape of the opposition's formation before reaffirming to his players one last time what was expected of them in both their offensive and defensive shape. He also liked to pose questions to his players about these formations, just to open a line of dialogue which would, in turn, keep the players' minds whirring. This was a trick he had adopted from Jock Stein. Stein often engaged in tactical conversations with his team ahead of games, just to ensure they were all switched on. If people are involved in the conversation, rather than just taking the position of a listener, they engage at a much higher level. It's interesting to note that a lot of players who played under Stein went on to have careers in football management. Same with Alex.

"It's important to maintain eye-contact and to look directly at the players because it adds intensity to the delivery of the message," Alex would write about his pre-match team briefings.

"There are some managers who will enter a dressing-room with a pack of notes. When they talk to players, they will use their notes as props. I cannot imagine how that is an effective way to communicate."

The delivery of the pre-match team talk had to be clear and it had to be concise. That way, if a player didn't perform as instructed, then the sword fell on him. It meant everybody knew where they stood. That level of clarity was paramount.

A line often repeated by Alex ahead of games was a very simple message, but one that would prove hugely effective over the years.

'All you gotta do is what I've bin telling you tae do. If you all do your individual jobs, we'll win!'

That was the consistent message he delivered to his players just before they headed to the pitch—and armed with a team talk that touched them, whether it be about their grandfather, their mother, the working class or geese, Alex was confident that they would take to the field to give their individual job all they could muster.

If he felt a player wasn't giving his individual job his all, then out came the hairdryer.

1978-1986

ALEX HUNG UP THE PHONE — HIS SMILE WIDE, HIS FACE RED WITH excitement — and decided there and then that the next thing he must do is call to Aberdeen chairman Dick Donald's office. He'd mostly had a good relationship with Donald and simply felt obliged to let him know that he was now leaving, in case the story leaked before he got the opportunity to tell him himself in person. After eight years as Aberdeen manager, toppling the Old Firm to win the League Title three times, winning the Scottish FA Cup four times, the Scottish League Cup, the European Cup Winners Cup and the European Super Cup, a major club in England had called. He'd had offers before, but not from a club of this magnitude. He couldn't turn them down. This was too great an opportunity for the ambitious Govanman—returning one of most decorated clubs to the perch of English football was the ideal football legacy for him to chase.

He knocked on Donald's door, then entered and found within seconds that his excitable body language and red face had said enough already.

'You've had an offer, haven'tchu?' Donald said.

'Aye, I have.'

'Too big to turn down?'

'Aye, t'is.'

'You prolly don't need to tell me which club it is… but go'un… I guess I will need ta knoo.'

'Arsenal,' Alex said.

'Arsenal?' Donald replied. 'Nooo.'

'Huh?'

'I'm no' lettin' y'go there.'

When Alex entered the Aberdeen dressing-room for the very first time, he didn't only tell the players that they were going to be the best team in Scotland, he would inform them, individually, that it was going to happen with, or without their input.

'I'm not gonnae change,' he said, spinning around the centre of the dressing-room with his finger pointing, 'you're gonnae change.'

Then he spelt out to them exactly how and why they were going to change. He would give the exact same speech to the Manchester United dressing-room some eight years later after Donald would talk him out of accepting the Arsenal job offer.

Firstly, the drinking culture *had* to go. That was inarguable. The reality of professional footballers being part-time drinkers was done as far as Alex was concerned. The pub scene had always fit like a glove within the routine of a professional footballer's life, which had been the case for just over a century, ever since the game was first invented. But Alex was having none of it. Not anymore. If Aberdeen were to topple Glasgow giants Rangers and Celtic to reach the pinnacle of Scottish football, then they would have to better them through hard graft, discipline and professionalism. He advised the Aberdeen players that they could drink as much as he drank when he was a player—one beer per week. That was their allowance. He would further tell them that he and his coaches had been to visit every landlord of every pub in Aberdeen.

'Any players o' mine enter any of those pubs, and I'll knoo aboot it,' Alex barked. He wasn't joking either. Though he may have been exaggerating. They didn't have spies in *every* pub in Aberdeen, but they weren't far off meeting that quota.

The Aberdeen players had heard tales of Alex's strict approach from their counterparts at St Mirren prior to the Govanman's arrival, so free-flowing are the gossip corridors of the professional game. But they never realised just how straight and stern he was until he was stood in front of them on that very first day. His eyes were bulging when he informed the players their drinking days were over, and his face was glowing with red blood cells. Alex was only thirty-seven at the time, but management had aged him beyond his years already, not just in terms of maturity, but in appearances, too. Whereas he was handsome and fresh-faced as a twenty-something year old footballer, by the time he had evolved into a thirty-something year old manager, it seemed as if he had aged two decades, not just the one.

Most players who played under Alex through the years will tell you he had a Jekyll and Hyde personality; that he could be shouting and screaming in the morning, and by the afternoon be cracking jokes or singing Neil Sedaka songs with his arm around them. But none of the first Aberdeen team that he inherited would tell you that. Because they only ever got to meet Jekyll. Hyde was... well, Hyde was hidden. For the first year at Aberdeen, Alex was a fireball—determined to show these household names just who was boss.

"I knew I had to develop the players' minds," Alex would write in *My Autobiography*. "The dominance established by the Glasgow giants (Celtic and Rangers), virtually since the beginning of professional football in Scotland, infects the mentality of the other clubs with resignation, an almost acceptance of their role as the supporting cast. But passivity of that kind is alien to me."

The squad Alex first inherited at Aberdeen included the likes of Gordon Strachan, Jim Leighton, Willie Miller, Joe Harper and Steve Archibald. Their long-held status as great footballers meant that managing them proved a different beast for Alex. But it was a beast he had long been anticipating handling for he had, years previous, decided how he would approach big players when the opportunity would inevitably arise.

The likes of the most experienced pros, such as Miller, Harper and Archibald didn't know how to take Alex's obsession with discipline. Archibald, who was tasked with playing in Alex's favourite position — the striker with the puffed-out chest — would prove to be a major headache for the manager. Once, having scored a hat-trick and then gone home with the match ball, a practice not allowed back then, (players were just allowed to walk off the pitch with the ball under the arm as a reward for a hat-trick before handing it back to the club) Alex summoned the striker to his office the following morning.

'Where's that fickin' ball?' Alex screamed at his star striker—who had single-handily won him and his team all three points the day prior.

Later that afternoon, Alex would be sitting having a cup of tea with Pat Stanton — the devoted and much-loved Aberdeen coach — when they both heard a wallop. A ball ricocheted above their heads, slapping from wall to wall of the pokey meeting room they were sat inside, smashing a fluorescent lamp in the process before bouncing to a stop next to Alex's feet.

'There's ya fickin' ball,' Archibald snarled.

He'd be fined two weeks wages. A light punishment from the Alex Ferguson disciplinary handbook, but likely light because Archibald was a vital member of the team. No one else in that squad quite had the attributes to play in such a key position.

Under Alex's hard-line approach, the Aberdeen squad cut down their socialising, though they didn't do so without a huge amount of sulking. Teaching old dogs new tricks, Alex felt, was one hell of a tough battle to win. Which is why he always held a penchant for managing players from the time they were teenagers, just so he could evolve them as both a footballer and as a personality in the ways he saw most fitting.

Aberdeen would have an average start to Alex's first season in charge—where they found themselves in the average position Aberdeen usually found themselves in: fourth, though they were to have long runs in both cup competitions.

However, aside from the exhaustion of having to play army

sergeant at the training ground every day, Alex's mental health was being stretched at this stage of his life for two other reasons. Firstly, he had decided to take St Mirren to a tribunal for unfair dismissal, just out of spite and to get one back on Willie Todd. But as the process was being dragged through the mud, with details being constantly leaked to the press, so too was Alex's reputation. Todd had said during the tribunal process that Alex's fining system in the dressing-room was illegitimate and had never been agreed upon by the club. On top of that, Todd brought a witness who testified Alex had sworn at a female member of staff. Alex was fuming that his ex-chairman was washing such dirty linen in public, though he only had himself to blame. There was no need for him to bring such a case against St Mirren. Certainly not when he had already agreed to move to Aberdeen before he was even fired. The disappointment of the tribunal, however — which deeply affected Alex — didn't come close to the heartbreak he was feeling as the tribunal reached a climax due to the fact that his father was slipping away from him. Alex Snr's insides were suffering from the dankness of his decades-long hard labour. As a mammoth football fan, he had dreamed about seeing one of his sons reach the pinnacle of the game. And although Alex went closest as a player with Rangers, Alex Snr never got to live out that dream. The season after he would pass away from stomach cancer, Alex would fly to the top of the game, by winning the first of his sixteen top league titles both north and south of the border.

'It's just one o' those things, Alex,' his dad said to him about his illness before he left his hospital ward one Friday evening. They would be the last words his father would ever say to him.

The month after Alex Snr's death, Aberdeen would lose the Scottish League Cup Final, and then get dumped out of the Scottish Cup semi-final before their league campaign stuttered to completion with Aberdeen finishing where they normally finished. Fourth. The declaration Alex made to his players on his first day in the job — that Aberdeen were going to be the best team in Scotland under his guidance — seemed rather ill-conceived and pretentious by the end of his first campaign. Some members of the Dons' dressing-room were openly discussing how long he would stick around, given the club had a reputation for chopping and changing managers readily. They weren't to know what Alex had been planning for season two, however.

What Alex thought of his first campaign — which proved long and brutal for him, but a learning curve of great magnitude none-theless — was that although he had inherited the best players he had managed in his career thus far, there were very few players who complemented each other in that side, particularly in midfield. Alex's midfield four during his first season read well on paper: Gordon Strachan, Dominic Sullivan, John McMaster and Drew Jarvie. But they were all too technical in order for Alex's tactical system to work fluidly. They all needed the ball at their feet in order to shine on a football pitch. Alex needed a different dynamic in the centre, a player who might have less technical ability but who would prove all of his value when his team were not in possession.

Aside from the recruitment of nineteen-year-old Neale Cooper— whom Alex felt was a total disciplinarian and in turn changed the whole dynamic of his midfield, the Govanman had already decided he was going to play his old hand again. He wanted to draft young-sters in to his first team set-up who could either light a fire under the arses of the seasoned pros, or, even better Alex thought, steal posi-tions in the starting XI from them.

In the summer of 1979, Alex recruited promising twenty-one year old striker Mark McGhee from Newcastle United and then drafted in teenagers such as Ian Angus, Doug Bell, Ian Porteous, Steve Cowan and Eric Black to add to the capture of Cooper. Five of those young-sters would go on to be integral players in the Aberdeen team that would send shockwaves through European football four years later.

Heading into season two with Aberdeen, Alex had the mix of squad he had always strived to create as a manager. Experienced pros being pushed for their starting berths by hungry teens who were being manufactured in the Alex Ferguson mould.

'Very scary,' is how Cooper would flippantly describe his memories of Alex during this era. 'He had a huge fear factor.'

'He had this very aggressive Govan manner and he intimidated the kids quite a lot,' Alex McLeish would reveal. 'On occasion he would produce this baseball bat to torment the kids, but it was all done in a light-hearted manner.'

It was a manner that worked. Heading into the 1979/80 season, Alex held the attention of his squad and informed them that if they applied themselves to meet his vision, they could conceivably become champions of Scotland that year. Some players had already seen the promise Alex had been building, but most of them raised their eyebrows at such an unattainable prediction. No team outside of Glasgow's big two had been crowned Scottish champions since Kilmarnock had won a very strange title back in 1965.

Alex sat his players around the training dressing-room the day before the season was about to start and attempted to galvanise them by pointing out predictions certain journalists had made in the newspapers.

'Look at this,' he would say, holding up a newspaper, 'more fuckin' predictions for Celtic to win the league. Look at this one,' he said grabbing another tabloid. 'Fuckin' Rangers this guy thinks will win it this year.' He picked up all the newspapers he had brought to the dressing room that day, then threw them to the floor. 'Not one journalist thinks we can win the title. Nobody outside of this room thinks we can win the title. So we're gonnae show 'em.'

Gordon Strachan would later say, 'He always did it. He would let us know everybody hated us. Especially the press. He would tell us, "The press don't even wannae come to Aberdeen to watch us play, they'd rather stay in Glasgow." And we bought it. We all fell for it. We were like eleven Tasmanian Devils running around the pitch for him.'

They were eleven Tasmanian Devils that would go on to achieve what Alex had predicted pre-season—they would shock Scottish football by pipping Celtic to the title on the last day of the season by one single point. What's most notable when looking through the results of that campaign is that Aberdeen had to visit Celtic Park twice. They won both times, using Alex's pragmatism disguised as attractive, fast-paced football in order to do so.

When the final whistle blew in the final game of that season, Alex ran on to the Pittodrie pitch in his club suit with his arms flailing in the air and then jumped into the arms of goalkeeper Bobby Clark, wrapping his legs around his waist and screeching celebratory profanities into his ear.

The whole squad, manager and coaches included, stripped in the dressing room and got into the large square bath where they would pop open a dozen bottles of champagne and swig them back in celebration. It had been a long time since players of Aberdeen had tasted champagne. Though they had to acquire a palate for it— plenty more bottles of the fizz were coming their way.

Over the next six seasons, Aberdeen would come out on top of the Glasgow giants two more times to claim two more league titles. They would also win four Scottish Cups in the space of five years—a stunning feat when its realised Aberdeen had only ever won the Scottish Cup twice in their entire history prior to Alex taking the reins.

'The whole city was buzzing,' Cathy would, unusually for her, tell a journalist back then. She preferred to stay out of the limelight and had no interest in even going to see a game, let alone commenting on one. But she did take the time to talk about the effect the team was having on the city in which she now lived. Her description was accurate. Aberdeen had never tasted success like this before. It has never tasted success like it since. It likely never will again.

The pinnacle of Aberdeen's football history occurred outside of the city itself, though it can be argued most Aberdonians were actually in Gothenburg on the night they would cause the footballing world to sit up and take notice.

'I'm pretty sure there was nobody in Aberdeen that night. Every man and his dog were saving up to go to Gothenburg,' Cooper would recall.

'I don't think any woman or family is getting a holiday this year,'

Cathy would tell the journalist who doorstepped her. 'Every man is saving for Gothenburg. I would hear them in the shops — the women — "I'm getting no holiday this year cos he's goin' tae the match."' In fact it was reported at the time that in the three days prior to the 1983 European Cup Winners Cup Final, Aberdeen Airport's Duty Free sold more alcohol than they normally do over the course of an entire month.

However, despite the undying support and the excitement Alex had brought to the city of Aberdeen, not even the most positive of Dons supporters could have felt there was further excitement to come. Getting Aberdeen to the European Cup Winners Cup Final was a victory in itself. It's a pity they were facing the might of Real Madrid in the final, supporters thought, otherwise they probably could've claimed the trophy. Even though Alex had masterminded a shock victory over German giants Bayern Munich in the quarter-finals of the Cup Winners Cup, there was still little reason for anything other than blind optimism to think they would see off Real in that final. But they did. In fact they battered them, even if it took 120 minutes for the battering to be confirmed.

Alex used the fact that not only were the Scottish newspapers writing off their chances but the entirety of Europe was too as a mental tool to implant within his players' heads in the build-up. 'Nobody thinks we can win this... except for every one of us,' he told them. Being underdogs played right into his hands. He approached Alfredo Di Stefano — once Alex's idol as a teenager, now the glorified manager of Real Madrid — at the Argentine's pre-match press conference to present him with an expensive bottle of the finest of fine Scottish whiskies.

'That was actually Jock's idea,' Alex would years later reveal. The Govanman had actually invited Jock Stein (who was by then the Scotland national team manager) to be a guest of his for the final. 'Jock gave me plenty of good advice on that trip without ever pushing himself too far forward. "Make him (Di Stefano) feel important, as if you are thrilled just to be in the final with him".'

The most accurate turn of phrase, if not the most pleasant, to describe the weather the night of that memorable final is that it pissed out of the heavens. For all 120 minutes.

Aberdeen simply played Real Madrid off the park, and went in front as early as the seventh minute through Eric Black. It may have been the early concession, or maybe it was the rain, perhaps it was the fiery atmosphere being created by half of the population of Aberdeen behind one of the goals, or maybe it was because Alex Ferguson totally set up to stem the threat of Real Madrid's best players. Maybe all of those elements combined. But Real Madrid heads dropped as the game went on, despite scoring a penalty to equalise on the quarter-hour mark, as Aberdeen brought the game practically into their penalty box. They hounded the Madrid players, ran rings around them. Yet a mix of the Ullevi Stadium crossbar, cat-like skills from goalkeeper Augustin and, in particular, the tackling and blocking of centre-back Uli Stielike (the only outfield Real Madrid player to perform anywhere near his usual standard that night) ensured Aberdeen didn't capitalised on their dominance. At ninety minutes, the game somehow ended 1-1, with a half-an-hour of extra time to be played. Aberdeen could've scored at least four over the next thirty-minutes, but John Hewitt's diving header, which arrived via a stereotypical Alex Ferguson-style counter attack, was the only goal they'd get. It would be enough, however. Aberdeen had shocked Europe. They were the European Cup Winner's Cup champions.

The job offers would come flooding in from south of the border straight after that famous victory, but Alex's head wouldn't be turned, not until Arsenal would call him up some three years later. In fact, in the immediate aftermath of the European Cup Winners Cup win, Rangers would call him up, telling him the manager's job was his if he wanted it. He didn't want it.

Before the Arsenal call would come in, Alex had two more league titles to win at Aberdeen (they'd win back-to-back titles in the two seasons immediately following the Gothenburg final, 1984 & 1985), two more Scottish Cups (1984 & 1986) and a Scottish League Cup (1986) to ensure that in the space of seven seasons at Pittodrie, Alex

Ferguson had led the parochial club to nine major trophies. To put those achievements into perspective, Aberdeen had only ever won five major trophies in their entire history until they appointed the Govanman in the summer of 1978.

As was usually the case, Alex's personal life was mirroring his professional life during this period. Having been fearful of leaving Glasgow, Cathy settled well in Aberdeenshire and each of the three boys had formed firm friendships at school. Alex, himself, had begun to form a very meaningful friendship of his own at this time. He had always adored Jock Stein, even though Stein was leading the club he was supposed to hate to monumental success. But after Celtic had shockingly sacked Stein in the same summer that Alex became boss of Aberdeen, Alex felt he could now reach out to him. They had long phone conversations, in which Alex would pick Stein's brain on two specific topics, one being tactics, the other mind-games. They would often meet up, sipping over a lemonade in a Glasgow pub.

"For any young manager seeking to further his education in football, Jock Stein was a one-man university," Alex would write in his first autobiography, *Managing My Life*.

Jock simply meant so much to him—almost like a godfather figure. Though instead of teaching him the ways of religion, he taught him the ways of football. Alex was actually at home when a friend of his rang to inform him that Jock's assistant manager at the Scottish national team, Jim McLean, had stood down from the position.

'Ye think he'll offer you the job?' Cathy asked Alex after he had given her the news.

Alex shrugged. He would spend the next forty-eight hours crossing his fingers until the phone finally rang.

'I'd like ya to be ma new assistant,' Jock said.

'Aye,' Alex replied. 'How much input can I have. Can a pick the team?'

'No. I'll pick the team. But I'm happy to listen to your input,' Jock replied.

'Fair enough,' Alex said.

The education from Jock was a big enough reason for Alex to commit to juggling his full-time role with Aberdeen to the part-time gig as the nation's assistant manager, that he didn't even ask what figures would be in his contract—highly unusual for a man who constantly obsessed about his wages.

At the time the Scottish squad read well on paper with names such as Graeme Souness, Kenny Dalglish, Alan Hansen, Graeme Sharp and Charlie Nicholas added to players Alex was already managing at Aberdeen in Willie Miller and Alex McLeish. Those names, coupled with the impressive management duo, gave the Scots a fighting chance of making the 1986 World Cup Finals that were being held in Mexico.

However, Scotland were pitted in a tough group with Spain, Wales and Iceland—and while there was only one automatic place in the World Cup Finals from that group, the runners-up would be offered a second opportunity via a play-off. Spain were expected to take the one automatic place, while the other three would vie for the play-off spot. Scotland and Wales may not have enjoyed as much of a passionate rivalry as Scotland and England did, but matches between these two British countries still proved to be intense affairs over the years. They would, of course, play each other twice in qualifying, with Wales getting the better of the Scots in Scotland, thanks to a lone Ian Rush goal. By this stage, the group had totally opened up and any four of the teams could still finish in any of the four positions.

By the time Scotland had to visit Wales, in which was the last game of the qualification process, both teams were on six points. A draw would be enough for Scotland to finish second as they had a better goal difference than Wales, but nobody wanted to call this match as there had proven to be relatively little between the two teams during the qualification process.

Mark Hughes would score a finely taken early goal to give Wales a 1-0 lead heading into the break. And when the Scotland players gathered in the dressing-room for their mid-point talking to by their manager, he was furious. Mostly with Gordon Strachan. Stein yelled at Strachan from the top of his voice for being wasteful in possession, then turned to goalkeeper Jim Leighton who seemed as if he was trying to catch hot lava and not footballs out on that pitch. Leighton would then admit to Stein in private that he had in fact forgotten his contact lenses that evening. The manager was livid. All Scotland needed to do was draw, yet they were being beaten by their Welsh rivals while their goalkeeper could barely see. Leighton received a rollocking from both manager and assistant manager. But there was no alternative. There was no goalkeeper on the bench which was very usual back then. The second half was intense, so intense that Cathy, watching on television from her own sitting-room, would comment that Alex looked so worried that she thought he might have a heart-attack. She was right in one sense, Alex was indeed worried, but not entirely about what was going on on the pitch. He was mostly concerned about the legendary manager sitting next to him, because Jock's face was overly pale and his breathing had become inconsistent.

Alex decided to have a quiet word with the team doctor, Stuart Hillis, asking him, discreetly, to keep an eye on the boss. So Hillis took his eye off the thrilling game playing out in front of him and, instead, stared at Stein. The sweat was constantly pouring from his large forehead, his skin was greying, and he was unusually quiet while he sat in the dug-out—especially so for a game of such magnitude. In fact, he stayed quiet all through the furore of Scotland winning a dubious penalty which Davie Cooper coolly slotted into the corner of the net. The game was finely poised at 1-1 and Scotland were only ten-minutes from making the play-offs of the World Cup. Those ten minutes proved to be an intense ten minutes, but as they ebbed towards their conclusion, Jock decided to get to his feet. He wouldn't be standing for long. As soon as he stood upright, his body collapsed. Alex grabbed him from one side, stopping him from falling, and Hugh Allan, the Scotland physio, grabbed him from the other. As injury time was being played out, with the game still poised, Stein was being carried down the tunnel by five medics.

Some of the Scotland players say they weren't aware their manager had gone missing from the dug-out, yet when the final whistle did eventually go, and Scotland had been confirmed as the country that would enter the World Cup play-offs, there was no celebrating. Alex didn't run on to the pitch. The players weren't jumping on each other. There was, for some strange reason, a sombreness to their 'victory'. Alex would congratulate them as they left the pitch and would then find out through medical staff when he paced down the length of the tunnel that Jock had suffered a heart-attack but was recovering well in a small medical room. Alex remembers feeling relieved by the news, and so headed back to the players to pass on the latest. But soon after, he would leave the dressing-room to get an update on Jock's condition when he heard a sniffling sound in the far corner of the tunnel. He walked towards the sound to find Graeme Souness with his hand over his face and his shoulders shaking.

'He's gone,' Souness sobbed.

An hour later, Alex would ring the Stein household from an office inside the Ninian Park stadium with the unenviable task of informing them that Jock had passed away.

'I didn't cry at the time,' Alex later recalled. 'I had to tell the dressing-room, the players, the staff. Poor Steely (Jimmy Steele— the team masseuse) was inconsolable. He had worked with Jock for years. No… I didn't cry because somebody had to remain composed. Then, the following day when I was driving from Glasgow airport back to Aberdeen, I had tae pull over in the lay-by because I knew I wasn't going tae get home before I cried. And I cried and cried. I sat there for ages crying. Then I recomposed maself, drove back home and as soon as I set foot inside ma house I saw Cathy and I just collapsed into her arms.'

In Jock's memory, Alex and the players would oversee Scotland's qualification to the World Cup by beating Australia 2-0 over two legs in the play-offs, and the Govanman would then be offered the job of taking Scotland to that World Cup in Mexico the following summer. At every turn, those few months Alex had as manager of

Scotland were largely sombre. Jock's giant shadow consumed the entire squad. They were handed a tough group in the summer show-piece, lumped in with West Germany, Uruguay and Denmark in which they would manage to accumulate only one point and finish bottom of the table before taking the long flight back to Scotland. Despite their disappointing showing on the world stage, the dream Jock dreamt in his final nights had been realised. He had led his nation to a World Cup Finals.

When Alex got his feet back under his desk at his Aberdeen office in preparation for the 1986-87 season, his phone, one morning, would ring. By the time he hung up that phone, his adrenaline would be rushing.

He made his way to Dick Donald's office and politely knocked on the door before being invited in.

'You've had an offer, haven'tchu?' Donald said.

'Aye, I have.'

'Too big to turn down?'

'Aye, t'is.'

'You prolly don't need to tell me which club it is... but go'un... I guess I will need ta knoo.'

'Arsenal,' Alex replied.

'Arsenal? Nooo.'

'Huh?'

'I'm no' lettin' y'go there.'

Alex was perplexed.

'Well... you're not gonnae stop me, are you? They've offered me the job.'

'I am gonnae stop you, Alex. And here's why,' Donald told him. 'I thought you were gonnae tell me you bin offered the Man United job. That's the only job you're gonnae leave here for. That's the biggest challenge in football. You're tailor-made for Man United. They suit yer football philosophy.'

ALEX AND HIS FOOTBALL PHILOSOPHY

ALEX FERGUSON'S FOOTBALL PHILOSOPHY WAS INSPIRED BY THREE legends of the game who had, just like he, grown up on the grey streets of Glasgow that web away from the banks of the River Clyde. Matt Busby. Jock Stein. Bill Shankly.

Busby had been Manchester United manager and on board the plane during the Munich Air Disaster in 1958 that claimed the lives of eight players in a time when a squad was pretty much made up of the just the starting eleven. Within ten years of the club almost being wiped out by that tragic airplane crash, he would rebuild the team with a string of young players to become the kings of not just English football, but European football. It was a jaw-dropping feat, steeped in long-term planning and patience. A year before Busby led United to European Cup glory, Stein had lifted the same big old trophy as Celtic manager with eleven players all raised in Glasgow. Well, one lived on the fringes of Glasgow, but the other ten all lived inside the border of the city. A team of local lads winning the holy grail of European football would never be achieved again, and still ranks in Alex's mind as *the* greatest footballing feat he's ever witnessed. He was twenty-five at the time and was just about to sign for Celtic's bitterest rivals Rangers. But Alex was enamoured by the way

Stein man-managed his players and could only watch on as they claimed nine league titles in a row, bending them around that famous night in 1967 when they became the first British club to ever reach the Holy Grail of European football. Shankly would be appointed Liverpool manager when they were in the old second division and far removed from the prestigious club they are today. Within ten days of being appointed as the Reds' boss, he would place twenty-four players on the transfer list and decide he was going to take a long-term approach in an attempt to cata-pult Liverpool to the big time. All twenty-four players would leave the club within eleven months, and as they each departed, Shankly was readily replacing them with younger and hungrier players. He would leave Liverpool sixteen years later having gotten them promoted as Second Division champions before going on to win three English league titles and the UEFA Cup—and in doing so setting the club up for what turned out to be two decades of dominance both domestically and in Europe. All three Glaswegians proved that the way to dominate British football was to run their clubs with a long-term vision that produced not only a constant conveyor belt of players but a conveyor belt of trophies.

Alex's fascination with Busby, Stein and Shankly is the reason he became addicted to salt and pepper shakers throughout his playing days. His football philosophy was being defined for him by the elder icons of the neighbouring hoods he knocked around in just as he was immersing himself in the professional game.

If Alex's philosophy can be summed up in one sentence it would be this: *At no point was he ever interested in just winning the next league title, he was only ever interested in competing for multiple titles over multiple years.* Creating a football club, not just a football team was Alex's chief objective. Just like his three heroes, he was genuinely only ever interested in long-term success.

Alex wrote in *Managing My Life*: "My aim in management has always been to lay foundations that will make a club successful for years, or even decades. Flash-in-the-pan achievements, such as good runs in cup competitions, or even the odd winning appearance in a final could never satisfy me."

Alex had decided upon his long-term football philosophy while he was still playing, and by the time he was twenty-six had already obtained his full coaching badges. While that seems a young age for a player to take their badges in today's world, back in the 1960s it was most certainly unique. But once Alex had signed his first professional playing contract at Dunfermline, he was adamant that he would never leave the game. He didn't want to return to being a landlord, and was hell-bent on not going back to laborious work as a shop steward in a tool-making factory. When Alex signed himself up for a career in professional football, he wasn't just signing up to play.

'Just before I signed ma first professional contract, I didnae think I was gonnae make it as a footballer,' he said. 'But once my opportunity came and I signed my first contract, I knew I was never gonnae leave the game. I couldnae leave the game. I was thinking about a career as a manager as soon as my career as a player began, really.'

Alex's belief in building a long-term strategy was evident as soon as he took the manager's job at East Stirlingshire and insisted on buying young and hungry players after he had inherited half a team. He did the same at St Mirren, where he fielded up to five teenagers in his first eleven. At Aberdeen, he would inherit an experienced squad, but having undergone an underwhelming first season with these household names, he would gut the dressing-room the following summer and replace them with very young talent in the shape of Mark McGhee, Ian Angus, Doug Bell, Ian Porteous, Steve Cowan, Neale Cooper and Eric Black. Those players would help Aberdeen to a level of unprecedented success for the club that remains head-scratching even to this day, and isolated from his United successes could arguably be regarded as equal to the feats of Alex's three heroes named above.

As soon as he was offered the Manchester United job, Alex

was under no doubt how he wanted to approach it. Dick Donald had been right. Manchester United were the perfect club for Alex Ferguson's football philosophy. They had wowed European football when Busby's team rose from the ashes of the Munich Air disaster to be crowned the continent's champions in 1968, and because of that, there already existed a precedence at the club that had been etched into history—a precedence that aligned perfectly with Alex's philosophy.

After his retirement, Alex would appear on American TV to be interviewed by Charlie Rose. He would tell the host: 'When I arrived at Manchester United I decided I had tae build a football club. Not just a team. In doing that, I had tae work really hard to develop a youth system that gave me a stream of players continuously year after year and which exists right up to this present day. At United we did buy. But we also had this great youth system in which we developed our own players. Time was the secret.'

Archie Knox, Alex's lieutenant who he had taken to Old Trafford with him from Aberdeen, has confirmed that the Govanman's long-term strategy had been put in place from literally their first week at the club.

'The first thing we did was we got all the scouts together,' Knox admits. 'And Alex was laying into them, saying we are Manchester United and we need to recruit all the best young talent in the country. At the time, United weren't even getting all the best talent in Manchester. The first thing we did was change that. The scouting for young players changed in the first week.'

As Alex and Archie were instructing their scouts — which three weeks later evolved to United hiring six more scouts to cover the Manchester region alone — a young player by the name of Ryan Wilson was turning up for his first training sessions with Manchester City even though he was a Manchester United fan. Wilson would go on to be the most decorated player in United's history, but the reason he wasn't training with the red team in the city at this time was simply because he hadn't been invited to. This was a measure of how poor United's scouting was inside their own city, where Wilson was now living with his mother having moved from Wales. Alex of course would personally turn Wilson's head once he had become aware of the winger, but it wasn't one of his scouts who had turned the manager's attentions to the player. It was actually a steward at Old Trafford. That's how lacking United's scouting system was in the mid-eighties. It took a steward to confront the first-team manager to ask, 'Why are City getting a free run at this wonderkid?'

Alex would recall well into his retirement: 'When I arrived, Old Trafford was a theatre with ghosts walking aboot it… memories. This had been the place where they created gods. Matt Busby doing what he did in bringing all the young players in, that is what I was good at, that is what I wanted tae do. This had been ma football upbringing, ma football life. So, it was question time for me… I started thinking, what do I need tae do tae resurrect this football club?'

What's interesting to note at this time is that while United still held a reputation as an academy club when Alex arrived (so heartfelt was the romantic story of how United rose from the ashes of the Munich disaster) the first team he inherited only had one player in it who was under the age of twenty-four. With just one youngster in the first team, coupled with a declining youth system, the famed academy Busby had given birth to even before the tragedy — which is where the nickname Busby Babes had originated from — was truly tapping on death's door by the time Alex was appointed in November of 1986.

When he retired, Alex had managed Manchester United for exactly 1,400 games. In every single one of those games, he named an academy graduate in the first team squad. But that wasn't necessarily an Alex Ferguson innovation at the club. That legacy had been set five decades before he'd even arrived, and continues to this day (United have by now named an academy graduate in every match-day squad for over 4,000 games in a row going back as far as October 1937). But it is inarguable that by the mid-1980s, that astonishing legacy was severely under threat.

'I went tae see a youth team game when I first arrived, and they were shocking. Shocking!' Alex admits. 'I realised at Manchester United that a proper youth system would not only work long-term, but it could become the spirit o' the place. The new spirit. Ma first job was to flood Manchester with scouts.'

These scouts would, over the next three years, unearth gems such as Nicky Butt, Paul Scholes, the two Neville brothers and David Beckham among others to add to Ryan Wilson who Alex had personally persuaded to turn red.

In retrospect, United of the mid-eighties was the perfect base for Alex to put his football philosophy into action. It genuinely was a tipping point for both the club and the Govanman. If Alex had taken the Arsenal job he had been offered in 1986 (he had also been offered the Spurs job which he turned down flat in 1985), there is little chance he would have created the legacy he ended up creating at Old Trafford. Alex moving to Manchester United was the right man, at the right club, at the right time. As he himself would often say: 'There's no doubt aboot that.'

Although he was disappointed with the state of affairs when he first arrived, Alex was hugely excited by the seismic job he had on his hands. He was about to oversee a rebuild, ideal for his long-term football philosophy.

There are a couple of reasons Alex loved developing teenagers

Firstly: 'They give you loyalty,' he said. 'You've been responsible for their upbringing. You've been responsible for their character-building. You've been responsible for their development as human beings. And all that work is repaid in the loyalty that a young player will give you back. It's almost family.'

Secondly, Alex knew that nothing lit a fire under the arse of a senior pro like a young player snapping at his heels who happened to play in his same position as him. The manager was well aware of this fear amongst established stars, and in fact had that fear himself in his later years as a player. As a result, he constantly set out to light fires under his players' arses to ensure they performed to their fullest.

Alex's football philosophy included having multiple ages in his dressing-room, and he purposely structured his squad equally in three different age categories: those over thirty years old, those between twenty-three and thirty and those below the age of twenty-three. As time went on, so too did his insistence on the diversity within his dressing-room. Not only did Alex try to have three players in his squad for every position on the pitch at different age levels, but he also made sure player contracts in certain positions ran down at separate times, too. He simply did not want his first team ageing together, and he didn't want their contracts running out at the same time, either. This way, it meant his recycling of the squad over the long-term could be effortless. He also insisted that his squad have up to four multi-use players in it, players who could operate in a number of different positions. He knew these figures would light a fire under every player's arse. Utility operators down the years such as Mike Phelan, Brian McClair, Phil Neville, Michael Silvestre, John O'Shea, Phil Jones and later Ashley Young weren't always first-team starters, but they were pivotal squad members in that their presence threatened the starting berth of more than one player at any one time.

While the structuring of Alex's new-look academy system at United is famous for graduating future club legends in the shape of Giggs, Beckham, Scholes, Butt and the Nevilles, the true lore of the Class of '92 lies in the fact that they all pretty much graduated into the first team together. But Alex's rejuvenated youth academy had been in full swing before these future megastars became household names and had already produced players for the first team such as Russell Beardsmore, Clayton Blackmore, Lee Martin and Mark Robins. The academy remains in full swing even to this day, despite the mess the club entangled itself in in the wake of Alex's retirement (which you read about in fine detail later). But because of the lore in which the Class of '92 is viewed, those who went before and those who followed such as Wes Brown, John O'Shea, Darren Fletcher, Jonny Evans, Darron Gibson, Danny Welbeck, twins Fabio and Raphael Da Silva, and Tom Cleverly coupled with peripheral breakthrough players like Michael Clegg, Danny Higginbotham, Ronnie Wallwork, Keith Gillespie, Jonathan Greening, Luke Chadwick, Kieran Richardson, Gerard Pique, Phil Bardsley, Danny Simpson, Fraizer Campbell, Federico Macheda and Paul Pogba (who all played in title-winning teams) tend to go largely unnoted. Any one individual's transition into a first-team player never really stood any chance of living up to six academy graduates from the same class being promoted together, even if those academy graduates named above would go on to win fifty major titles between them for the club (more than the total of the Class of 92's haul of major trophies).

There is of course no argument that the Class of '92 thoroughly deserve their place in United folklore given the longevity they each gifted the club. When their breakthrough is considered in isolation, they were six players all entering the first team at roughly the same time. And although it was a rare occurrence that all of them were named in the starting eleven, they did essentially comprise six players out of a possible starting eleven. Two-thirds of an outfield football team. For over a decade. All developed from within—costing the club zero in transfer fees.

One statistic that sums up how impressive the conveyor belt at United's academy eventually became under Alex's watch (though it didn't gift the club itself much) lies in the fact that at one point, twenty-nine out of the ninety-two league clubs in England boasted a Manchester United academy graduate in their squads. That means almost one-third of all professional football clubs had players in their ranks that had all graduated from the same school.

On top of promoting players into his first team from the academy, as well as selling on the ones who didn't quite cut the mustard, Alex also held preference for buying young players when he entered the transfer market. Future stars such as Wayne Rooney, Cristiano Ronaldo, Roy Keane, Rio Ferdinand, Ole Gunnar Solskjaer, Nani, Anderson, Javier Hernandez, Phil Jones, Chris Smalling and David De Gea were all twenty-three or younger when Alex snapped them up. Some of them were still only teenagers.

The main reason Alex liked to develop young players was because it allowed him to transition his team while continuing to compete for multiple trophies over multiple years. This is also the reason he kept his tactics pragmatic and readily adaptable. It made no sense to his overall aim of long-term success to have a definitive playing philosophy tactics-wise. Everything *had* to be constantly interchangeable and evolutionary. These are the reasons, essentially, why Alex personally handpicked David Moyes as his successor in 2013. Moyes had proven he could work under very similar circumstances at Everton where he constantly cycled and recycled through teams using pragmatic tactics so that high standards could remain consistent over the long term. When Moyes took over at Everton in 2002, the club were in dire straits and in danger of losing their Premier League status. They had just about avoided relegation and finished 16th or 15th in the league four times out of the previous six seasons. On those other two occasions, they had finished 13th and 14th. They were in the bottom seven for seven years running. When Moyes came in, inspired by the Glaswegian giants that went before him — Busby, Stein, Shankly and now Alex himself — he was unshakeable in his desire to adopt a long-term strategy. He would lead the club to an average finish of seventh in the Premier League over the next eleven years, often finishing fifth—well away from the threat of relegation and into European football on five separate occasions. He did it on a shoe-string budget, too. What was most impressive to Alex was that Moyes had made huge strides by promoting young players from the academy such as Wayne Rooney, Leon Osman, Ross Barkley, Jack Rodwell and James

Vaughan among others, coupled with signing relatively unknown young players with potential who he eventually turned into household names in the shape of Tim Cahill, Seamus Coleman, Steven Pienaar, Leighton Baines and Mikel Arteta among others. The superstar managerial names the media had tipped to follow Alex, such as Jose Mourinho, Pep Guardiola and Jurgen Klopp, while all largely hailed by the Govanman, were never in the running for the Old Trafford hotseat. It made no sense for Alex to build all he had built, only to hand the baton on to managers who had such strong football philosophies that they relied on the immediate. Mourinho worked in three-year cycles where he had proven to buy physically large and established pros to carry out his philosophy. Those players would all age at the same time which happened to coincide with the Portuguese either leaving the football club or being sacked. By the time Alex was retiring, Mourinho had lasted an average of 1.9 years at the clubs he had managed. Since Alex's retirement, that average has barely risen after the Portuguese spent two years at Chelsea, two and a half at Manchester United (after he had been appointed by Ed Woodward in 2016 which you can read about in detail in a later chapter) and eighteen months at Tottenham Hotspur. Likewise, Pep Guardiola, who Alex hugely admires, had gone on record as saying he would only ever last up to four years at any one football club. The Spaniard had admitted in 2012: 'Three or four years at a big club like Barcelona is an eternity.' He stepped down from his role at Camp Nou, citing stress and exhaustion and had to take time out of the game. As astonishing as his feats were at Barcelona, the short-termism of his reign didn't endear himself to Alex in terms of considering the Spaniard as his successor. Nor did his public admission that he wouldn't stay in one job more than four years (even though he proved years later, at United's rivals City that he could last longer than that). Separate from the United job, Alex was a huge fan of Guardiola and did indeed dine with him in a restaurant in New York City in January 2013. But this meeting was personal, not professional, and the Spaniard was never offered the job at Old Trafford. The problem for Alex wasn't that Mourinho and Guardiola had proven they were interested in short-term stints at the clubs they had been at, but more so the fact that they were both insistent on a strict tactical philosophy that really only could rely on one cycle.

Jurgen Klopp was viewed in the same manner by Alex. Although he, just like Mourinho and Guardiola, had won major trophies, he did so with a very strict philosophy that is almost, if not certainly, impossible to continue past one cycle. Klopp led Dortmund to great success by winning back-to-back German League titles in 2011-2012 (the first time they had done so for sixteen years) but Alex was under no doubt that Dortmund weren't destined for any long-term dominance under the German. Latterly, Alex was hugely impressed when Klopp transitioned Liverpool to fantastic success in winning the Champions League and the Premier League in consecutive seasons. But again, he wasn't sure Liverpool were set up for success past that one cycle. A lot of their key players were ageing at the same time. So too were their contracts. On top of that, Klopp's insistence on a punishing pressing tactical approach is an almost impossible footballing philosophy to cycle through. It relies too heavily, like Guardiola and Mourinho's great teams, on established players in the prime of their career who can outrun their opponents. The only way to cycle through such a strict tactical approach is to continually buy new, established players in the prime of their careers once the previous established players had run their course. There exists no conveyor belt behind them. And, therefore, there is little to no scope for long-term success with these philosophies unless, of course, there exists a bottomless pit of money at a club that could allow the manager to continuously buy established player after established player.

Alex would write in *Leading*: "While you might be able to buy your way to short-term success, it does not work over the long term. That requires patience, and the construction of a complete organisation."

He would also say in a separate interview: 'You can't have long-term success if you only have a short-term strategy.'

This is not to say Alex isn't a huge fan of these managers, nor their footballing philosophies, and he certainly wouldn't play down their fantastic successes as managers, given the lifespan of managers in the modern game. Alex genuinely respects the philosophies adopted by the modern greats such Mourinho, Guardiola and Klopp, but at no point did he believe their footballing philosophies suited the Manchester United he had built. When Alex walked through the door at the club for the first time in 1986, he admitted he wasn't interested in winning titles in the short-term. He was only ever interested in building a football club that could compete for multiple titles over multiple years. It's painfully ironic that in the years after he retired, United would turn into the club he had been trying to avoid them becoming by not appointing a short-termist big-name manager to succeed him. United did eventually go down the route of appointing short-termist managers with a strict football philosophy in Louis van Gaal and Mourinho. It meant that by the time Ole Gunnar Solskjaer would eventually be appointed as United's temporary manager in 2018, the Norwegian would inherit a squad with some promising youth team players, some established Alex Ferguson players bought to suit his philosophy, a couple Moyes had brought in, a number of established players bought to suit Louis Van Gaal's philosophy, and some established players bought to suit Jose Mourinho's philosophy. The squad was a mish-mash, a mess. Gone were the three players for every position, gone was the balance of ages for every position, gone were the four utility players who could threaten the place of multiple stars in the first-team, gone was the conveyor belt of youth team players nipping at the heels of every established pro, too.

When Alex had heard that Moyes was about to be sacked at

Manchester United after only ten months in the job (which you can read about in detail in a later chapter) he was beyond livid. He knew as soon as he heard that news that Manchester United were about to U-turn on everything he had built.

Alex would write in *Leading*: "Prioritising a long-term strategy for the club was absolutely crucial, and at United we always had to be thinking about the composition of the team a few seasons ahead. So we had to have a conveyor belt of talent… It is much easier to produce a consistent level of high performances when you nourish youngsters, help them develop and provide a pathway to long-term success."

That conveyor belt of young talent, for a multitude of reasons — whether it be threatening the place of an established pro in the first-team, or becoming a first-team regular for twenty three years like Ryan Giggs — was crucial to Alex's philosophy. Moyes had proven his methods aligned. The bigger-named managers hadn't. In fact, what they had proven thus far in their careers was the complete opposite. Moyes wasn't just the chosen one in Alex's eyes. He was the only one. He was certain that if his fellow Govanman be given time, he could continue benefiting from the conveyor belt already in motion at Manchester United.

As far as Alex is concerned, the club lost their way and almost lost their identity, not the day he retired, but on the day David Moyes was sacked, for that is when United sacrificed competing for multiple titles over multiple years for *desperately* trying to win their next title instead.

It was quite literally everything Alex's football philosophy opposed.

1986-1992

<small>ALEX HAD BEEN TO OLD TRAFFORD A NUMBER OF TIMES BEFORE, BUT HE'D</small> never stood in the centre circle of the pitch and swivelled around in slow motion to take in the breadth of the famous stadium.

'Bloody hell,' he said.

He was already smitten. And because of his passion for studying "young history", was all too aware of the rich traditions instilled deep within the fabric of this specific club. When he would leave that centre circle for the final time some twenty-six and a half years later, to the thunderous applause of seventy-eight thousand fans, he would have pocketed Manchester United thirteen Premier League titles, five FA Cups, four League Cups, two Champions Leagues, one European Cup Winners Cup, a Super Cup, a Club World Cup, had the north stand (the largest stand of the largest club stadium in Britain) named after him and had a solid bronze statute sculpted by the great Philip Jackson standing proud — forever — outside the red bricks of that very stand. At the time Alex Ferguson took over Manchester United in November of 1986, they lagged way behind Liverpool in terms of league titles won. Liverpool had amassed eighteen. United only had seven. When he would retire in May of 2013, Liverpool would still have eighteen. United would have twenty.

Although Dick Donald had told his manager that the only club he would allow him to leave Aberdeen for was Manchester United, the adored chairman was still heartbroken by how the move eventually materialised. It was, rather cruelly, all done behind his back. Manchester United went behind his back. And his own manager went behind his back. It should also be noted that all of this was also done behind the back of then Manchester United manager, Ron Atkinson. After two hush-hush, wink-wink phone calls that occurred during the late morning of, November 5th in 1986, Alex found himself pulling in to the services station off the motorway in Hamilton some five hours later. He had chosen the location himself, feeling it would be discreet. At bang on seven p.m, a Land Rover pulled up behind his Mercedes, with four middle-aged men inside. One of them got out, walked to Alex's Merc and opened the door before sliding into the passenger seat. It was Martin Edwards—the Manchester United chairman. In the Land Rover behind them remained Bobby Charlton, Mike Edelson and Maurice Watkins—the entirety of the Manchester United board of directors at the time. Alex drove, while the Land Rover followed, to another destination he, himself, had chosen—Cathy's sister's house in Bishopbriggs in the north suburbs of Glasgow. Again, he thought it would be discreet.

It was in the living room of Bridget Holding's modest Glasgow terraced home that Alex Ferguson would agree to become Manchester United's manager.

Donald was furious when he found out the move, that he genuinely had hoped would occur one day because he adored Alex so much, had happened in such a cloak and dagger manner. And so, Alex would depart yet another club having fallen out with his chairman. Though it must be added that he and Donald became close friends again before Donald's death some seven years later, aged 82.

Cathy, while proud her husband had secured such a seismic move in terms of his career, wasn't exactly jumping for joy. She, and especially the three boys, had settled more than comfortably in Aberdeen.

'No, I was nae happy,' Cathy said, not long after she moved

south to Manchester in 1988—eighteen months after Alex's had initially moved down. 'But there was no way he was gonnae turn that job down, I wouldnae expect him to. But I was so settled in Aberdeen at the time, y'know.'

Alex initially moved in with his assistant manager, Archie Knox, (who had been Alex's assistant at Aberdeen and who he had promised he would bring with him if, or rather *when*, he got a move to a big club), to a small two-bedroomed house just outside central Manchester. It was fine. For a couple of weeks, anyway, until Alex almost burnt the house down by placing a box of matches on top of a grill he had just lit. The grill lit up, sizzled and then exploded like a firework, causing Alex to jump backwards.

During his first day as manager of Manchester United Alex would be stunned twice. Firstly, when he entered his office for the first time, he found most of the floor space was taken up by what looked like a futuristic coffin. After making an enquiry, he would find out it was a sun bed and that his predecessor, Ron Atkinson, liked to take ten-minute sessions for a quick touch up for his tan whilst the players took a breather between morning and afternoon training. The second thing that stunned Alex was the fact that the players he inherited, including some of the biggest names in British football, were, to a man, woefully unfit—certainly in comparison to the squad he had just left up in Aberdeen. What was so striking was the fact that this squad read like a list of who's who. So many of the players were household names and considered to be elite pros. Among them were Bryan Robson, Paul McGrath, Norman Whiteside, Kevin Moran, Remi Moses, Frank Stapleton and Gordon Strachan. Strachan had forewarned Alex that he was in for a shock when he'd finally get to the training ground after his appointment was made public, because Strachan — having worked under Alex at Aberdeen — was well aware of the Govanman's insistence for peak physical condition. Strachan had a love/hate relationship with Alex and it was such a conflicting and complicated debate in Strachan's mind at the time that he wasn't sure whether he was or wasn't happy with Alex's appointment as Manchester United manager.

'At the time, I remember,' Strachan would joke years later, 'it was in the papers that Fergie would only ever leave Aberdeen for either the Manchester United job, or the Barcelona job. Well, I remember always thinking I hope the Barcelona manager gets sacked.'

By their second week in the job, Alex and Archie concocted a training regime that was so tough that the players were instantly incensed by their new management team. The murmurings around the training ground in the very early days was that the players much preferred the easy ride of it they had been experiencing under Atkinson, even if they had sunk to second from bottom of the league table by the time Alex arrived. While the players were undergoing their new pre-season under their new manager — in the middle of a freezing November — Alex began to study the famed Manchester United academy. After all, he'd heard so many great stories down the years. But it turned out that these stories were just that. Stories. Tales of years gone by. The Manchester United academy may have been the envy of every club in Europe some twenty years ago, but it wasn't enviable any more. Yes, the underage teams at the club were competitive in their respective competitions and had been continuously, but they weren't doing exactly what they truly should be existing to do: producing talent for the first team. So, the second act Alex carried out as Manchester United manager, after laying down a new training regime for his players, was to send each of the club's scouts on a mission to cast their nets as wide as they possibly could. Their remit was impossible, but it was crystal clear: bring me the best teen talent the country has to offer.

Alex would tell Martin Edwards, as his first season at Old Trafford progressed sluggishly with mixed results, that only six of the playing squad he inherited were worthy enough to play for the club. Edwards would raise his eyebrows, but that's all he would raise. Since Mark Hughes had left United for Barcelona the previous year, Atkinson had spent almost £2m (a huge amount in the mid-eighties) trying, but ultimately failing, to replace him. Atkinson had eaten through the club's transfer budget on the likes of Alan Brazil (£700,000), Peter Davenport (£600,000) and Terry Gibson (£650,000) before eventually being sacked in the midst of all three strikers flopping. There would be no money for Alex to splash on players. He had been told this up in Bridget Holding's front room when he had agreed to become the club's manager.

So, with little to call on from a depleted academy and next to no money in the kitty for transfers, Alex had to work with what he had. And what he had was a dressing-room filled with household names, but household names who were coasting through their careers seemingly content to live in the giant shadow Liverpool's success was casting, not just over the country, but over Europe. As was the case when he took over at Aberdeen, Alex told a listening dressing-room that sitting by and watching Liverpool winning trophies wasn't gonna happen under his watch. 'That kind of passivity is alien to me,' he barked, mirroring exactly what he had said to the Aberdeen squad eight years earlier while referencing the Old Firm.

From second from bottom when he took over, Alex would eventually lift United to eleventh place in his first season, though not many were impressed by the feat. Some fans were already whispering that the Scot might be in over his head down south. And the media were sharpening their claws almost weekly too, feeding that narrative to the fans. To be fair to the fans and journalists who were calling for Alex's head in his earliest years, they simply couldn't have foreseen what was coming because all the progress being made at the football club was being carried out in the shadows. Alex told Martin Edwards and Bobby Charlton as his first season as manager was coming to an uneventful conclusion that it would take five years for the club to win the league title. The first team simply had to be dismantled and a new team had to grow in its place, he informed them. To initially work with what he had, Alex gave the Manchester United dressing-room the same treatment he had given the Aberdeen dressing-room when he first walked in. He told them the club was going to be successful under his management whether they were part of it or not. And he informed them he had been to all of the pubs he knew they frequented and had put spies in place in each of them. Though with Manchester being a much bigger city than Aberdeen, this plot was much more difficult to carry out. And so Alex didn't quite get a reign on the drinking culture at United as swiftly as he had done at Aberdeen. On top of that, the drinking culture, Alex sensed, was much worse at United than it had been up north. He'd have loved to have taken a bulldozer to the Manchester United squad he inherited as soon as he realised what he had to work with. But he simply couldn't. There weren't any kids in the academy ready to take their place. On top of that, Edwards was being very shy when it came to opening the purse strings.

In his second season (1987-88), Alex would lead those players to a second-placed finish behind champions Liverpool. And while that sounds like an impressive jump from eleventh, Alex was as equally frustrated through that second campaign as he had been through his first. However, the consistency of the team's results — certainly by the end of the season — negated the negative headlines some-what and the discontent from supporters quietened to a silence. They wouldn't be silent for long, though. One of the main reasons for United's impressive and consistent league performances was one player Alex did manage to net in the transfer market—Brian McClair. Alex had been a fan of the clever Celtic forward and persuaded Martin Edwards to splash £850,000 on him after giving the green light to the sales of players such as Frank Stapleton, who Alex felt was not only too unfit, but too timid to be one of his strikers, and Jesper Olsen who Alex simply didn't consider skilful or quick enough to be one of his counter-attacking wingers. Olsen and Stapleton had been among the fan favourites at Old Trafford, but not many eyelids were blinked when they were sold. Alex took relief from that. And so he began plotting how he could sell the likes of Paul McGrath and Norman Whiteside the following summer without receiving a backlash from the supporters. Those two players — an Irishman and a Northern Irishman — were considered elite stars, but Alex simply wasn't happy with their levels of discipline. He was aware they were readily slipping by the spies he had set in place in the pubs in Manchester, and worse, they were leading some of the more promising young members of the first team astray by inviting them for drinks in the evenings after training sessions. His frustrations with those players would intensify over the course of his third season at the club—undoubtedly the most frustrating experience he had in all of his twenty-six and a half years at Old Trafford.

Cathy and the boys had moved, full-time, to Manchester after Alex had purchased a beautiful home in Wilmslow — a remote town, thirteen miles south of Manchester's city centre. Mark, Darren and Jason, being the cocky and cheeky teenagers they were (replicas of their old man), didn't take long to settle in school. Mark had actually been a passionate United supporter as a kid, years before his father had become manager. And although he played football at a high level, a career similar to his dad's was out of the question. As it was for Jason, who, although a huge football fan, was more interested in academia. Darren, however, did have what it took to have a career in the game, and would join the Manchester United academy. The three boys settled into life in Manchester as seamlessly as possible. Cathy took a while, but she eventually settled in the city she still calls home to this very day. A quarter of a century later, when Alex would eventually retire, there was no question of them moving back to Glasgow. Cathy didn't just settle for Manchester when she moved down there in 1988, she settled in Manchester for life. However, as was unusual during Alex's career thus far, his settled home life wasn't mirroring what was happening on the pitch. The 1989 season got off to such a bad start that the unrest in the stands at Old Trafford grew in volume from whispers to shouts. 'He doesn't know what he's doing!' was a particular line that was often volleyed towards the dugout in between the many bouts of silences at home games. 'Bring in Clough!' was another.

Lifelong season ticket holder Chris Robinson said a decade later — just as United were en route to an unprecedented treble of Premier League, Champions League and FA Cup victories: '1989 is certainly the worst year of football I've seen at United. They were poor. They were not worth watching and the crowds reflected that. There was a lot of people calling for Fergie's head in the autumn of 1989.'

In fact it was in the autumn of 1989 — a couple of months after Alex had finally taken a bulldozer to the United squad he had inherited by selling McGrath, Whiteside and Strachan — when one supporter, Pete Molyneux, unfurled a thirty-foot banner from the midsection Old Trafford's famous Stretford End.

It read:

3 years of excuses and it's still crap.
Ta Ra Fergie

As the banner was slowly unfurled, a large number of home fans cheered. Even though a PR move from the club tried to convince supporters that Alex's development was yet to be seen because it was cooking in the academy, most simply weren't buying it. The first team had started the 1989 campaign just as poorly as they had started the 1988 season, though this start was confounded by a 5-1 thrashing at the hands of local foes Manchester City. The result turned most United fans blue. It sickened them. They were, by now, convincing each other that the manager simply had to go. The newspapers agreed. So much so that they set a specific date for Alex's sacking. January 7, 1990. Just after Christmas. With United already languishing in the bottom third of the First Division table, all they had left to play for during that campaign was the FA Cup. But they'd been pitted away to Nottingham Forest in as tough a third-round tie as they were likely to get. Given the form of both clubs, United were heavily backed to be beaten. And if that was the case, United's chance of any glory would be over by the half-way point of the season. And so, too, it was assumed, would Alex's job.

The story of Mark Robins heading home the only goal in that game against Forest to save Alex's job is a story that has been well worn. But it's a story that isn't technically accurate. Martin Edwards — to his credit — had visited Alex's office at The Cliff on the

Wednesday before the Nottingham Forest tie to tell him the press were wrong, that he wasn't going to lose his job if Forest beat them on Saturday. Alex was grateful for the vote of confidence.

However, thirty-one years after the famous Mark Robins goal — in 2017 — Edwards would finally go on record as saying he simply hadn't made up his mind back then.

'I am always honest,' he would say, reflecting on January 1990, 'and although I told Alex that his job wasn't on the line at Forest, I don't know whether, if we had gone out of the cup that game and our league position hadn't improved, how long more I could've gone on supporting him. I really don't know.'

It may have been the Mark Robins headed goal that found itself in United folklore, but it was a well-taken rifle of a finish from none other than left-back Lee Martin (one of the first academy players Alex had promoted into the first team) that should be mostly celebrated. Martin scored the only goal of a drab FA Cup Final replay against Crystal Palace (in stark contrast to the thrilling 3-3 the two teams had been involved in on a glorious summer's day the Saturday previous) to claim Alex's first piece of silverware as Manchester United manager.

The FA Cup win reduced the volume of the protests within the stands of Old Trafford to mere whispers once again, and despite inconsistent form in the league the following season (in which they would finish sixth) United fans would be treated to a mirror-image of Alex's most successful campaign as a manager thus far—the winning of the European Cup Winners Cup. Still, despite a glorious run in Europe's secondary competition, there was a little bit of unease in the stands of Old Trafford, mainly because Darren Ferguson had been promoted from the academy and the word 'nepotism' was often muttered under the breaths of some die-hard supporters. With Arsenal and Liverpool running away with a title charge, (Arsenal eventually winning this one) United's focus that season turned to the European trophy Alex had famously lifted previously with Aberdeen.

United came through tough ties against Legia Warsaw and

Montpellier to set up a grand finale with the mighty Barcelona. And, replicating the success he had at Aberdeen, Alex's men would claim the trophy by slaying a Spanish giant. Mark Hughes (who Alex had bought back from Barcelona) and Steve Bruce grabbed two goals in the second half of a technically hard-fought game to see off a team that included great names such as Ronald Koeman, Eusebio, Julio Salinas and Michael Laudrup. The back-to-back trophies hushed the last remaining disgruntled fans at Old Trafford so much so that not even the word 'nepotism' was being mentioned anymore as Darren racked up more first-team opportunities. But despite the silverware, Alex wasn't happy.

'It was clear we had become a cup team,' he reflected. 'Our league form was, well it was scratchy. We were still sitting back and watching Liverpool rise tae the top all the time. So we needed to do something aboot that. I was determined after we'd won the Cup Winners Cup that we just had tae concentrate on the league. We'd done what everyone said we had tae do... we'd won cups. Now it was time to win a league.'

The lucrativeness of the cup wins persuaded Edwards to open up his tight purse strings. And in the summer of 1991, Alex would purchase Peter Schmeichel (a relatively unknown goalkeeper from Brondby) and Andrei Kanchelskis (an even less known right-winger from Shakhtar Donetsk). He also promoted the gem from his academy that he had specifically drawn a path for—Ryan Wilson, who had since changed his surname to Giggs, his mother's maiden name.

Four years later, George Graham (who took the Arsenal job Alex had turned down in the summer of 1986) would ask him while they were socialising, 'Remember you kept banging on about that Wilson lad in your academy, whatever happened to him?' He was dead serious. Alex sniggered before answering. 'Oh, that lad? He changed his surname,' he said.

'To what?' Graham asked.

'Giggs.'

Alex was determined to win the last ever First Division title (before it rebranded as the Premier League in 1991-92), simply because he had promised Edwards and Charlton that he would win the league in his fifth year. This was his fifth year. Alex felt the writing was on the wall, specifically because he predicted the great Liverpool team that consisted of warriors such as Steve Nicol, Ronnie Whelan, Ray Houghton and Ian Rush was crying out for refreshing, and simply hadn't had any. His prediction, which would have sounded crazy in the summer of 1991, turned out to hit the bullseye. Liverpool had a poor campaign by their high standards and were never really in the hunt for the title for the first time in over a decade. They eventually finished sixth. But it was another great rival of Manchester United's who would thwart Alex's destiny of winning the title just as he had predicted in year five. Leeds United. They were, at this stage, under the guidance of Howard Wilkinson — a good friend of Alex — and with a front two of Lee Chapman and Eric Cantona pulling the strings, they looked unplayable at times. By the turn of the year into 1992, the two Uniteds were the only horses in the race, though Sheffield Wednesday who eventually finished third — thanks to the great goalscoring form of striker David Hirst — would likely contest that.

United would hold a lead over Leeds for most of the campaign and with only six games to go were clear favourites to lift the trophy that had evaded the club for nigh on a quarter of a century. Alex would blame their collapse over the next six games on injuries. Bryan Robson and Mark Robins had both been long-term absentees through that campaign, but they were to be joined in the treatment room by Paul Ince, Paul Parker, Danny Wallace and Lee Martin within the space of the first two weeks of April—right at the most pivotal time of Alex's reign thus far. But injury excuses aside, what derailed United the most was the form, or lack thereof, of Mark Hughes. The Welsh striker hadn't scored in fourteen games and without his goals, the victories dried up. Back-to-back defeats over the Easter period, firstly to Nottingham Forest and then to West Ham three days later, helped Leeds to top spot—a position they wouldn't surrender over the next four games. Despite Alex's excuses over injuries, Leeds were simply worthy winners of the last ever First Division title, whereas United simply buckled under the pressure in the final stages of the campaign. They did, however, have success in the League Cup by beating Nottingham Forest in a tense final thanks to a lone Brian McClair goal. It was the first time United had ever won that competition, but it was scant consolation for missing out on the league title.

Alex would have a meeting with Martin Edwards after a two-week break following that campaign where he would insist on purchasing a new striker. He felt Hughes was by now past his wonderful best and needed replacing. David Hirst was Alex's first choice for this role. He had been top scorer for Sheffield Wednesday over the previous two campaigns and had just been called up to the England squad. The problem Alex faced was that Owls boss Trevor Francis was adamant that the player wasn't for sale. Edwards officially bid £1.6m in July for the striker which was rejected without hesitation, before he increased that offer to £2m a week later. That bid was met with the same negative response.

'How much will you accept?' a desperate Alex asked Francis during a pleading phone call on the eve of inaugural Premier League season kicking off.

'Alex,' Francis replied before sighing, 'how many times do I have to tell ye? Hirsty's not for sale.'

Alex would turn his attentions to Alan Shearer, who, despite being only twenty-one, was proving to be a handful for even the most experienced of defenders, and was netting goals with relative ease for Southampton. Shearer would give Alex the signals that he was interested in the move, but ultimately decided upon signing for Blackburn Rovers instead, whose rich owner Jack Walker offered him a much more lucrative contract than he would have got at Old Trafford.

Dismayed, Alex had to opt for the third striker on his list—Dion Dublin. It worried Alex that Dublin hadn't had top division experience, but his talents were clear and obvious when he played for Cambridge United against Alex in an FA Cup tie a year prior. The fee for Dublin was a cool £1m which would look like a bargain at first. The lanky striker scored a late winner against Southampton two weeks into the campaign, right in front of a roaring Stretford End to become an instant cult hero. But in the next match — at Selhurst Park against Crystal Palace — he would collapse under a challenge from Eric Young that snapped his leg in two. Despite the heartbreak — or leg break as it literally was — United were holding their own in the table by November, but Alex was worried there wasn't enough goals in his team to win the title he had promised Charlton and Edwards he would deliver.

'Maybe we could sign Peter Beardsley,' Alex said to Edwards during a meeting on the tenth of November in 1992. Edwards was taking notes while discussing what sort of fee Everton might accept for the former Liverpool striker when his phone suddenly rang. It was Bill Fotherby on the other end of the line—his mirror equivalent at Leeds United.

'We'd like to sign Denis Irwin,' Fotherby presented to Edwards.

A perplexed Edwards placed the call on speakerphone and asked the Leeds supremo to repeat himself.

'We'd like to sign Denis Irwin.'

Alex scoffed. And as Edwards was politely telling Fotherby to forget about such a move, a thought popped into Alex's head. He grabbed a pen from Edwards' desk, tore off a slip of paper from the copybook he had been jotting notes in during the meeting and scribbled on it. Then he pushed the thin slip of paper under his chief executive's nose who looked down at it, then back up at Alex with his eyebrows raised.

'Ask him about Cantona.'

ALEX AND HIS TRANSFERS

THE OFFICE WAS MODERN AND OVERLY LIT—AND THE LONG GLASS conference table that stretched almost the entire length of the room reflected the strong light back into their eyes. Alex sat in the chair at the head of the table and leaned his elbows onto the glass to stare intently at the greasy-skinned teenager across from him.

'You gottae come back on the plane with us tonight,' he pleaded. 'I made a phone call at half-time, and we want you at Manchester United.'

It was true. Alex, rather than instruct his players in the dressing-room, had spent most of half-time on his mobile phone which was highly unusual, even if it was during a pre-season friendly. They were now sat in the brand-new offices upstairs in the main stand after Manchester United had been beaten 3-1 in a game played to officially mark the opening of Sporting Lisbon's brand-spanking-new Jose Alvalade Stadium.

The teenager could speak broken English, but he understood fully what the great manager was saying to him despite the thick Scottish accent. Through Sporting's president Dias Da Cunha, who spoke perfect English, the teenager would firstly apologise to Alex, then inform him that he couldn't travel to Manchester. Not tonight. Not without his mother. He wouldn't feel comfortable, even if he was in the company of the household names he looked up to such as Ryan Giggs, Paul Scholes, Roy Keane and Ruud van Nistelrooy.

Alex, hugely excited, agreed the teenager could travel to Manchester the following day with his family. The reason the manager was so excited was because he had just witnessed this teenager make his experienced United defenders look drunk. Alex had already done due diligence before this friendly took place (it was actually United youth scout Jim Ryan who had first noticed Cristiano Ronaldo sixteen months prior) and had been given indications that the winger would love to sign for Manchester United. But although Alex was hugely excited, he also felt a tinge of panic because he was aware Arsenal and Liverpool had been scouting the teenager. Before this friendly, Alex hadn't considered Ronaldo physically mature enough to fit into his United team just yet and had already scheduled in signing him the following summer—in 2004. But he couldn't wait another year after witnessing the player dancing around his defenders under the floodlights of the brand spanking new Jose Alvalade Stadium that night. In fact, he couldn't wait another day. But he'd have to.

Ronaldo would fly into Manchester airport twenty-four hours later with his mother and sister. And when he scribbled his name on the straight line across the bottom of the contract put before him, Alex had signed the greatest player he'd ever sign in all his years in management.

'Cristiano is the best player I've ever signed, no doubt aboot that,' he would admit. 'I wasn't s'posed to sign him until the following year, and we'd been tracking him for some time. But when he played against us that night, he gave John O'Shea a terrible time and I just knew we couldn't wait any longer. I'd seen him a couple of times before then, but that night I knew he was born to play at Old Trafford.'

Ronaldo may have been the best player Alex ever signed, but that's not to say he was the Govanman's greatest ever piece of business in the transfer market. That accolade goes to a man who can arguably be considered the complete opposite of Cristiano Ronaldo in almost every respect. Born in Cork, quiet as a mouse and a gentleman who preferred to stay in the shadows where the spotlight couldn't find him, Denis Irwin is always the first name that comes to mind when Alex is asked, as he often is, who his best ever signing is. Not the best player he's ever signed. But the best signing he's ever made.

'We used to call him eight out of ten Denis,' Alex recalls. 'Because he would produce the same level every game. Every game for twelve years, Denis was incapable of putting a foot wrong.'

When once probed in a Q&A by a fan on what his best accumulative eleven would be from his time at United, Alex once answered: 'Ach, that is absolutely impossible. You look at the strikers I had going back to McClair, Hughes, Cole, Cantona, van Nistelrooy, Saha, Solskjaer, Yorke, Sheringham. Then on to Wayne Rooney, van Persie, Chicarito (Javier Hernandez)... how do you pick from that? Cantona and somebody else? I dunno. The midfield might be a bit easier... you have Keane, Robson, Scholes —they were fantastic players. Beckham, Ronaldo, Giggs... But in all honestly, I would say Denis Irwin would be the one certainty to get in my eleven.'

Irwin had been bought by Alex in 1990 from Oldham Athletic for £625,000 and would stay at the club until 2002 having won every trophy he had competed for: seven Premier League titles, two FA Cups, a League Cup, a Champions League, the European Cup Winners Cup, the European Super Cup and the Intercontinental Cup, all while staying in the shadows out of fear the spotlight might find him.

Of course, signings such as Steve Bruce (£820,000 in 1987), Lee Sharpe (£500,000 in 1988), Andrei Kanchelskis (£625,000 in 1991), Peter Schmeichel (£500,000 in 1991), Eric Cantona (£1.1m in 1992), Roy Keane (£3.75m in 1994), Ole Gunnar Solskjaer (£1.2m in 1996), Ronny Johnsen (£1.2m in 1996), Quinton Fortune (£1.5m in

1999), the teenager with the greasy skin (£12.5m in 2003), Ji Sung Park (£4m in 2005), Nemanja Vidic (£7m in 2006), Patrice Evra (£5.5m in 2006), Antonio Valencia (£16m in 2009) and Javier Hernandez (£6m in 2010) can all be considered amongst Alex's most shrewd purchases for their respective outlays given their impact at the club. Yet, as far as Alex is concerned, Irwin is the best piece of business he ever conducted in the transfer market.

That list of shrewd transfers (which leaves out his biggest name and biggest budget signings) suggests Alex may have been the shrewdest of all football managers when it came to the transfer market. But he didn't always get it right. There exists a lengthy list of players who didn't quite live up to their expectations after Alex had snapped them up.

Neil Webb (£1.5m in 1989), Jordi Cruyff (£2.3m in 1996), Karel Poborsky (£3.25m in 1996), Jesper Blomqvist (£6.3m in 1998), Bojan Djordjic (£1.4m in 1999), Juan Sebastian Veron (£24m in 2001), David Bellion (£3m in 2003), Eric Djemba-Djemba (£5m in 2003), Kleberson (£7.5m in 2003), Gabriel Obertan (£3.6m in 2009) and Bebe (£7m in 2011) are all players Alex feels didn't represent good value — if any in Bebe's case — for their respective outlays.

But it is two big-name signings that United pumped multi-millions of pounds into that he felt most let down by. And they may well be two names that surprise Manchester United supporters, given that they won multiple major trophies as regular first team members.

Dimitar Berbatov is a player Alex feels could and should have shone brighter at Old Trafford. The Bulgarian, still seen as a cult hero at the Theatre of Dreams (especially so as he scored a sublime hat-trick against Liverpool in front of the Stratford End) hugely frustrated Alex during his time at the club. Having observed him closely as a Spurs player, Alex genuinely assumed he was purchasing a Cantona-esque striker. In fact, if Alex was to design the type of No.10 he adored, most of the traits Berbatov had would have been included. The problem was, Berbatov strangely lacked the self-belief Alex had assumed he had in abundance once he arrived at Carrington. And his lack of mobility when off the ball would constantly grate on his manager.

Alex would write in *My Autobiography*: "I signed Berbatov in the summer of 2008 because he had that lovely balance and composure in attacking areas… (but) he was extremely lacking in self-assurance. He never had that Cantona or Andy Cole peacock quality, or the confidence of Teddy Sheringham. Berbatov was not short of belief in his own ability, but it was only based on his way of playing. Because we functioned at a certain speed, he was not really tuned in." It pained Alex, due to his frugality, that United had splashed £30.75m for Berbatov in 2008, only to sell him for less than ten percent of that outlay just four years later (when the Bulgarian was signed by Fulham for £3m).

But Alex's most disappointing signing, ahead of Berbatov, was Owen Hargreaves. The Canadian-born England international had been outstanding at Bayern Munich where he occupied a sitting midfield position with great discipline despite being a technically gifted player in possession. Alex would snap him up for £17m in 2007, but the midfielder would end up only participating in thirty-nine games before being let go for free in 2012. What's interesting is Alex had a negative gut feeling about Hargreaves just before he sanctioned his purchase, but none-theless followed through with it.

"I studied his playing record and felt a tinge of doubt. I didn't feel a strong vibe about him… it turned out to be a disaster. Owen had no confidence in himself whatsoever. He didn't show nearly enough determination to overcome his physical difficul-ties for my liking. I saw him opt for the easy choice too often in terms of training."

In fairness to Hargreaves, he suffered from severe knee and thigh problems, though the thigh problems can be put down to his knee never feeling ideal. These injuries plagued his Manchester United career, but it was the lack of positivity in how Hargreaves handled these injuries that truly irked his manager.

"He went everywhere in search of cures: Germany, America,

Canada. I felt he lacked the confidence to overcome his injuries. It went from bad to worse. He was away in America for the best part of a year."

But even when Hargreaves was at Carrington, Alex wasn't best pleased with his willingness to be as great as he possibly could be.

"I would say to him, 'How are you this morning?' 'Great, boss,' he would reply. 'But I think I'll do something on my own. I'm feeling it a bit.' When I signed him, there was something about him I didn't like. The thing every good leader should have is an instinct. Mine said to me, 'I don't fancy this.' When he came over to Old Trafford for the medical, I still had some indefinable doubt. He was very hail-fellow-well-met. Almost too nice."

It was unusual Alex would have signed a player who he had a negative gut feeling about. His due diligence before sanctioning a purchase was mostly comprehensive and intricate. The asset Alex most looked for in a player was discipline over ability. Always. A player had to prove to Alex that he could carry out the orders set down by his manager first and foremost. Secondly, Alex needed a player to prove to him that he could make the right choices when in possession of the ball. Decision-making was key. A player had to be aware of all of his options. If he took the wrong one, Alex would fume, even if the passage of play did work out in the player's favour. Yet when Alex opted to buy a player, the equation of his decision was often made up of more than what was proven on the pitch. Alex would delve deep into a player's background — his upbringing, his friends, his lifestyle — before deciding whether or not he was a right fit for his dressing-room. It was a player's upbringing that particularly intrigued the Govanman.

He would write in *Leading*: "Before we signed players, especially youngsters, I always tried to understand the circumstances in which they had been raised. The first ten or 12 years of anybody's life have such a profound influence on the way they act as adults."

As previously mentioned, Alex would then use that knowledge of a player's background to motivate them in the dressing-room.

Yet the fact that Alex went into intricate detail before buying players is contradicted by the manner in which he bought Bebe—a young Portuguese winger whom he signed out of nowhere for £7m in 2010. Bebe — who had a strange bi-ability of being an outrageously good player one minute and then looking like Bambi on Ice the next — had been scouted, unofficially, by super-agent Jorge Mendes. Mendes brought the player to Alex and informed him he should snap him up now, for £7m would seem like peanuts in a few years when all major clubs would be gunning for his signature. Alex watched video clips of Bebe and based on them — but more so the judgement of the trusted associate and agent of Cristiano Ronaldo — he asked the club to pay the transfer fee. Bebe would go into United's reserves where he would constantly confuse coaches. He scored a beautiful volley in one game that some staff at the club have labelled the greatest goal they've ever seen scored in a Manchester United shirt. Yet on most occasions he looked lost on the pitch, as if he didn't understand his role as part of a team. It seemed pretty early on that Bebe was an outstanding street footballer. But that didn't count for much at the top level of the game. In early 2012, Alex had words with Jorge Mendes, informing him how disappointed he was in his recommendation. But he shouldn't have been disappointed with Mendes. He only should have been disappointed with himself. Signing a player based on *YouTube* clips and the recommendation of a super-agent is far removed from the manner in which the manager of the most famous football club in the world should go about his business. In fairness to Alex, the Bebe transfer was far from the usual manner in which he went about his transfer business. Bebe would go on loan to two different clubs over the next two seasons before United managed to convince Benfica to part with £3m for his services.

One of the most high-profile flop signings Alex made was that of world-class midfielder Juan Sebastian Veron. The Argentine cost United £24m from Lazio in 2001 in a move the football world lauded. He seemed like an ideal Old Trafford player within the first month of him turning out for the club. But pretty soon, Alex would learn that the playmaker was the wrong fit in his midfield. Veron simply didn't have the discipline to carry out his manager's orders—one of the traits Alex usually demanded before green-lighting a transfer, but somehow missed this time.

'What a footballer,' Alex would admit. 'Talent-wise there was absolutely nothing wrong with him. He had two fine feet, he could run, his control was magnificent, his vision was brilliant, but he just couldn't fit into the team. He was the sort if you played red versus yellow on the training ground, Veron would play for both teams. He just played everywhere. He went everywhere he liked. If I managed him for a hundred years, I wouldn't know where to play him.'

Alex would end up selling the midfielder to Chelsea for £15m, meaning United took a £9m hit on a player their manager had assumed would be just as world class at Old Trafford as he had been at Lazio.

Another transfer that ended up frustrating Alex was that of lesser-known youngster, Nick Powell. Alex would tell anybody who listened to him about a year before he retired that Powell was going to be "some player."

The midfielder had been snapped up from Crewe Alexandra and Alex was certain he had unearthed a gem. The Govanman would write in *My Autobiography*, having just retired and left Powell for Moyes to develop: "He is an absolute certainty to be in the England team one day."

That prediction would embarrass Alex. Powell would end up not in the England team, but in the lower divisions with Wigan Athletic, Hull City and Stoke City. In fairness, Powell had represented England at all underage levels up until senior level when, for reasons unknown, his eliteness somehow deserted him.

There was another signing Alex would predict great things

for. Centre-half, Phil Jones. Alex had watched Jones play for Blackburn Rovers at just nineteen years of age and was bowled over by his maturity. Jones was literally bossing his defensive line throughout the game, yelling at players much more experienced than him that they were slightly behind his holding line. So impressed, Alex would order a detailed scouting report on the centre-half; both a player review and a lifestyle review. Both would come back filled with praise for the young star.

Alex would watch him three more times, once at Old Trafford where he acted as captain for Blackburn as they impressively held United to a 1-1 draw, even though he didn't have the armband. After that game, Alex would green light a £16.5m transfer.

After just six weeks of training with United, as they began the 2011-12 season, Alex was so impressed with his new centre-back that he would remark: 'Jones, arguably, the way he is looking, could be our best ever player. I think he may be one of the best players we've ever had, no matter where we play him (Jones could play right-back, centre-back and as a defensive midfielder). At 21 years of age, he is going to be a phenomenal player. He has such a massive influence, with his instinct and reading of the game. He has a real drive aboot him.'

Alex would also say, on a separate occasion: 'He is so good. He's gonna be one of the greatest ever at United. He could be our next Duncan Edwards.'

Edwards, a victim of the Munich Air Disaster at just twenty-one years of age, had been beyond mature for his age: tall and stocky, a man when he was supposed to be a boy. He could also play in a number of different positions. The comparison was meant to be the highest compliment Alex could have given Jones. Instead, it turned out to be a stick pundits could beat the player with as his career at United took hit after hit. Despite turning himself into a Manchester United and England regular, Jones would suffer seventeen different injuries in the space of five years and couldn't possibly live up to the billing his former manager had laid out for him. Sadly, the player turned down the opportunity of a lucrative testimonial game having remained with United for ten years—for fear supporters wouldn't turn up given his multiple injuries.

The most frustrated Alex would become in the transfer market, however, was in his repeated attempts to replace talismanic goalkeeper Peter Schmeichel who left United in the summer of 1999—just after the club had clinched the unprecedented treble. Alex had always earmarked Edwin van Der Sar to replace the Great Dane, but for some reason his head was swung by the romantic notion of re-signing Mark Bosnich on a free transfer—who had been a former youth prospect at the club before going on to play for Aston Villa for seven years. Bosnich, a talented goalkeeper in a number of different respects, would let Alex down with his lack of discipline and party lifestyle. Alex's detailed report before signing Bosnich had noted the keeper's party lifestyle as an issue, but Alex still sanctioned the purchase because he felt he could help the Australian to mature. He couldn't, as it happened. And before the end of the keeper's first season at the club he was being replaced by reserve shot stopper Raimond van der Gouw. The next summer, with van der Sar having signed a long-term contract with Fulham, United signed Fabien Barthez. The reason Alex green lit the colourful Frenchman's transfer was because he felt United were missing a character in goal following the loss of Schmeichel that neither Bosnich, nor van der Gouw had filled. Alex would love working with Barthez, but he considered him less than a good enough goalkeeper in the Premier League. While disappointed with Barthez there would be opportunity for another goalkeeper purchase, Massimo Taibi, to get game time. But he embarrassed himself on his debut at Old Trafford when he let the ball slip under his legs. Then, having grown fully frustrated with Barthez, Alex signed the strong-minded Roy Carroll. The Northern Irishman would eventually oust Barthez as the number one and proved to be a consistent, if far from spectacular, Premier League keeper for United. Alex would then make another keeper purchase in the shape of Tim Howard — a man who suffered with Tourette's and large bouts of depression — from MLS side MetroStars in 2003. Like Carroll, Howard would prove to be a steady pair of hands more often than not, but lacked the consistency to be a great. He would, for the most part, be United's number one for two seasons until Alex decided to opt for the player he should have signed all along: Edwin van Der Sar. It meant United had endured a six year merry-go-round in search of Schmeichel's replacement. It didn't look good. But in truth, United won three Premier League titles during the goalkeeper debacle as well as an FA Cup. It was quite telling that when it came to replacing van der Sar some six years later in 2011, Alex allowed goalkeeping coach Eric Steele to choose the Dutchman's successor. It was Steele who had been scouting David de Gea for years, planning for van der Sar's departure. Alex, interestingly, would have preferred to sign Manuel Neuer, but Steele managed to convince him that De Gea had all the potential to become world class and, given his mess up at the start of the century in trying to replace Schmeichel, Alex decided Steele was best placed to make the judgement.

While most of the above signings paint a bleak representation of Alex's dealing in the transfer market, there were of course many more successes than there were failures. He, however, doesn't like to take full praise for the players brought into the club. That is reserved for the multiple scouts who worked for him over the years (Les Kershaw and Alex's brother Martin were considered the best of his scouts). Manchester United's successes in the transfer market was not so much an homage to the Govanman himself, but more so the scouts who had an eye, not just for a good player, but for an Alex Ferguson player.

Alex, oddly enough, literally went through an A-to-Z of signing players for Manchester United. The first player he ever bought was Viv Anderson. The last: Wilfried Zaha. Alex made 105 signings in his twenty-six and a half years at Old Trafford.

The best player he bought: Ronaldo. The best signing he made: Irwin. The most disappointing: Hargreaves. His personal favourite? Ole Gunnar Solskjaer.

Solskjaer was as close to Alex as any of the hundreds of players he managed over the course of his career. He had plucked the player from Norwegian side Molde in 1996 for just £1.5m after growing frustrated in his pursuit of Alan Shearer. Solskjaer would score some of the most iconic goals in United's history, even if he spent most of his time at the club as a back-up striker. The Norwegian would use his lunch breaks at Carrington to pick Alex's brains on tactics and training drills. And the two of them formed a life-long bond that Alex developed with very few of his many players. When Solskjaer felt it was time to hang up his boots, eleven years after signing for the club, Alex didn't want to let him go and so offered him a role as United's first team striker coach. After a year, Alex felt Solskjaer's abilities as a coach were wasted in just working with strikers, so he was given the job as the United reserve team manager—a role he would stay in for three years until Molde — the club United had purchased him from fifteen years earlier — offered him the chance to become their first team manager. Alex was heartbroken in both a personal and a professional sense when the Solskjaer family headed back for their homeland. But seven years later, Alex would play a key role in appointing Solskjaer as United's first team manager (which you can read about in detail in a later chapter).

The records and indeed collation of trophies prove that Alex, much more often than not, called it right in the transfer market.

He would write in *Leading*: "If you take a closer look at all my signings — over many years — the money was well spent."

Alex, due to a frugality inherited from his mother's tight purse-strings, hated wasting the club's money. Even when he did green-light the splashing of big amounts, he had to be certain the spend would bring in value.

"Some of my churlishness about spending comes from my upbringing. My parents made sure that my brother and I never wanted for anything. But there wasn't a lot of spare money sloshing about our tenement flat in Govan. Put it down to my Scottish roots, but I always tried to treat club money as if it was my own."

That is why the low-money signings such as Schmeichel, Irwin, Bruce, Solskjaer, Cantona, Keane, Johnsen, Fortune, Park, Ronaldo, Vidic, Evra and Valencia are his favourite dealings in the market much, more so over the bigger named and certainly bigger spend on signings such as Berbatov (£30.75m), Hargreaves (£17m), van Persie (£24m) and Veron (£24m). The big splash on players such as Rio Ferdinand (£30m) and Wayne Rooney (£30m) Alex feels were fees well spent given the players' relatively young age and the fact that they ended up spending the majority of their playing days at the club.

The greasy skinned teenager Alex signed for £12.5m? He would be sold six years later for £80.9m. It represented a £68.4m profit—on top of the years Ronaldo shone as brightly as any player had ever shone, even Best, Charlton and Giggs, at Old Trafford. But Alex didn't want that profit. He didn't want to sell Ronaldo at all. The greasy skinned teenager he once signed had turned into a handsome specimen under Alex's watch, but his ambition of turning out in the all-white strip of Real Madrid had never been a secret between the pair. Ronaldo would leave with Alex's blessing, and during his goodbyes, Alex told the best player he ever managed that he was certain he would end up back at Old Trafford one day. In September 2021, Alex — by now eight years retired — would play a pivotal role in securing the return of Ronaldo.

What's interesting to brush over in this chapter are the players Alex would have loved to have signed but failed to over the years. Despite missing out on some major names in the game, it was his failure to sign Sheffield Wednesday striker David Hirst that pained him most. He was desperate to land the player in both 1992 and 1993, but Wednesday manager Trevor Francis would barely even answer Alex's calls—so intent was he to keep the player at Hillsborough. Another huge let down for Alex was losing out on Paul Gascoigne in the summer of 1988 when he genuinely believed a deal had been agreed with the infamous and talented playmaker. Gascoigne told Alex over the phone one Friday evening in August of 1988 that he had agreed the terms of the contract laid out to him and that he was definitely going to sign for Manchester United the following week. On the Sunday, Alex would learn through sources that Gazza had put pen to paper on a four-year-deal with Tottenham Hotspur for the same wages. Alex couldn't understand it. He was totally perplexed as he not only thought Spurs to be a far inferior club to United, but because he felt Gascoigne was making a disastrous decision in moving to the country's capital. Upon doing his due diligence, Alex would find out Spurs had offered to buy Gascoigne's mother a £40,000 house in London. And that swung him. A £40,000 house—when Alex would have offered that and more in extra wages to secure the talent had he not rushed into signing a Spurs contract on impulse that Sunday.

Alex said: "Paul Gascoigne was the best English player since Bobby Charlton. Unfortunately, we didn't get him and looking back now, he made a big mistake. He recognised that himself years later. We had Geordies at United: Bobby Charlton, Bryan Robson, Steve Bruce, even Gary Pallister was from Middlesbrough. We had people who would have taken care of him, particularly Robson who was fantastic with young players. Instead, he goes to an island in London, and you're easily swallowed up there as a young lad. I think it was a big mistake by him."

Gazza wasn't the only Geordie who would frustrate Alex in the transfer market. Over three separate summers he tried desperately to sign Alan Shearer to no avail. Southampton opted to keep the striker when Alex first made contact about securing him in the summer of 1991. Twelve months later, Alex would enter the market for him again and would end up livid that the striker opted to sign for Blackburn Rovers instead who had

offered a better salary and signing-on bonus. Alex could understand some personalities opting for the bigger pay day, but he
thought Shearer a more determined and intelligent man than that
and couldn't come to terms with why that player in particular
would choose money over medals. Four years later, Shearer then
chose to sign for his boyhood club Newcastle United over
Manchester United. Alex was again left shaking his head. Shearer
has gone on record as saying he has never regretted turning
Manchester United down. Given that the Red Devils secured
eight league titles, five FA Cups and a Champions League in all
the years Shearer played since he first turned down the lure of
Old Trafford, Alex finds it very difficult to believe Shearer talks
about having no regrets with sincerity.

In future years, Alex would miss out on more big-name
attackers in the shape of Ronaldo (the Brazilian one), Ronaldinho,
Gabriel Batistuta and Patrick Kluivert, all because the club
refused to pay the wages demanded by these megastars. The
closest they came to landing one of those players was in 2003,
when Ronaldinho looked destined for Old Trafford. Then United
chief executive Peter Kenyon had agreed a deal with Ronaldinho's representatives and told Alex over a phone call while he was
in France holidaying with Cathy that the contract was all but
signed. The Brazilian icon would have his head turned days later
by the new money at PSG however, and ultimately opted to
move to the French capital over Manchester.

Though instead of signing Ronaldinho, United signed Cristiano Ronaldo. Instead of signing Shearer in the early nineties,
they signed Cantona. And instead of signing Shearer in the mid-
nineties, they signed Solskjaer. On occasions, thanks mainly to
Alex's network of scouts, the backup option proved to be the best
option over the long-term.

Despite not splashing cash to land megastars such as Ronaldinho, United weren't backward in spending money. Alex would
break the British transfer record five times in all his years at Old
Trafford (Gary Pallister for £2.3m in 1989, Roy Keane for £3.75m

in '93, Andrew Cole for £7m in '95, Juan Sebastian Veron for £24m in 2001 and Rio Ferdinand for £30m in '02), but rather bizarrely, United were only the highest spending club in three out of the twenty-six and a half years he was in situ.

Yet, rather than the signings Alex made over his long tenure at Old Trafford, it was the players he sold that made the boldest headlines.

If United fans were shocked in the earliest part of his career when the Govanman proved his audacity by unceremoniously dumping the likes of Paul McGrath, Kevin Moran and Norman Whiteside from his dressing-room, then that truly was only a flashing sign of what was to come. United fans still hadn't learned Alex's cut-throat ways by the summer of 1995 when they felt outraged that he had sanctioned the shock sales of Ince, Hughes and Kanchelskis (which you can read about in more detail the next chapter). Strangely enough, despite all of his success, Alex would continue to stun and frustrate fans and the media alike with his player sales.

In fact, the media would be so shocked by one sale that it not only became headline news on the back *and* front-pages of the national papers, but also the lead story on BBC News in the same summer that Britain and America were going to war in Iraq. David Beckham was leaving Manchester United.

Beckham's reaction, by standing up to his manager, after the football boot split his brow wasn't the reason Alex sanctioned his sale. In fact the boot was kicked in anger because Alex had long since been losing faith in a man he had nurtured from the age of fourteen. He didn't kick that boot towards Beckham because he was frustrated with his performance that day. He kicked it out of sheer frustration with Beckham's life choices. Alex had, for almost that entire season, been hugely irritated by the player's need for acclaim in fields beyond football.

What really riled Alex was that Beckham had signed up an agent called Simon Fuller who was notorious in the celebrity world (Fuller is or has been the agent of The Spice Girls, Simon

Cowell, Lisa Marie Presley and S Club 7 among others (the 'S' in S Club stands for Simon)). Fuller was ahead of his time in marketing his clients; getting them as much exposure his charming ways could muster in the celebrity pages of tabloid newspapers. His ways were designed to help his clients flourish from their own celebrity brand. The way Alex saw it, Beckham should only have been striving to appear on the back pages of newspapers, not in the mid-section posing with the likes of Tom Cruise and Jennifer Lopez. And certainly not on the front pages, photographed on red carpets alongside his wife. Alex blamed Becks' wife Victoria for turning the player's head and rather rudely used to call her just 'Spice' when referring to her rather than by her name (bizarrely unusual given his fondness for remembering even the tiniest of details about the family members of his players). Even though Beckham's commitment and performances rarely dipped while he was at United, Alex didn't want the player's celebrity status setting any sort of precedence in his dressing-room, so he sanctioned his sale to a huge outpouring of grief from United fans worldwide in June, 2003. The fact is, the manager's mind had been made up months prior. Beckham's increasing celebrity status spelt the end of his United career.

Alex would write in My Autobiography: "The minute a player thought he was bigger than the manager, he had to go. David thought he was bigger than Alex Ferguson. There is no doubt about that in my mind. It doesn't matter whether it's Alex Ferguson or Pete the Plumber. The name of the manager is irrelevant. The authority is what counts."

Becks signed for Real Madrid for £23.5m that summer and went on to have an astonishing career at AC Milan, PSG and LA Galaxy up until he was thirty-eight. But he was heartbroken by Alex ousting him from Manchester United—the club he had supported since he was a boy.

'When I joined Manchester United, I never wanted to leave,' Beckham recalls. 'When I was told they were selling me I realised my dream was over. And in all honesty, I couldn't watch Manchester United for two years, I was that gutted.'

Aside from leaving the club of his dreams, Becks was hugely heartbroken by the breaking down of the bond he had with Alex. He often did, while playing under him as well as after the Govanman had sold him, refer to Alex as a 'father figure.' Alex, meanwhile, rather dismissively didn't speak to Beckham for five years after he left the club. Beckham handled his departure like a gentleman. Alex continued to act rather petulantly about his former right-winger. However, they would make up for lost time when Beckham appeared in a charity game at Old Trafford. Alex approached him in the corridors of the famous ground, and they embraced as if no time had passed. To this day they remain close.

The same can't be said of Alex's relationship with Roy Keane —another player he dumped from his dressing-room with little warning. They didn't remain friends at all, and the Corkman is still quick to have a pop at his former manager when given the platform today. But the story of Keane and Alex's breakdown in relationship is so juicy that it is reserved for a chapter later in this book.

One other sale that shook the United fanbase was that of goal machine Ruud van Nistelrooy in the summer of 2006. Alex was a massive fan of the Dutchman, but his ego began to take control in his final season at the club—and Alex wasn't having any of it.

The crack in their relationship began after United had signed Cristiano Ronaldo in 2003. Van Nistelrooy had had one too many run-ins, not directly with Ronaldo, but with assistant manager Carlos Queiroz who he would constantly lambaste during training sessions such was his frustration with the young Portuguese winger. Van Nistelrooy was aghast that most of Unit-ed's attacks were centred around the pace of Ronaldo and a final ball into the box for van Nistelrooy to finish off no longer became the focal point of the team. Alex simply decided to put fewer crosses into the box, so deadly was Ronaldo proving to be by cutting inside the full-back, rather than going outside him and crossing like Beckham had mastered over so many years from that side of the pitch. Van Nistelrooy loved playing with Beckham. He couldn't stand playing with Ronaldo. That all stemmed from his own ego. His moaning went so far that Gary Neville had to have words with the Dutchman that turned into a blistering stand up row. Neville roared at van Nistelrooy, shouting at him that he wasn't the only player in this team and that he needed to calm his arrogance. The Neville row was one of many van Nistelrooy had with teammates or coaches in what proved to be his final season. Alex began to wonder if he should part with the Dutchman, given that he was causing so much unrest in his dressing-room even if he was, arguably, the best centre forward in the world at the time. But Alex wouldn't have to wonder for long. At the end of that season (2005-06) United would play Wigan Athletic in a Millennium Stadium-set League Cup final. United's back up striker at the time was Louis Saha who had to play second fiddle to van Nistelrooy for much of the season. Except in the League Cup, where Alex often fielded his second team coupled with some promising youth academy players. He told van Nistelrooy in the lead up to the cup final that he was going to stick with Saha, but did concede to the Dutchman that he would get on at some point. Except he didn't get on. United trashed Wigan 4-0 in that final, but van Nistelrooy's face was bull-like when the players went to receive their winners' medals. And then, as the players were parading the cup in front of their fans, the Dutchman decided to walk off the pitch and down the tunnel to get changed.

The following week in training, as United were heading towards another Premier League title win, news came through that Cristiano Ronaldo's father was gravely ill. Alex gave the Portuguese time off to return to his home town of Madeira to grieve. When he came back, van Nistelrooy stuck a late boot into Ronaldo in training, and as the winger was complaining, van Nistelrooy said: 'What you gonna do. Complain to your daddy?'

Most witnesses in training that day believe van Nistelrooy

was referring to Carlos Queiroz, and not in fact Ronaldo's actual father. But nonetheless, that episode was the straw that broke the camel's back. The Dutchman's time at Manchester United was over. He had caused way too many arguments in his final season with a number of different personnel at the club. Alex often wondered why van Nistelrooy was so volatile that year and seems to think that either the Dutchman had already been touted by Real Madrid and was gunning to sign for the Spanish side or simply that his ego couldn't handle the adulation Ronaldo was receiving from all quarters.

Many years later, during one frosty evening in January of 2010, Alex's phone rang. When he picked up, his former Dutch striker was on the other end.

'I just wanna say sorry for how I acted in my final season with you,' van Nistelrooy said. Alex accepted his apology, but never received a full explanation as to why the Dutchman's ego had gotten so out of hand.

Van Nistelrooy would go on to be just as prolific for Real Madrid as he had been for United, but Alex never regretted letting him go. It was for the benefit of his dressing-room overall.

The only real regret Alex has ever had in selling a player was reserved for another Dutchman, Jaap Stam.

Stam had been a rock at the heart of United's defence for three seasons (helping them to that treble win in 1999), but upon returning from a bad Achilles tear, Alex and then assistant coach Steve McClaren both noticed that he had lost a yard of pace in training. He then had consecutive underwhelming performances for the team which bizarrely coincided with Lazio making a bid for him out of the blue. The money on offer was £16m, and Alex — assuming he had insight that the Dutchman's body was on the way down — accepted it. But Stam would prove that he hadn't been affected fully by his Achilles injury, that he was just taking time to readjust back into full-time football life and would be a smash hit at Lazio. Selling Stam was an instinctual decision—one Alex has since regretted.

'Jaap Stam was the one, definitely. Aye, I made a mistake there. He continued to play at a high level long after we let him go.'

Although Alex has since praised Stam and Beckham and van Nistelrooy for continuing to perform at an elite level after being let go by Manchester United, he genuinely never felt any sense of sorrow when cutting them from the club. He felt no sorrow for McGrath or Whiteside or Keane or Ince or Kanchelskis either. He only ever felt sorrow when it came to letting go academy players who he had deemed not quite good enough to make the breakthrough at United. Over his twenty-six and half years at the club, he had to deliver such news to almost a hundred teenagers—all who shared the same dream of playing in front of a packed Old Trafford.

It still to this day hurts Alex to recall letting talent players such as Ben Thornley and Michael Clegg in particular (though it was injuries rather than ability that ended their dreams) as well as Josh King, Robbie Brady, Chris Eagles, Oliver Norwood and Paul McShane among others that their time was up.

'That was the worst,' Alex admitted. 'Having to tell a young lad that he wasnae gonnae to make it at Manchester United. That was absolutely terrible. No doubt aboot it, having those conversations were the worst moments in my years as a manager.'

He wouldn't feel bad about letting one academy player in particular go, though. The lanky Frenchman was head and shoulders above everyone else as the shining light in United's academy for three years running and looked an absolute certainty to be a future world class star, even if Alex had reservations about his off-the-ball movement. But when Paul Pogba hired super-agent Mino Raiola to help him negotiate a better contract at Manchester United, Alex became aware he had a player on his books that was more interested in the bottom line than he was about the successes of his football team. Raiola would meet with Alex to discuss a new contract for his player, only for Alex to call the meeting to a conclusion within three minutes. Raiola was being not only outrageous in his demands for his player, but also strangely arrogant in how he went about those demands.

'Paul Pogba?' Alex would simply say years later. 'He just had a bad agent. A scumbag.'

Alex would write in *My Autobiography*: "There are one or two football agents I simply do not like, and Mino Raiola is one of them. I distrusted him from the moment I met him. He became Zlatan Ibrahimovic's agent while he was playing for Ajax, and eventually he would end up representing Pogba, who was only eighteen years old at the time. We had Paul under a three-year contract, and it had a one-year renewal option which we were eager to sign. But Raiola suddenly appeared on the scene and our first meeting was a fiasco. He and I were like oil and water."

It didn't matter how good a player Pogba was; he was shown the door for lacking the willingness and desire Alex insisted a player had to have if they wanted to play for Manchester United. Six months later the Frenchman signed for Juventus on a free.

Bizarrely, in a transfer that went some distance to proving how much Manchester United had departed from the Alex Ferguson way in the midst of his retirement (which you can read all about in a later chapter), the club, under Jose Mourinho, would spend £89.9m to bring the Frenchman back to Old Trafford.

That signing — completed three years after Alex's retirement — made the frugal Govanman squirm.

1992-1995

It was the dawn of a new era. The Premier League had been born (a rebrand in which Sky Sports had invested £304m in for the rights to broadcast live matches over the next five years) and just as it had all kicked off to a tidal wave of optimism and excitement, Eric Cantona would sign for Manchester United.

Alex couldn't believe it when Martin Edwards hung up from Bill Fotherby and nodded.

'He said they might be interested in selling him.'

Alex slapped his hands and rubbed them together.

'Perfect,' he said. 'Ring him back in an hour and make an offer.'

Edwards did as his manager requested, and within a five-minute phone call managed to haggle Fotherby down from £1.5m to an agreed £1.1m for the services of the Frenchman. The following day, Cantona arrived at The Cliff training ground with a cheap toiletries bag under his arm to undergo the first part of his medical.

Because the transfer came out of the blue, rumours began to circulate as to why Leeds would sell such a talismanic figure to their rivals. It was speculated at the time that Leeds sold Cantona because he had had an affair with his strike partner, Lee Chapman's actress wife, Leslie Ash. But that's all that was—speculation, a rumour; a rumour that went way too far, even appearing in national newspapers. The truth is, there is no conspiracy to be had over the Cantona-to-Manchester United transfer more so than any other transfer that has ever occurred in the game. Cantona was allowed to sign for Manchester United simply because Leeds manager Howard Wilkinson felt the Frenchman didn't fit in well with his squad. Cantona was a complex character to deal with, and quite odd to boot. He was interested in paintbrushes and easels and the many different facets of artistry. The gritty British-born players that made up the bulk of the Leeds dressing-room, such as Chapman, David Batty, Gary McAllister, Chris Fairclough and Gary Speed simply couldn't relate to him. Cantona was an outcast at Leeds United. He didn't enjoy being there. And most of the players, certainly the manager, didn't enjoy having him there. And so, despite the Frenchman playing a pivotal role in Leeds' league title win the previous season, Wilkinson thought it appropriate to move him on in an attempt to harmonise his dressing-room. In fact, by chance he had held such a conversation with Fotherby the very same week his chairman happened to call Martin Edwards about the availability of Denis Irwin. It is mere coincidence that Alex wrote down Cantona's name in the middle of that conversation.

Alex was buzzing about his new capture, and in his programme notes for the Manchester derby that would take place the week after Cantona had signed, he would write, with predictive powers: "Eric is a great entertainer. The reason I am more confident about the success of this transfer than is being expressed in some quarters is that Manchester United are tailor made for a player of this Frenchman's temperament. They don't call Old Trafford the Theatre of Dreams for nothing. We have a unique stage here, just right for his talents."

Cantona would light up that stage. He would stay at Old Trafford for six seasons and within those six seasons would lead the club to five league titles. The only title United didn't win during that period — in which Blackburn were crowned champions in 1995 — happened to be the season the Frenchman was banned by the FA for eight months after attacking a Crystal Palace fan in the front row of the Main Stand at Selhurst Park (which you can read about later).

'Right, we're gonnae win this fuckin' title,' Alex would tell Cantona and his new teammates in the middle of November 1992. United, having finished as runners up the previous season were among the favourites to win the inaugural Premier League, but the season hadn't got off to a great start. Sheffield United had beaten them on the opening day of the campaign and draws against clubs they were expected to beat, such as QPR, Ipswich Town and Middlesbrough, had the fans whispering about Alex's credentials in the stands once more. But he was confident the players would put their disappointing start behind them, certainly now that Cantona had been added to the ranks. He was everything Alex adored in a striker; chest puffed out, back to goal, a wonderful first touch, and a born entertainer. If Alex could design his perfect player, he'd design Cantona. It wasn't just the Frenchman's ability to control games that excited Alex, it was his willingness to practise. Cantona didn't end training when he was expected to end training. He would stay out for an extra ninety minutes on the training pitch; quite often calling on academy players to assist him. The academy players he would ask to cross balls in for him for extra training included spotty-faced teenagers named Nicky Butt, David Beckham, Paul Scholes and two brothers called Neville.

It was another academy player those spotty-faced teenagers were all aspiring to follow into the first team. Ryan Giggs had become an ever-present on the left-wing by the start of the Premier League rebrand and was lighting up Old Trafford in a way that was clearly reminiscent of the legend of George Best.

'I remember the first time I saw Ryan play,' Alex would recall. 'It was like he was gliding across the ground. Not running. Gliding.'

'The first time I ever saw him play,' Gary Neville would recall, 'I thought, Oh my God. If that's the level we have to get to around here, I'm done. I'll go back to Bury.'

'We were nowhere near him,' Paul Scholes would say. 'We weren't even in the same bracket as Ryan.'

Cantona, in 2011, said, 'When I arrived Giggs was playing. He had just got in the team. And now I am retired fourteen years, he is still playing.' The Frenchman laughed. 'That tells you all about Giggs.'

With Giggs on the left, hit signing Andrei Kanchelskis on the right, and Cantona pulling strings in between the two of them, Alex's pragmatic approach of nullifying the opposition before breaking out quickly was orchestrated with such finesse, and at such a pace, that the fans inside Old Trafford were on their feet more often than they were seated.

Suddenly, from only scoring seventeen goals in sixteen games (which included a dumping from the UEFA Cup by minnows Moscow Torpedo on penalties following two scoreless legs) and not knowing where their goals were going to come from, everybody in the team was scoring. Even Mark Hughes found his finishing boots again following the arrival of Cantona.

United went on such a consistent run of results in the December and January period that by the first of February they had tightened the gap on early pace-setters Aston Villa and Norwich City to just one point. And, having thrown away the league title over the Easter period the season prior, Alex was determined that wouldn't happen again. He demanded consistency in the final months of the campaign, ranting and raving at his players that there was to be no repeat of the 1991-92 season.

'We said we'd win the last First Division title. But we threw it away. We sure as hell won't throw away the first Premier League title. Undastood?'

There were lots of unique tests during the final quarter of that campaign — but none more so than United's trip to title rivals Norwich City on April fifth. If United had been beaten, their bubble would likely burst just as it had done twelve months prior. However, victory over the Canaries would catapult United to the top of the table. Alex pulled a masterstroke leading into that game. He started with Lee Sharpe on the left wing and played Giggs through the middle with Kanchelskis on the right. The speed of these three players running with the ball, coupled with Cantona's devastatingly quick brain just ahead of them, saw United roar to a 3-0 lead by the twenty-first minute. They were in such control of what was deemed a 'six-pointer' by half time that Alex simply told his players to go out and enjoy the second half. They did. There was a carnival atmosphere amongst the away supporters that evening in Norwich. It seemed as if they'd crossed a bridge—a bridge that had snapped in half when they tried to cross it the previous Easter. In fact, it was in the Easter weekend in 1993 when United fans would begin celebrating as if they'd won the title. After finding themselves 1-0 down to Sheffield Wednesday in front of a packed and tense Old Trafford, talismanic captain Steve Bruce etched his name into United folklore by scoring two headed goals in injury-time to gift United all three points. Soon after the game had finished, the stadium announcer called out the results of games taking place elsewhere. The players were heading for the tunnel when it was announced that Aston Villa had been held to a scoreless draw by Coventry City. Two weeks later, Villa would stutter again; losing 1-0 at home to Oldham Athletic —a result that would confirm Manchester United as English football league champions for the first time since the same day in May, 1967 —precisely twenty-six years in the waiting.

United's next game — the penultimate game of the season — at home to Blackburn Rovers, was played in front of a carnival atmosphere that consisted of repetitive chants of 'champions' and the odd interlude of Queen's smash hit *We Are The Champions*. Giggs would cap off a stunning season by scoring an audacious thirty-yard free-kick before Paul Ince and then Gary Pallister would score to round out a 3-1 victory. It was Pallister's only goal of the season. In fact, he had been the only outfield player not to score over the course of that campaign when United got a free-kick twenty-yards from goal at the tail end of that game against Blackburn.

'Let Pally take it,' captain Steve Bruce roared out over the crowd's repeated chants. Nobody expected him to score; certainly nobody expected him to curl the ball around the wall to nestle it into the far bottom corner. But he did. Alex beamed with pride as club captain Bryan Robson and team captain Steve Bruce lifted the new trophy together. He was particularly proud of the fact that, sitting amongst the electric crowd, was Sir Matt Busby. Alex stood on the edge of the pitch and raised both of his clenched fists towards Sir Matt in celebration, then both Glaswegians joined the players in the dressing-room to pop open multiple bottles of champagne.

If the club's first league title win in twenty-six years didn't announce United as being back on the perch of English football with enough volume, then their winning of the domestic double — of both Premier League and FA Cup — the following season screamed it from every Georgian and Victorian rooftop in the country.

The 1993-94 campaign was largely flawless for Alex, but for three separate episodes. Firstly, Cathy was genuinely furious with her husband for selling Darren Ferguson to Wolverhampton Wanderers half-way through the season.

'Why would you do that… sell ya own son?'

She was perplexed. The decision to sell Darren would only be perplexing to a non-match-going parent of said player, in truth. United had just won the battle against Blackburn Rovers and their millionaire owner Jack Walker to sign energetic Irish midfielder Roy Keane from Nottingham Forest. Keane was a no-nonsense, in-your-face, twenty-three-year-old and there was no hiding the fact that he had the potential to be a world-class midfielder, primed for taking over the role of Bryan Robson who had stood down from the club after the first Premier League win. Keane matched Robson quality for quality. Darren Ferguson didn't even come close. It was quite telling that Darren didn't leave United for another Premier League team. He would drop a division, to play for Wolves in Division One before seeing out most of his playing career at Wrexham in the lower divisions of English professional football.

With Keane now controlling the engine, Cantona having his two hands on the steering wheel and Giggs and Kanchelskis flipping through the gears, United were — inarguably — streets ahead of the rest of the teams in England.

They sped to a second title in a row, holding nearest challengers Blackburn off with relative ease and eventually winning the league by eight points. They sped by teams in the FA Cup, too, until a dramatic semi-final clash against Oldham Athletic almost caused them to crash. It took a miraculous, last-gasp Mark Hughes volley in the 120th minute to take the original tie to a replay where United turned in a much classier performance to knock four goals past the Latics. They would score the same number of goals against Chelsea in a one-sided Wembley final a fortnight later, in which Cantona turned in one of the best individual FA Cup Final performances of any era.

The second flaw in that double-winning season, however, aside from Cathy getting herself into hysterics because Alex had the cheek to sell their own son, was the fact that United failed so miserably in Europe. After winning the title the year previous, the Red Devils were back in the European Cup (rebranded as the Champions League in the same season England's First Division was rebranded as the Premier League) for the first time in over a quarter of a century. In fact, the last time they had been in this competition, they'd won it—with Sir Matt Busby leading the team he built in the aftermath of the Munich Air Disaster to a tear-inducing win over Benfica in an epic Wembley final on 29th of May, 1968. But that level of history wasn't about to replicate itself. United would be dumped from the Champions League by Galatasaray on away goals as early as the second round. Alex was hugely frustrated, but not necessarily by that two-legged result. English teams, in particular, were feeling the pinch of the three-foreigner rule that applied to teams competing in Europe in those days mainly because their squads were built on a diet of British and Irish born players. The rule meant the likes of Ryan Giggs and Mark Hughes (Welsh), and Denis Irwin and Roy Keane (Irish) along with Brian McClair (Scottish) all counted as foreign players, alongside Peter Schmeichel, Andrei Kanchelskis and Eric Cantona. The majority of the team Alex had built weren't English, and he therefore had to change his sides dramatically when competing in Europe. The three-foreigner rule would frustrate Alex up until it was dismantled in 1997. It would take Alex two years thereafter to win his first Champions League. He would then go on to compete in three more finals (winning another one) which remains a record for any manager who has ever competed in Europe throughout football history. He also appeared in seven semi-finals—another record. The argument that Alex Ferguson failed in Europe can easily be dismissed when it is taken into consideration that no manager has ever bettered him in European competition in the history of football. Yet those early years — when the three foreigner-rule applied, and United were getting dumped out of Europe by the likes of Galatasaray and later IFK Goteborg — still casts long shadows over his legacy in the minds of some.

The third disappointment for Alex that season — and by far the saddest of all — occurred when Sir Matt Busby passed away on 20th of January, 1994, aged 84. Despite a long illness, everybody took heart in the fact that Sir Matt had lived long enough to see United be crowned English champions once again, but unfortunately, he did not live long enough to see the club claim a first historic double. The double was seen as the holy grail that only a few had ever achieved. In the entire twentieth century up until that point, only three clubs had ever reached that holy grail; the brilliant Tottenham Hotspur team of 1960-61, the great Arsenal side of 1970-71 and the even greater Liverpool team of 1985-86. Despite only three teams reaching the holy grail in the space of ninety-three years, Alex would go on to win three domestic doubles before the century would end (1993-94, 1995-96 & 1998-99).

Even though United had proved to be undoubtedly the best team in England in 1993-94, Alex was seriously looking over this shoulder with concern. Jack Walker's millions had helped Blackburn to become a major threat, and despite United holding them off for an easy run to the title in '94, Blackburn's spending was worrying him. Ahead of the 1994-95 campaign, Blackburn manager Kenny Dalglish would snap up Chris Sutton to complement an already in-form Alan Shearer up front. Alex was certain their partnership would flourish, and flourish with a consistency that would see Dalglish's side crush other team in the division.

As was predicted, the two teams jostled for the top spot all through the winter and by the turn of the year into 1995, a cigarette paper wouldn't have slipped between them in the table.

At the end of January, United faced a tough encounter away to Crystal Palace with the home team trying to rile up the champions in any way they could. They truly got under United's skin, and by half-time neither team had broken the deadlock—just as Palace had planned. After being read the riot act at half-time by Alex, the United players took the pitch full-blooded. Too full-blooded, it would seem. Palace defender Richard Shaw, who had done a fantastic job of keeping Cantona quiet during that first half, finally got the reaction he was aiming to get from the Frenchman two minutes into the second half. After feeling frustrated throughout, Cantona lashed out at the defender, kicking him in an off-the-ball incident that saw referee Alan Wilkie immediately reach for his red card. The sending off caused a melee on the pitch, with both sets of players forming a chest-to-chest huddle just outside the centre circle. While that was going on, Cantona was being led to his early bath by United coach Norman Davies when a Crystal Palace fan, Matthew Simmonds, ran down the concrete stairs of the Main Stand of Selhurst Park to hurl abuse at him. 'Fuck you, you dirty French bastard. Fuck off back to France,' witnesses have claimed Simmonds shouted. Two weeks later, Simmonds would admit to only shouting, 'Off, off, off. It's an early bath for you, Cantona.' It's difficult to believe Simmonds' version, given what happened next. Cantona pulled himself away from Davies and sprinted towards Simmonds. He then dived, feet-first, over the advertising hoardings, landing his studs into the shoulder of the 'fan'. Cantona, after getting to his feet, then threw a punch, that luckily missed the Palace fan's jaw. If the punch had landed, Cantona surely would have faced sterner punishment. As it was, Manchester United — within twenty-four hours — released a statement saying they would ban Cantona until the end of the season (four months), assuming that would be punishment enough.

The FA had other ideas, however, and doubled United's original suspension—meaning Cantona would not only miss the second half of this campaign, but a chunk of the beginning of the next.

It was a good job Alex had, just ten days before Cantona's moment of madness, purchased striker Andy Cole in a move that had shocked the football world. The transfer seemed to come out of nowhere, though it wasn't a secret United were looking for a new partner for Cantona. They preferably wanted an English striker to skirt their way around the foreigner rule that was still frustrating Alex in European competition and were expected to sign Nottingham Forest's Stan Collymore. But when Newcastle United manager Kevin Keegan personally rang Alex to enquire about a player who had come through the academy to relative success, Keith Gillespie, Alex cheekily ad-libbed. He was reluctant to let Gillespie go, such was the winger's potential. But he was Northern Irish, after all, which only added to the headache when it came to European competition.

'Aye, I'll let ye have Gillespie,' Alex told Keegan, cheekily, 'but I want Andy Cole in return.'

It was an outlandish suggestion, given that Gillespie had made few appearances in the United first-team while Cole was scoring goals at such a rapid rate for Newcastle that he was being compared to the club's all-time great, Jackie Milburn. Astonishingly, Keegan's fondness for Gillespie ran so deep, that he eventually agreed a deal with Alex (United would pay £6m in cash plus Gillespie) much to the ire of Newcastle fans. The Toon Army were so incensed by the transfer that they protested outside St James's Park the day it was announced.

However, despite Cole finding the same sort of form he had shown for Newcastle as soon as he arrived at Old Trafford, without their talismanic Frenchman, United were to be pipped to the title by Blackburn Rovers on the final day of the season, denying Alex three titles in a row and forcing him to act slightly quicker than he had planned.

'I wannae sell Hughesie (Mark Hughes), Incey (Paul Ince) and

Andrei (Kanchelskis),' Alex told Martin Edwards in a post-season meeting in late May, 1995.

Not for the first time, Edwards stared back at Alex with one eyebrow raised. The three players Alex wanted to get rid of had all played key roles in the trophies the club had collected over the previous campaigns. On top of that, Edwards immediately feared that selling these three stars meant they would need replacing—and that would cost him more than a fair chunk of the club's revenues.

'Nah, they dinnae need replacin' in the transfer market,' Alex told Edwards.

'Huh?'

'Y'knoo all the talent wiv bin cooking these past years in the academy?'

'Yeah.'

'Well, they're cooked.'

ALEX AND HIS MAN-MANAGEMENT

WHEN ALEX FIRST START MANAGING AT EAST STIRLINGSHIRE, THE players he convinced to sign for the club in his debut summer of 1974 were offered a maximum of £30 in playing fees and expenses each week. The last big contract Alex signed a player to in 2010 was for £300,000 a week—when he convinced Wayne Rooney to perform a U-turn on a shock transfer request.

The Govanman managed in Scotland and England through a mouth-watering dialling up of financial investment in the professional game, and while he may have etched a legacy for himself in winning an unprecedented number of trophies as a manager, his true lore can be underlined and bolded in the fact that he evolved from managing teams of part-time tradesmen to managing teams of multi-millionaire celebrities—and he was hugely successful with them all.

His canny ability to suck the very best performances and desires from the men he managed — no matter who they were, where they came from, or how much money they earned — is, without doubt, the most ingenious attribute Alex possessed as a leader. He truly was an innovator in man-management and used a multitude of fascinating techniques to lead the unique individuals he had under his rule for four decades in football management.

There are two key attributes Alex naturally possesses that enabled him to master man-management. Firstly, he has an eidetic memory (all four Fergusons he grew up with: Alex Snr (his father), Lizzie (his mother), and Martin (his brother) were considered to have good memories and possess great attention to detail, but Alex's brain was dialled in to a unique spectrum in this regard, even for a Ferguson). To this day, even post brain haemorrhage, Alex has an incredible knack of remembering even the smallest of details from way back when. Ask him to recall the starting eleven from his first match as manager at East Stirling-shire, and he'll reel the names off within eleven seconds. He'll probably also inform you of the score in the game, precisely who scored, and in what minute those goals arrived. The second natural attribute he possesses is the fact that Alex is a humanist (a trait all four Fergusons he grew up with had, but particularly his mother). He is fascinated by people. He likes to get to know people, and specifically to understand what makes them unique. When placed in the company of somebody he hasn't met before (be it meeting a new player for the first time, inviting an opposition manager for a post-game drink or even sat next to a stranger at a charity function) Alex is not backward in coming forward. He is undoubtedly a questioner.

When it came to meeting new players for the first time, his first queries wouldn't be about football. They were always personal.

'Where d'ya grow up, son?'

'What yer parents do for a living?'

'Your grandparents?'

He'd go back as far in the lineage as the player's under-standing could stretch. And once detailed with as much history of the player as he could unscrew, that information would go into his memory bank to be recalled whenever necessary (as detailed in a previous chapter where he would use his understanding of a player's heritage in the dressing-room just to unearth an extra will in their performance). Simply put, Alex's man-management techniques were always geared toward unearthing an extra fraction of a percent in every player's performance. And his humanist nature married his eidetic memory to genuinely make players consider him more than just a football manager.

Rio Ferdinand, for example, will never forget the time his grandfather fell ill, and given that Alex had asked about Rio's background when he first met him, coupled with meeting his grandfather on two occasions in social settings, Alex sent a bottle of the grandfather's favourite whisky to his home address. He also sent a bouquet of flowers to Rio's mother, whose father it was who was ill.

He had not only remembered Rio's grandfather's name from two brief meetings, but also recalled they were talking about drinks at the function they first met at, when Rio's grandfather — because questioned by the questioner — revealed what his whisky preference was. When the bottle of whisky arrived at his home address — many years after that conversation had taken place — with a note signed by Alex Ferguson, it picked Rio's grandfather up no end during the toughest battle of his life. This is just one anecdote to show how Alex married his two natural skillsets to manage his players, and yet it's an anecdote that when considered in isolation, has nothing to do with football. Alex must have met a new personality after every single game he played and managed in. To recall a player's grandfather's favourite drink having only met him fleetingly on two occasions proves his unique memory skills. But that is only one anecdote of thousands along the same lines over the years.

'It's the little percentages like that that make a big difference,' Ferdinand admits.

On a daily basis, Alex would marry his memory and humanist abilities in casual moments during training. If a player was heading towards the training pitch from the Carrington changing rooms and Alex happened to be walking with him, that player would be probed with personal enquiries.

'How's your mam and dad's health?'

'Your brother still working down in London?'

'How're Stacey and Dylan getting on in school?'

His probing never sounded pretentious, always natural, always with genuine interest. Alex perfected his man-management skills through a multitude of caring conversations, so much so that many former players have often used the deep phrase 'father figure' to describe their relationship with him.

'He was a father-figure for me for so many years,' Beckham recalls. 'He brought me to the club I loved as a kid and I was successful at the club, so he gave me everything I have in my career.'

'My dad left when I was fourteen,' Giggs has admitted. 'I had two mainstays in my life: my grandfather and the manager. There was definitely that father-son relationship there.'

Darren Fletcher is another player to use the 'father figure' reference when talking about his former boss. He once said: 'He's more than just a football manager. He's a father figure and an inspiration to everybody. It's these small little things that go so far that most people will never understand.'

Cristiano Ronaldo, Rafael da Silva, Rio Ferdinand, Nicky Butt and Phil Neville are among other players who have described Alex with a similar paternal comparison.

For the likes of Giggs, the Nevilles, Butt, Scholes and Beckham, of course, the paternal influence of their manager began when they were indeed just kids. Most of the class of '92 were signed by Manchester United by the age of just fourteen. In fact, Beckham and Giggs literally signed on the day they turned fourteen—the age in which a player could first sign professional contracts back then.

It wasn't a case of them signing paperwork and posting it back to the club. Alex literally knocked into one of their houses on their birthday with his gift tucked into the inside pocket of his coat, a gift almost all boys dream of—a professional football contract.

Giggs's fourteenth birthday wasn't the first time Alex had knocked on that modest front door. Lynne Giggs — Ryan's mother — had welcomed Alex for cups of tea on at least four previous occasions as Alex tried to lure the Welsh wonder from under the noses of Manchester City. Alex formed a bond with Lynne and when it came for her son to choose which team to sign for on his fourteenth birthday, there was only ever going to be one winner.

Beckham was invited to Alex's office for his fourteenth birthday, where his present was waiting for him on his soon-to-be boss's desk. The teenager turned up to sign his birthday present in a black blazer just like the senior pros at United wore at the time and a black and red striped tie with the Manchester United crest emblazoned on it. Alex was wearing a very similar get-up and exited the office before coming back in with a birthday cake. After the signing, Alex would host the Beckhams for dinner where he would probe them about their family history and heritage as far as their memories could stretch. Although Beckham was a much-sought-after teen player, he was only one of hundreds of much-sought-after teen players Alex signed over his years. And he learned all about their families in as much detail as he learned about the Beckhams.

Leaning about the history of his players and their family was all intertwined with Alex's favourite pastime: "young history". In much the same way he could reel off details about the American Civil War, he could also do so with each of his players' backgrounds.

Possessing the wherewithal to tap a player on the shoulder before they entered the tunnel ahead of a vital ninety minutes to ask: 'Your grandfather gonnae be watching back home on tele in Uzice?' (As he would have asked of Nemanja Vidic) is an extremely powerful tool of motivation to use at such a pivotal time. Alex's question would, from the outside, seem like such a small step to take... what with it being a sentence comprised of just eleven words. But the impact of those eleven words would make its way on to the pitch. The intention behind them would have been years stored in the Govanman's memory bank. Vidic had big admiration for his grandfather. Stored in the memory bank! Vidic's grandfather lives on the outskirts of the small city of Uzice, Serbia. Stored in the memory bank! Vidic would take to the field to defend in honour of his grandfather, buoyed by the extra percentage that otherwise would have been lacking but for Alex's eleven-word question just as the player was heading to the pitch. It was gaining those extra percentages more than anything else that gifted Alex all the success he unwrapped over his years in football management.

On evolving his leadership qualities from dealing with part-time tradesmen to full-time multi-millionaire celebrities such as Vidic, Alex once said: 'I've managed to adapt and help players adapt. I was here before agent power, before freedom of contract, before the really big money from TV kicked in. Part of ma job is to make sure these lads keep their feet on the ground. I hammer it into them that their work ethic is what got them through this door in the first place, and they must never lose it. I say to them, "When you're going home to your mother, you make sure she's seein' the same person she sent ta me, because if you take all this fame and money the wrong way, your mother'll be disappointed with you".'

Alex readily preached that latter point to academy players on an ongoing basis. But of course, it wasn't just first-team players or academy hopefuls who were under Alex's management at the club. The branches of the Manchester United tree spring out in all manner of directions. And Alex, being the natural leader he was, hung from every branch.

The personal assistant he inherited when he first joined the club was a jovial, short, blonde woman with an infectious snorted giggle. Her name was Lyn Laffin. Alex treated her with the same personable touch as he did his players. He knew all of Lyn's family's names and would regularly ask about their well-being. Lyn was a devoted disciple at the church of Alex Ferguson, so much so that she remained his PA into his retirement, until she sadly passed away in early 2020. Alex was heartbroken by her passing and genuinely views her role in his career on a par with the assistant managers he had by his side in the dug-out, such as Archie Knox, Brian Kidd, Carlos Queiroz, Steve McClaren and Mike Phelan.

Similarly, Alex had a fantastic relationship with Kath Phipps who worked on the reception desk at Old Trafford and who has given over fifty years of her life to the club. Although he would only pass Kath twice during the day, on his way in and then out of work, he always had time to stop and talk to her and insisted she and all the other staff who operated behind her desk at the forefront of the club were just as responsible for results come Saturday afternoons as the players were. He reserved his best wit, however, for dinner lady Carol Williams whom he used to trade barbs with while queuing with his tray at Carrington. Some say Carol was the only person at the club who could get away with ribbing the boss unmercifully. Albert Morgan — United's kit man for twenty years — might have rivalled Carol for Alex's sharpest wit, however. Albert and Alex often played tricks on each other over the years, and deep into both of their retirements the Govanman was constantly on the phone to Albert as his wife, Debbie, fell gravely ill through 2019 and 2020.

'I was caring for my wife for the last few years of her life, so it's been so hard since she's been gone,' said Albert. 'But the gaffer has been unbelievable. There aren't words to describe what he's done for me. He's been absolutely wonderful for me, and for what I've gone through.'

It is inarguable that the Manchester United family during Alex's reign was a tight-knit family, from the front desk all the way to the football pitch, and so anytime United won a title, Alex would insist the following day that the trophy be passed around all staff members at the club—starting at the reception desk, then downstairs to the laundry workers, up to the physios and yoga instructors, to the dinner ladies, to the groundsmen, to the office staff, the PAs, the security guards, the coaches and then back into the hands of the players.

"Every time we won a trophy it was passed around the whole staff," Alex wrote in *Leading*. "We got the champagne out, the trophy out, and we all celebrated together. Because it was their trophy as much as ours."

In fact, Alex intercepted the original £60m architectural plans for Carrington Training Ground when it was first scheduled to be built in 1999—getting himself heavily involved in the layout of the complex. He simply wanted every department to work alongside each other in as close proximity as possible, rather than divided into separate sections. It works a treat. Everybody at Carrington knows everybody's name, and that tradition is still adopted by new players as soon as they come into the club. All of the staff who work at the club are to be viewed as their equals. They are all playing for the same team. It was a harmony that was created at the club through Alex's meticulous man-management.

It genuinely did not matter whether he was managing a player valued at over £80m or a part-time security guard on a couple of hundred pound a week, Alex Ferguson managed his staff to a level where they were proud to be led by him, and honoured to follow him.

'Whereas Steve Jobs is Apple, Alex Ferguson is Manchester United,' David Gill once said.

The greatest myth that exists about Alex is that he ruled with an iron fist. That perception couldn't be further from the truth. Alex's tenure as a manager could actually be scored by an in-tune whistle or an out of tune chorus; for Alex, more often than not, could be heard whistling or singing around the corridors of Carrington, or before that, Manchester United's old training ground The Cliff. There existed only three places in which he ever raised his voice: in his own office where he may berate players or staff for underachieving; in the dressing-room, where he truly could let fly; or on the touchline, where players or referees could be burnt by the flames of his wrath. But for the most part, Alex was in great form because he consciously wanted an air of positivity to spread throughout the club. An outsider could be forgiven for holding the opinion that Alex's face was regularly purple with rage and his thick Scottish accent routinely ranting and raving because they viewed so much footage of him on the touchline. But that opinion opposes the truth. Alex was light-hearted, personable and loved to joke in the workplace. Once, of course, everybody was toeing the line as he saw fit.

Alex's long-time assistant coach Rene Meulensteen once said: 'There was a unique harmony among the players and staff and there was no envy or jealousy as we were all pulling together. There wasn't one day where we didn't crack up with laughter—and the boss was usually the instigator.'

It's difficult, if not impossible, to get past the fingers on one hand when attempting to count the number of players who wouldn't paint Alex's management with praise, which is a very low number considering he managed hundreds of players over the course of his career. One of the players who may not be quick to praise him is his former captain Roy Keane. Though, so conflicting and dripping with dry sarcasm are the Corkman's views that it's difficult to know his true feelings on his former boss. Alex's relationship with Keane is so interesting, however, that it has been reserved for a later chapter in this book where it can be delved into in finer detail. But one former player who certainly holds disdain for Alex is goalkeeper Jim Leighton. Alex, in 1989, had to let Leighton know forty-eight hours before an FA Cup Final replay that he would be dropped for the showdown against Crystal Palace having played in every round of the competition up until that point (including the original FA Cup Final the prior Saturday), and his fellow Scot, who Alex had managed at Aberdeen as well as at Manchester United, took the news so badly that he hasn't spoken to him since that day.

Though in truth, it was highly unusual for Alex to fall out with a player. There were certainly voices raised and arguments aplenty, but one key element of Alex's man-management that remained consistent until his final days in the game was that he thought of every day as a fresh day. And if, for example, he had let rip at Ryan Giggs in the dressing-room, the next day Alex would wait on Ryan to come out on to the training pitch before putting his arm around him.

'How's your mother keeping?' he'd ask.

The question would begin a personable conversation that purposely signalled the end of the previous day's argument.

'I never let it (an argument) go into the next day,' Alex says. 'That is something every player can say about me, no doubt aboot it. The next day, it was over. We were all back on equal footing. I made sure of it.'

Ryan Giggs can confirm such a managerial approach.

'There were some stand up rows, definitely, yes. In the dressing-room. He'd fine me one week's wages, maybe two weeks' wages. But the great thing was, the next day he'd get you and it was all over and done with. Let's move on. With the boss there was always that fear, but ultimately there was always that respect.'

Interestingly, in 2012 when Alex became the subject of a module at Harvard University, the essence of the lectures on his leadership skills centred around the fine line between fear and respect, which is a line module creator professor Anita Elberse feels Alex strolled along as if he were a master tightrope walker.

Elberse — the Harvard University's Business Professor who was granted an all-access pass at Manchester United in 2012 that nobody outside the club had ever received — observed Alex in multiple meetings with his staff and players, joking around in the cafeteria, barking orders on the training ground, and preaching in team briefings as she gathered evidence for her module on the Govanman.

'We got accesses to the club that are normally closed off. We had a chance to speak with a range of people he has worked with, from the club's CEO to his assistant coaches, the players, the kit manager, his long-time personal assistant, the dinner ladies and those who wash the team jerseys,' she said. 'For me, all of those experiences and interactions proved valuable to understanding Sir Alex's day-to-day approach. What is apparent is that his man-management is remarkable. He is a true master at motivating those around him. Many people at the club spoke about the family atmosphere he creates. I think, ultimately, that allowed players of all different backgrounds to thrive. What became apparent was that he holds everybody he works with to the same high standards. But will tailor his approach for different personalities.'

The latter point didn't need to be unearthed by a business professor, in truth. Each of his ex-players had long since arrived at that same conclusion. They, to a man, will admit every player received a different degree of man-management. Alex would admit each personality *deserves* a different degree of man-management.

Giggs, who had been under Alex's wing since the day of his fourteenth birthday on November 29, in 1987 up until Alex's official retirement date of May 31, 2013, is perhaps the player who bore the biggest brunt of Alex's rage. Criticism in the dressing-room and in team briefings was often aimed at the Welshman, not because the player underperformed more than any other, but because he had the personality and stature to accept it. It was conscious man-management. Alex knew that his players learned that if he could rant and rave at his boy wonder over a couple of misplaced passes then *every* player was vulnerable.

'He regularly picked me out for a rollicking,' Giggs said. 'I think it was because he knew I wouldn't sulk for long and he would get a reaction on the pitch. But he was making an example of me, definitely. I got it more often than the rest. One pre-season in America he went for me in front of everyone. I was fuming and pulled him later. He said it was a ploy because he knew the younger players would know that if he could have a go at me, then nobody was safe.'

Wayne Rooney — another strong character in the dressing-room — was another player who received more than his fair share of the infamous hairdryer treatment.

'Sir Alex was clever like that,' Rooney would admit. 'He knew who he could have a go at and who best to leave alone. He always knew an argument would bring the best out of me. It wouldn't work with Nani. Sometimes he would have a go at me, and through me he was really having a go at Nani. That's how he worked.'

In 1993, as soon as Giggs walked through the door to attend the club's end-of-year awards do, Alex stormed over to him, huffing and puffing about the fact that his tie wasn't done up properly and his top button was undone and, 'How dare you turn up so casual to an official club function'. Fifteen minutes later Eric Cantona arrived at the same do, dressed in a white linen suit and sky-blue shirt. The top two buttons were undone.

'See, lads,' Alex said to his players while patting Cantona on the back, 'Now this is style.'

Alex would write in *Leading*: "You might think that team-mates would resent another player who was treated differently... but once in a while someone would appear who required something special. Eric Cantona fit into that category. I would always make a point of talking to him every day, on the training ground, or in the cafeteria or in the dressing room. He was a sensitive person who was easily bothered by all sorts of things, but he loved talking about football and that was always a way I could help restore his spirits."

Lee Sharpe has often told the tale that after Cantona had jumped into the crowd at Selhurst park to attack a fan, the players raced into the dressing-room at the end of the game to witness the manager berating the Frenchman. Instead, Sharpe says, Alex laid into the whole team for such a tepid display and then at the end of his rant, simply turned to his captain and said, 'Eric, you cannae be doing things like that, son.'

Cristiano Ronaldo is another high-profile player who was treated uniquely by his manager. When the Portuguese first arrived at the club, dancing around the ball and falling at even the inkling that a defender might be about to commit to a tackle, he began to get a deserved reputation for diving. Alex was vehemently against diving and had berated players for doing it in his earlier years. But with Ronaldo, he didn't say a word. Instead, he defended him to the hilt.

When Sky Sports reporter Geoff Shrives asked Alex in a post-match interview about the player's keenness to go down, Alex batted the question away and then as soon as the cameras were off berated Shreeves with a rollicking he usually reserves for the dressing-room. Shreeves was stunned. Alex would ban Shreeves for interviewing him for the rest of the season.

Alex would approach the subject with Ronaldo not by telling him to stop diving, but by opening up a conversation with him that he knew he would enjoy.

'Who d'ya think's the best player of all time?' he asked.

'Maradona,' Ronaldo replied.

'See what I like about Maradona, or Pele, or Di Stefano,' Alex would say, 'they were the best of all time because when they got kicked, they just got up. All us fans remember that about them. That's why they are remembered as the best ever. They were men.'

The message filtered through. The diving would be curtailed.

Years later, upon hearing the news that Ronaldo's father was ill back in Portugal, Alex would pull the player aside and order him to fly home.

'But we are in an important moment in the season, boss,' Ronaldo replied.

It didn't matter. Ronaldo was told that family is more important than football and that he was to take a few days off.

'When he told me that, I thought, "This guy's unbelievable". He was a father figure for me.'

And there appears that phrase again. Father figure.

In truth, it wasn't just high-profile players or key stars such as Cantona and Ronaldo who were treated differently. Peripheral members of Alex's dressing rooms over the years such as Liam Miller, Kleberson, Diego Forlan, Gabriel Heinze, Denis Irwin, Tim Howard and Lee Sharpe all had vastly different personalities, and therefore required a totally different degree of man-management.

The most basic day-to-day examples of Alex differentiating the personalities of his dressing-room could be found in the simple phrases he would use with certain individuals.

Faced with a need to confront a sensitive personality, such as Ronaldo or Cantona or even Tim Howard or Liam Miller, Alex would say, 'That was rubbish, that,' but then make sure to follow it up with 'for a player of your ability.'

"That was for picking them back up after the original blow. Criticise but balance it out with encouragement," Alex would write in *My Autobiography*. He also admits to using phrases like 'What are you doing that for? You're better than that!' to get points across to these types of personalities, and 'You're coming inside the player, we talked about going outside him. I know you know that, because you are one of the best players at taking instruction.'

Some sensitive players such as those named above needed the compliment to accompany the criticism in order to up their game, whereas strong-minded personalities such as Giggs, Keane and Rooney needed the rollicking to kick them into gear.

One particular trait Alex held zero patience for, however, no matter the personality, was lateness. He absolutely deplored anybody being late, especially his players. Punctuality was a discipline everybody had to perfect at Manchester United. There simply was no alternative. Another aspect Alex insisted on was that every member of the playing squad and staff wore blazers and club ties when representing the club. He would often say to his players, 'We are Manchester United. We simply must not allow our standards to drop to the level of other clubs.'

These traditional authoritarian ways proved to be a key attribute to his man-management. He was insistent that United could only ever be the best club in the land if they firmly believed they were the best club in the land. And he religiously drilled into his players and staff that United simply *had* to be the best club in the land. His psychology in this regard worked wonders. Players under Alex genuinely felt they were much better than they actually were. His man-management, no matter how seemingly minimalist or insignificant, constantly raised the percentages of his players' and staffs' performances.

What's interesting is that one of the most fascinating facets of Alex's man-management was his ability to lie.

In 1984, at Aberdeen, the Govanman began taking steps away from training sessions on the advice of Archie Knox. Alex's assistant manager suggested the boss would learn more about his players if he observed their input from a distance. It was advice Alex disagreed with at first but as soon as he gave in and took his first step back, he began to see mass benefits.

'Watching is an underrated activity in management and it costs nothing. A regular observer can spot changes in training patterns, energy levels, and work rates,' he said. 'The key is tae delegate the direct supervision to others and trust them tae do their jobs, allowing the manager to truly observe.'

He realised he could man-manage his players better this way and evolved this into overstretching the truth on many occasions. At first he began to see that if a certain player looked fatigued in training he could use that to make a decision of dropping him, by detailing what he had observed in training, even if the player himself hadn't noticed. And as football evolved to a stage where squads were filled with up to thirty players, Alex would use his powers of 'observation' to let players down when he knew in advance that they would be dropped for a game.

'Yer running is a little reliant on your instep of the right foot,' he would lie to a player. 'I think you might be tight in the left side. Best not risk a tear. What we'll do is, we'll leave you out of the team for the next two weeks, get you back for the West Ham game away.'

He would use the powers of his observation to convince players why they should take some time out from the first team without feeling as if they were dropped. Though quite how much the players believed his lies is up for debate. Certainly, the players who had played under him for the most amount of time had cottoned on to his ways.

Nicky Butt once asked his best mates when the Class of '92 met up for a reunion dinner in 2012, 'What was the best excuse the boss ever gave for dropping you?'

'That it was too hot,' Scholes answered before Messrs Butt, Beckham, Giggs and the two Nevilles burst out laughing.

'Sharpe always does well at Villa Park,' Giggs would answer to note why he rarely played away to Aston Villa.

'He used to say to me,' Butt said, 'that in the summer, pitches were too nice and that I came into my own on a heavy pitch, so November, you'll be a key player.'

'I remember him telling me once,' Gary Neville said, 'that I was being dropped for a game at Chelsea because there were rumours they had some Combat 18 fanatics in the crowd…'

Neville then recalled a scenario in which most Manchester United players down the years would have found themselves in at some point.

'I remember him coming up to me, I think it was a Thursday before a game on a Saturday and said, "I'm not gonna be playing you on Saturday, son. I've got a game for you. Two weeks on Saturday… just the game for you." I was like… so I'm not playing for four games? And he was like, "You make sure you prepare for that game. I'm gonna need you for that game." So I thought, yeah he needs me for that game. And then I'm thinking, have I just been dropped for four games or have I been told I'm really important for this one game?'

Wayne Rooney would surmise: 'As a manager he was the best, but his man-management was something. He knew how to speak to players, how to get a reaction. He's the only manager that could leave someone out and make them feel good about it —he was incredible.'

Alex didn't rule with an iron fist because he knew such an approach would be counterproductive. The Alex observed by millions of football fans on the touchline over the course of an intense ninety minutes of Premier League action is not, nor anywhere close to, a true reflection of Alex the manager.

He would write in *Leading*: "I always got more out of players by praising them than by scorning them with criticism. Foot-ballers, like all human beings, are plagued by a range of emotions that run all the way from profound insecurity to massive over-confidence. Trying to measure where, along this spectrum, each of these players was on any particular day was very important."

Javier Hernandez, who Alex had brought over from Mexico when he was just twenty-one years of age, once detailed the effects of Alex's man-management by saying: 'When I arrived to sign he wanted to have dinner with myself and my family. The way he presented himself and the way he treated you like a human... the way he treated my family, for me it was like, yeah, I will kill myself on the pitch for sure. For sure! If he treats my family that way, man, I will vomit after every game if it helps him to win games and championships.'

It was through these calculated man-management approaches that Alex convinced his players to take to the pitch and give the extra percentages in their performances. And, of course, it was the accumulation of all those little extra percentages, more than anything else, that readily helped his teams collate an unprece-dented number of trophies. Whether those players were earning £30 a week, or £300,000 a week truly was inconsequential.

1995-1998

RYAN GIGGS, NICKY BUTT, PAUL SCHOLES, DAVID BECKHAM AND GARY & Phil Neville aren't collectively known as the Class of '92 because that is the year in which they broke into the Manchester United first team. 1992 is the year they won the FA Youth Cup together—when they essentially came of age and Alex realised he would be able to rely on them as first team starters in the not so-distant future. Giggs was so far ahead of every other player who came through the academy that he had actually made the first team as early as 1990 as a wispy and lanky sixteen-year-old. Butt also made the jump slightly earlier than the others and was already competing with Roy Keane and Paul Ince for a place in central midfield by the second half of the 1994/95 campaign. But Scholes and the two Neville brothers, well… they didn't really impose themselves in the first team until the beginning of the 1995-96 season even if they had made an appearance in the odd cup tie over the previous months. However, Alex had been so impressed with the temperament and discipline they had proven to have in the academy that he was certain they wouldn't let him down. So, in the overcast summer of 1995, and in a move that stunned Manchester United fans, he would inform stalwarts Mark Hughes, Paul Ince and Andrei Kanchelskis they were all free to move on.

When no signings were forthcoming to replace that trio by the time the season was due to kick-off, United fans were seething. They had no idea who was going to replace the legendary figures who had been sold. The fans would find out when Alex named his team for the first game of that league campaign away to Aston Villa, with Scholes and Butt picked in what looked like a very makeshift midfield, and Gary and Phil Neville in both full-back positions while Beckham and another academy graduate John O'Kane were named on the bench. Villa would tank United 3-1 with relative ease.

'Ye can't win anything with kids,' Liverpool legend Alan Hansen would comment on *Match of the Day* that very night. That quote would become a phrase adorned across the T-shirts of match-going United fans for years to come. Those "kids" would go on to claim a second domestic double for Alex that very season — despite losing their first game so comprehensively — before going on to win thirty-nine Premier League titles between them. Butt and Scholes would vie for a midfield position alongside Roy Keane to replace Ince; Beckham would prove to be a direct replacement for Kanchelskis on the right-side of midfield (although *direct* is an odd way to label it given that they are total opposites in every facet of how they approach that role) and the Neville brothers would battle it out for starting berths on each defensive flank. Trying to oust Denis Irwin from left-full was proving difficult for Phil, though Gary had managed to push Paul Parker out of the side quite early on to become a main-stay at right-full.

United fans would soon get over the shock of losing three of their favourites, but what may shock them to learn is that Alex was giving serious consideration to stepping down as manager of Manchester United that summer. After agreeing to sell Ince to Inter Milan for £6m, he was on the end of a battering from the British press because they couldn't quite believe he was willing to allow the English international to move on. Alex was usually able to take the criticism that came his way. After all, this wasn't his first rodeo with regards negative headlines. But what really riled him that summer was the fact that nobody at Manchester United went out of their way to support him. He was on holiday in the United States with Cathy in June 1995 when the main bulk of the criticism was being thrown his way. From there, he made a phone call to Martin Edwards in an attempt to dampen the flames of negativity. But rather than agree to support his manager publicly, Edwards questioned Alex and suggested the slating from the press may be somewhat justified.

'Perhaps we've made a big mistake,' Edwards told him.

Alex was fuming when he hung up that hotel phone. After all the planning and plotting he had done over the years to ensure academy kids could seamlessly graduate into the first team — while at the same time constantly keeping Edwards in the loop — he couldn't believe his chairman was getting cold feet at the last minute. Although Cathy was in the States for a relaxing holiday, she found it nigh on impossible to enjoy herself with her husband animated and agitated.

'I should fuckin' resign,' Alex said to Cathy during that holiday.

'Don't be so bloody stubborn,' she told him.

They would seriously debate the matter for a day and a half, until a phone call made to their beach-side hotel in the early hours of the following morning pushed Alex's stubbornness into perspective. It was Ken Merrett on the other end of the line, an employee of Manchester United. Stephen — Alex and Cathy's nephew — Merrett informed them, had been killed in a road traffic accident. He was just nineteen years of age. Alex and Cathy immediately packed their bags and booked the earliest flight they could to Glasgow so they could comfort Cathy's sister Bridget and her husband John.

The tragedy afforded Alex the opportunity to park his ego. He no longer considered what the press were writing about him as significant; no longer cared that TV pundits were scolding him for selling Ince, Hughes and Kanchelskis. And within a matter of two days, in the midst of comforting his grief-stricken in-laws, Alex made up his mind. The devastating reality that Stephen's potential would never be realised screamed at him. He wasn't going to dive into the transfer market like the press were daring him to. He was going to trust the 'kids'; he was going to trust his own judgement; he was finally going to trust the plan he had put in place the moment he set foot inside Manchester United.

As if they were intent to prove Alan Hansen wrong in the least time possible, the United youngsters would help the team to five wins from their next five league games after their opening-day defeat to Aston Villa to top the table by the end of September.

However, despite the return of talismanic leader Eric Cantona — who made his comeback from his eight-month ban against Liverpool at Old Trafford, in which he scored one and assisted the other United goal in a thrilling 2-2 draw — United couldn't quite match Newcastle United stride-for-stride as the season headed into the New Year. Kevin Keegan had rejuvenated not just the football club in the northeast, but the entire city. By mid-January of 1996, despite United looking unbeatable at Old Trafford, Newcastle had managed to stretch their lead at the top of the Premier League to twelve points.

Bizarrely, United had managed up until that stage of the season just one point from a possible fifteen whilst wearing their away strip. It was a grey strip. The grey strip Alex forced his players to change out of at half-time when they were 3-0 down at Southampton. They'd still go on to lose that particular game at the Dell, 3-1, but their away form improved dramatically in the second half of that campaign after the grey strip had been binned. Then marketing manager of the club, Edward Freeman, would some years later suggest the club lost over £200,000 in revenue for Alex binning that strip—a huge slice of the club's annual revenue back then. Alex had been called to a meeting about his decision to ditch the Umbro jersey, but he was not for turning—insisting that football results came above everything else.

With a new kit, United's results away from home changed so dramatically that by the time it came to Easter, they had overtaken Newcastle at the summit, and — after beating old rivals Leeds United 1-0 at Old Trafford (a match in which Leeds played particularly well in and were unfortunate to walk away without at least a point) — Alex used his post-game press conference to heap pres-

sure on his title rival Keegan. He suggested that Leeds wouldn't play
as well when they travelled to Newcastle the following week. He was
right. They didn't. And Keegan's team won 1-0 while in cruise-
control. But Keegan would go on live TV straight after that game
and, clearly riled and shaking, would point his finger down the lens
at Alex, furious at the Govanman's suggestion that Leeds wouldn't
try against his players. 'I'd love it if we beat them, love it,' Keegan
said. Alex knew there and then, watching the drama unfold, that
Manchester United were going to win the title (a story you can read
in more detail in the next chapter.). He was right. Two weeks later,
United's young players who had graduated through all the underage
teams at the academy would lift their first Premier League trophy.
That wasn't all they'd be lifting, as they had an FA Cup final to look
forward to a week later—against Liverpool.

That FA Cup final was played on a glorious sunny May day at
Wembley, when the pitch had been cut into the new-wave of
bladed-sliced squares — like a chess board — for the very first time.
It was while standing inside one of those chess squares that Alex,
who was talking to his assistant manager Brian Kidd at the time, first
saw the Liverpool players arrive at Wembley. He was astonished to
see them decked out in all-cream suits, so much so that he immediately turned to Kidd and said, "One-nil". That's the exact score in
which United would win that game, thanks to a fantastic late half-
volleyed goal by Cantona who simply had a sublime season while
pulling the strings of all the young players around him.

It would have seemed, to the joyous United fans who were celebrating another domestic double (the second double in three
seasons), that all was rosy at their football club. But that couldn't
have been further from the truth. Astonishingly, during that fantastic
push from February to May, Alex was at loggerheads with club
chairman Martin Edwards yet again. And... yet again, the row was
over Alex's contract. He simply felt he was owed a better deal,
having overachieved on the plan he had put in place nine years
prior. Not only was he winning trophies, but he was winning trophies
with half of the outfield players he was picking every week having

graduated through their academy ranks—saving the club millions of pounds in transfer fees. When Alex spoke to Edwards and realised that the contract extension he would be offered would fall well short of what he expected, he told Edwards, face-to-face this time, that he was thinking of leaving the club at the end of the campaign. The Football Association of Ireland had been in touch. They were sounding Alex out over replacing their legendary manager Jack Charlton who had just stood down. They were willing to offer him £300,000 per year. Alex was only on £200,000 at United. Although he was never likely to take the proposal from the FAI, Alex informed Edwards of the offer and told him he was contemplating it. Then, as the season drew towards its thrilling conclusion, the English FA announced Terry Venables would be stepping down as the national team manager in the summer of 1996—after the European Championships that were taking place on home territory. This was a lottery win for Alex. Not only did he have the Irish job to use as a bargaining tool against Edwards, but the English job, too. Graham Kelly was the FA's chief executive then and his first port of call when looking for a national team manager was the Govanman. And, unlike the Irish job offer, Alex was somewhat tempted. Well, the truth is, it was Alex's brother Martin who was most tempted. He genuinely tried to convince his brother that he should take the England job. Intrigued by Martin's insistence in this regard, Alex agreed to talk with the FA. Edwards had been dutily informed that these talks were happening and, convinced Alex might leave, went ahead and sounded out his replacement for the Old Trafford hot seat. His choice was none other than the outgoing England boss, Terry Venables. Had Alex accepted the England job offer, Venables would have been appointed his successor at United in 1996. As it was, Alex would stay after Edwards matched the amount the FA were willing to pay him—£650,000 a year. Over triple his current salary. And by quite some distance the biggest wage any manager was receiving in the Premier League. For all he had achieved, Alex felt the mammoth contract was justified. He has claimed since that there was no way he would have ever seriously accepted the

England job. He truly was using the interest as a bargaining tool against Edwards.

The stability of his massive new five-year contract, however, meant Alex headed into the 1996/97 season with a renewed vigour and with his academy graduates now maturing into mainstays of his team selection. On top of that, UEFA had decided to forgo the foreigner rule in Europe—meaning Alex could field his strongest side in the Champions League for the first time since his arrival at Old Trafford. He was convinced his side could compete with the best of the best, once the playing field was levelled. His heart would be broken ten months later though when United — who had an impressive Champions League campaign — would crash out at the semi-final stage to Borussia Dortmund. Two hours after that defeat, his heart would crack some more. Cantona would pull him aside while travelling home, asking for a quiet word. He told his manager that he was going to quit playing football at the end of the current campaign because he wanted to be an actor. And although Alex had won the Frenchman around when he talked him out of quitting two years prior, he knew for sure this time that Cantona had his heart set on a new life. The fiery passion he had for the game had been extinguished.

'We're gonnae win this Champions League really soon. Stay. Be part of it,' Alex tempted Cantona with.

'I know you'll win the Champions League soon,' Cantona replied. 'But I won't be part of it.'

And so, after winning yet another Premier League title in May of 1997 (their fourth title in the first five Premier League campaigns), Alex said goodbye to the player he distinguishes as the most unique player he ever managed.

Cantona's last season — the 1996-97 campaign — proved to be largely uneventful by his standards. United had romped to the title, having got in front by October and remaining there until they were crowned champions in late April—holding nearest challengers Newcastle United at arm's length all the way. United were knocked out of the FA Cup in the fourth round by Wimbledon, meaning they didn't make it to a third successive final, and then, as already mentioned, were dumped from the Champions League in the semi-finals on the same day Cantona asked Alex for that quiet word.

While broken-hearted, the manager wasn't shocked by Cantona's resignation and had already lined up a dream replacement for the Frenchman... just in case. Alex was a huge fan of Teddy Sheringham, feeling he was the perfect striker for his favoured tactical set-up. But he also knew trying to prise him away from Spurs would prove tremendously difficult. It was a transfer that United did eventually manage to seal, however, with some suggesting they paid over the odds for the then thirty-one-year-old when they were negotiated up to £4.77m after they had originally bid £3.5m, and Spurs insisted they were holding out for £5m.

When Sheringham was asked why he moved to Old Trafford, he said: 'It's simple. I want to win trophies.' Spurs fans were livid with such a statement, and would take great pleasure when, for the first time in the Premier League era, Manchester United would go through a season trophyless in 1997-1998.

It wasn't necessarily that United were feeling the loss of Cantona. After all, Sheringham had proven to be a shrewd replacement for the Frenchman. It was actually another Frenchman who had been most responsible for United's first trophyless season in years. A Frenchman Arsenal had appointed as their manager the year previous. Arsene Wenger was innovative. He was changing the game up.

Whereas Alex had insisted on a no alcohol rule, in an effort to ensure his players were fitter than the opposition, Wenger took it to another level entirely. Alex had been hearing on the grapevine that Wenger had even banned ketchup from the canteen at the Arsenal training centre. The Govanman was intrigued by the Frenchman, but he was also shocked. He didn't expect him to turn Arsenal into champions in such a swift amount of time and in fact had been rather dismissive of the Frenchman when he first arrived in London. United ran them close that season — literally until the final match of the campaign — but the Gunners would ultimately win their first

Premier League title by a single point, thanks, in the main, to the goals of Dennis Bergkamp and Marc Overmars who had proven to be the flair players of Wenger's new continental-looking side. But it was the partnership of Patrick Vieira and Emmanuel Petit in midfield that impressed Alex the most.

What he wasn't impressed by was the manager, however. He took a dislike to Wenger not because he outmuscled Alex's United that season, but because he refused the tradition of meeting managers for a drink after Premier League games. Alex fumed the first day Wenger turned down his invite to his office in Old Trafford, and then had words with other managers such as George Graham (then at Spurs), Ron Atkinson (Sheffield Wednesday), Harry Redknapp (West Ham) and Joe Kinnear (Wimbledon) to confirm Wenger had snubbed them, too. Wenger instantly became enemy number one for Alex, and they would both vie for each league title over an eight-year period until a certain Portugueser arrived in England christening himself The Special One and eventually coming between the Govanman and the Frenchman. Over the eight seasons — between 1996 when Wenger first arrived and 2005 when Mourinho came between them — United would win five league titles to Arsenal's three.

But it was the first of those three Arsenal won that riled Alex more than any other Premier League loss. He would complain to all who would listen that Arsenal only pipped United to that title because his squad suffered too many injuries during that campaign. New captain Roy Keane missed most of that season after tearing ligaments in his right knee in a match at Elland Road. And his replacement in the side, Nicky Butt, would then miss out on multiple games due to a niggling eye problem that produced constant uncontrollable headaches. But the truth is, Arsenal won that title not because Roy Keane strained his right knee or because his replacement had eye problems, but because they were the best and most consistent team in England that year.

In search of a different approach in attack, to ensure Arsenal wouldn't be the best team in England the following season, Alex persuaded Martin Edwards to part with £12.6m for the services of Dwight Yorke—the Aston Villa striker who played with such unique flair that Alex thought he would be perfect in his side. Alex would also tighten up at the back, by bringing in man-mountain Jaap Stam from PSV Eindhoven for a fee of £10.2m. The manager convinced Edwards that if he were to make those two signings that summer — pricey as they were — then United would almost certainly win more trophies.

'We can win it all,' he told his chairman. 'Next season, we can win it all.'

He would tell his dressing-room that, too—insisting that they were now such an established team (with the Class of '92 now in the 23/24 aged bracket) that they shouldn't fear any team in Europe, let alone England.

However, the signing of Yorke, in particular, ultimately meant the end for somebody Alex had held so dear: his assistant manager and Manchester United legend Brian Kidd. Kidd wasn't a fan of Yorke and had actually insisted, behind Alex's back to Martin Edwards, that United should instead look to sign West Ham's number nine John Hartson.

Alex was flummoxed, not just because he couldn't believe Kidd would miscalculate exactly what type of striker the team now needed, but more so because his assistant had gone behind his back. They would make up after this, with Alex helping Kidd to negotiate a new contract, but the fracture that formed from Alex's humiliation that Kidd would go behind his back never fully healed. And when Kidd was approached by Blackburn Rovers to become their new manager six months later, Alex agreed to let him go. This contrasted with the summer prior, before the Dwight Yorke argument, when Everton had offered Kidd their manager's position, only for Alex to talk his right-hand man out of the job.

Having searched high and low for a new assistant, Alex was eventually won over by the constant praise one young coach in particular was receiving from those within the game Alex respected the most. In fact, it was his old buddy Jim Smith who sang Steve

McClaren's praises so much that Alex finally decided who should replace Kidd. By this stage, Alex's search was down to two promising coaches: McClaren and the then Preston North End manager, David Moyes.

'If you take McClaren, you won't regret it,' Smith promised Alex. 'In all my years in the game, I've never seen a better coach.'

'Steve, let me ask you this question,' Alex said, when he interviewed the then Derby County assistant manager. 'Do you think Manchester United can win it all?'

'I do,' McClaren said.

'Great,' Alex told him. 'Then let's win it all.'

ALEX AND HIS MIND GAMES

WHEN PHILIP JACKSON WAS COMMISSIONED IN 2011 TO SCULPT A bronze statue of the Govanman to stand proud outside the soon-to-be-named Sir Alex Ferguson Stand, the renowned artist genuinely paused to contemplate portraying Alex tugging back the left sleeve of his sports jacket while eyeballing his watch.

A portrait of Fergie Time.

Some argue that Fergie Time is a myth. It's not. Fergie Time is a construct. Of course, Fergie Time is a myth in terms of Manchester United getting more injury-time than any other club. Through the Premier League years up until Alex's retirement in 2013, Old Trafford amassed an average of 4:31 minutes of injury-time per match. It was twenty seconds less than the Premier League average of 4:51 minutes, and the Manchester United home ground hosted only the twelfth most amount of added time in Premier League games through that period. St James's Park was first. The Newcastle United home ground hosted 5:17 minutes of injury time on average per game over the same years in which they competed in the Premier League.

'I didnae know how much time was on ma watch, no,' Alex would say with a grin stretched wide across his face after he'd retired. 'I used tae tap ma watch for three reasons. And none of them had anything tae do with the referee, really. Sometimes it might have a small impact on a referee… I dunno. But that's not why I was doin' that.'

The three reasons, Alex would admit, that he often ran to the touchline tapping his watch was, firstly, to signal to his own players the urgency required; secondly, to signify to the fans the urgency required; and thirdly, to signify to the opposition that they were set for an onslaught. Manchester United won, by far, more points than any other club in the final minutes of games through Alex's reign and, as previously noted in this book, amassed 183 points from turning deficits into wins in the final minutes of Premier League games alone. They didn't achieve those wins because they had more time to play with compared to any other club. It was all psychological. Fergie Time was simply Alex's most powerful and impactful mind game.

'I never looked at ma watch,' he insists again. 'I didnae know how many minutes. But it got a message to the opponents, which is the little trick.'

Alex knew that when he ran to the touchline barking at the referee while tapping at his watch, United's supporters would rouse and as a result their opponents would brace themselves for the forthcoming onslaught. That meant retreating to the edge of their own penalty area from where they would desperately try to hold out until the final whistle. Playing the final minutes against a team desperate to hold out is a much easier route to winning a game than those final minutes being played out as an even contest.

Alex Ferguson's Manchester United won thirteen Premier League titles—and the total of the championship win margins between United themselves and the second placed teams totalled 94 points over those thirteen title wins. Which makes the fact that United earned 183 points by scoring late goals to claw back losing positions through Alex's tenure all the more head-scratching. Without the late winning goals in Fergie Time, it is likely Manchester United wouldn't have claimed so many titles. Yet the tapping of his watch was such a small psychological trick that it only cost the Govanman two seconds out of his working week. It only cost two seconds, yet it bought multiple victories, even titles.

Aside from American History, Alex is also well read on psychology. He has particularly taken pleasure in reading about the mental side of competitive sports (his favourite book on this subject is *What it Takes To Be No.1*, by the late, great American Football coach, Vince Lombardi. Incidentally, Alex's favourite Lombardi quote is, "We didn't lose the game. We only ran out of time").

The way Alex viewed football was very simple. Any one player on the pitch only ever had the ball at his feet for between three-to-four percent of any one game, on average. Preparing a professional footballer for that three-to-four percent was the easy part. It was the other ninety-six percent plus that Alex fixated on. For any one player, a football match is played mostly not with the foot, but with the mind. Preparing, training and evolving his player's mental state was paramount. That's why he placed so much emphasis on man-management. It's why his legacy became synonymous with mind games.

Not only did Alex try to alter the mind of his own players, he dabbled with trying to get inside the minds of his opponents, too.

For him, it was fun. But he's not exactly sure how big an impact his attempted mind games had on his opposing managers.

'The mind games are definitely overrated,' Alex once told broadcaster Dan Walker in an interview. 'It's a bit of a myth, aye.'

Yet, contrastingly, those closest to Alex give no hesitation to revealing that he thrived on trying to niggle at the opposition's mind ahead of competition. He saw his pre-match press conferences as a platform in which he could at least attempt to live inside their heads in the build-up to a game. Most times he would be ineffective, but there is to be no argument over the fact that Alex riled up some of his opponents on occasions. And although his mind games never worked on Wenger, nor on Mourinho who was even better than Alex in this regard, they did work on some.

Perhaps the most famous result of Alex's attempted mind games was the time he stressed his good friend Kevin Keegan out so much that the legendary Newcastle manager visibly shook and began to snap while being interviewed on live TV. Keegan would point down the camera lens after Alex had wound him up by suggesting Leeds United wouldn't put as much effort into beating Newcastle as they had done against Manchester United.

'This has really got to me…' Keegan said. 'You can tell him now if he's watching this, we're still fighting for this title, and I'll tell you, honestly… I will love it if we beat them, love it!'

What's not known about that tale is that Alex actually felt bad afterwards. All he wanted to do was drop a little bit of doubt into the Newcastle dressing-room. He was hoping his little mind game may shave off a fraction of a percentage in the Newcastle players' performance—or even raise a fraction of a percentage in the Leeds' players' performance. What he didn't expect was to see Keegan looking stressed and pressured on live TV after-wards. Six weeks after Keegan's on-air meltdown, Alex would meet him in London where he would host the Newcastle boss for dinner. At one point, when posed with the question of Alex's mind game and Keegan's subsequent on air 'moment' on live TV, the Newcastle manager would wrap both of his hands around the Govanman's neck and mock strangle him. They both laughed uncontrollably. But by then, United had claimed yet another league title as Newcastle — who had been strong favourites and twelve points ahead at one stage — lost their way.

There is one on-air managerial meltdown that Alex did revel in however, only because he didn't personally like the man involved or have any relationship with him—unlike Keegan who Alex deeply respects. In January of 2009, Alex was wary of the threat of Liverpool who had rejuvenated under Rafa Benitez and were causing United problems by bettering them atop the Premier League table. Alex opted to add pressure to Liverpool's lead by suggesting they were only top because they had a better run of fixtures due to having more time to recover between games—which was a bizarre conspiracy and one of his weaker attempts at trying to live inside the heads of his rivals.

Regardless of how weak it was, Benitez would react by embarrassing himself at his next live press conference. The Spaniard was so wound up by Alex's suggestion that he would unfold an A4 sheet of handwritten notes in front of the media and begin to reel off a list of what he continuously labelled "facts". Only Benitez's facts weren't facts at all. To start with, the Spaniard discussed a two-match ban and £10,000 fine that Alex had once received for confronting referee Mike Dean using 'improper conduct'. Ten seconds later, Benitez was discussing another time he alleged the United manager used improper conduct to a referee and wasn't charged. The Liverpool boss then said, "He was not punished. He is the only manager in the league who cannot be punished for these things." Literally seconds after pointing out an occasion Alex *had* been punished for the exact same thing. Incidentally, Alex holds the record for having the most amount of fines and bans handed down by the FA for improper conduct.

Benitez would go on to say, 'All managers need to know that only Mr Ferguson can talk about the fixtures, can talk about referees and *nothing* happens. We need to know that I am talking about facts, not my impression!'

As journalists cringed in the silences between his inaccurate 'facts' (perhaps, in fairness to the Spaniard, lost in translation), Benitez looked uncomfortable and began to stutter through the remainder of his notes.

Alex had been tipped off by a journalist that a colleague had been prompted to pose a specific question to Benitez at the start of that press conference which would ignite the rant. So, Alex and some of his staff purposely watched the press conference on Sky Sports News, all while scoffing and sniggering.

Liverpool were top of the table at this point. Two days later, they would lose against Stoke and Manchester United would climb to the summit—a position they wouldn't surrender for the rest of the campaign.

Alex knew that if a manager looked weak in front of the press, then that would have a psychological effect on his players, even if it did just shave off a fraction of a percentage in their efforts. But in truth, he didn't set out to rile Keegan, nor Benitez with his attempted mind games. Their awkward moments in front of the world's press were all on them. Alex was aware that most of the time his psychological ploys yielded no reaction at all. But that didn't stop him trying. Just in case...

It can be argued that it was Jock Stein who introduced Alex to the ways of mind games, but the truth is Alex is so deeply psychological himself that even in jovial times his goal is to wind people up. That's how he joked with his players, how he joked with his staff, how he joked with other managers (he once unwrapped an expensive bottle of wine Sam Allardyce had given to him pre-game in anticipation of their post-game drink in Alex's office. The Govanman then wrapped a bottle of Ribena with Big Sam's wrapping and left it on his desk. When the opposing manager called by for his post-match drink, Alex thanked him for the bottle again, unwrapped the Ribena and then snarled 'What the fuck, Sam?' Allardyce bolted out of the room, fuming at his staff.) Winding up is even how Alex jokes with his wife. His sons. And his best friends. He enjoys that type of humour. It gives him his kicks. So, despite Stein's intervention with regards mind games in the lead up to the 1983 European Cup Winners' Cup Final, it is quite likely Alex would have eventually ventured down the road of winding up his opposition.

'Take him a bottle of the finest Scottish whisky,' Stein instructed Alex in the lead up to Aberdeen's Cup Winners' Cup Final. 'It'll make him think you're just thrilled to be there… to even be in a final with him.'

Three days later, during the press briefings ahead of the match, Alex would approach Alfredo Di Stefano with an expensive bottle in a wooden gift box. Di Stefano was taken back by the gesture, and the following day his Real Madrid team filled with superstars would be bettered by a parochial club from northeast Scotland. Quite how much Alex's gift to the opposing manager played a part in the victory is impossible to quantify, though it is unlikely to have made a big difference. Regardless, that is the tale of how Alex first became conscious, and thereafter obsessed, with attempting to win a psychological war against his opponents before a ball had even been kicked.

On the day of a game itself, Alex always tried to get into the heads of his opposite number, or indeed the heads of his opposite number's players, by using a very basic intimidation practice.

'He always used to stand in the tunnel before every single game, outside the dressing room, and shake every single one of our players' hands,' Gary Neville recalls of Alex's most subtle mind game. 'But I didn't realise until I was the captain what he was doing. He was looking down the tunnel so the opposition players saw him and the referee saw him. It's a bit of intimidation. He was an overpowering figure. This idea of winning in the tunnel before you've even gone out on the pitch, there was an element of that with him in terms of the psychology. When handshakes were introduced, he used to say, "Make sure you look into the eyes of every single player you shake hands with when you walk down that line. Hold it strong and look right into their eyes. And you know something, one or two of them will fold, because there's a sternness in it—it's a message or challenge." He did these things, techniques, that didn't maybe work all the time, but he was always looking for that advantage.'

Of course, the impact these minor mind games had on the

opposition — whether they be implemented just ahead of kick-off, or at his press conferences on Friday mornings — is impossible to quantify. But given there exists evidence of opposing managers falling for Alex's mind games so much that they lived it out live on TV, it is arguable that his efforts went at least some way to scratching away at a fraction of percentages in his opposition's performances.

What is inarguable, however, is that the mind games Alex played with his own players had a major impact throughout his career. While Fergie Time is the construct that gifted his teams a never-say-die attitude, it was one simple line — repeated often — that the Govanman himself feels helped the teams he managed to unprecedented success.

Between November and December each season — whether United be top of the table or lagging behind — Alex would readily say in press briefings, 'We are always much stronger in the second half of the campaign... everybody knoos that.'

It was a simple line that lacks any form of impact in isolation, but Alex is convinced this little psychological ploy lived inside the heads of not just the opposition, but his own players. He liked to remind everybody that United would be the better team from January onwards. And the more he convinced everybody around him that this was the case, the more it became a reality.

He would write in *Leading*: "If we came out of Christmas week in fifth place, it was not a complete disaster because over the years, it became folklore within the club that United always performed better in the second half of the season. We would always say, 'The second half will look after itself'. Of course, it was a bit more complicated than this, but it buoyed spirits to have that outlook."

Alex is certain that this mental shift, which afforded his players a positive mindset just as everybody else was doubting them, was as crucial to winning league titles as the tapping of his watch. In truth, both are parallel psychological manoeuvres in that they gift the United players a never-say-die attitude while possibly implanting a detrimental connotation inside the minds of the opposition.

If United were beaten — which usually happened around six to eight times per season, out of approximately fifty-five to sixty games played — Alex would drill into his players that the next game always gave them the opportunity to put the bad result to bed. It was a psychological ploy that he had read about and began to master. As soon as a defeat was confirmed, and the players and coaches were back in the confines of the dressing-room, Alex — after handing out a tongue lashing to the individuals he felt were most responsible for letting the team down — would swiftly and consciously move matters forward. It had to move forward. There was no need to look back. Certainly not at a negative.

'We've another game on Wednesday night. Gives us a chance to make up for this… we'll win Wednesday, you hear me?'

United very rarely lost two games in a row during the Premier League years, and in fact not once in his final fifteen years as a manager did United lose three games in a row. He would very often use a defeat to mentally challenge his players and in doing so ensure another loss wasn't around the corner. This psychological trick worked a treat—and is at least a mind game that is quantifiable, given the recorded results.

Aside from his own players, as well as the opposition, Alex also tried his mental gymnastics on match officials. When he first started managing in Scotland, he would go on record to the press as saying that he felt referees always favoured the Old Firm in their officiating. He tried the exact same tactic when he came down to England—suggesting Liverpool always benefitted from the decisions of referees. He, of course, didn't believe that to be the case. But he did enjoy attempting to live inside the heads of match officials—just in case it may play out to his advantage in some guise. However, he has suggested that he held absolutely no influence over the decisions of referees, no matter how much he tried to.

'This is a guy (me) who has the worst record of any manager in the history of English football, fined around a hundred thousand pounds by them, suspended so many times ... that's some influence, I must say,' he has said in the past.

Regardless, Alex did often attempt to get inside the mind of the referees in the middle of games. If he felt the opposition had an influential player in their ranks, somebody who would flap and flail and moan at match officials, Alex could be heard shouting across the pitch, 'Referee, you're better than this. Don't let Vieira ref this match. This is *your* match.' The goal here was to dilute the influence of the opposing player—but once again, this is an almost impossible mind game to quantify. Though former Premier League referee Mark Clattenberg has come close to admitting that United may have benefitted from Alex's psychological prowess over the years.

When Liverpool manager Jurgen Klopp began complaining in the post-Ferguson years that United were getting favourable decisions from match officials, seeing as, at one point, they were getting more penalties than any other team, Clattenberg — who was no longer working in the UK — wrote in a newspaper column: "Jurgen does not like losing, he never has. He gets prickly. But he is wrong to suggest there is an aura around United that sees them given favourable decisions. There used to be when Fergie was there, but that has eased massively since he left."

This admission is perhaps the nearest we'll ever come to realising Alex's mind games did indeed have an impact on match officials.

Of course, there were occasions that Alex's mind games didn't have any desired effect at all.

In 1995, he once said — as Blackburn were atop the table — that they would have 'to do a Devon Loch for us to win the title'. In fact, he mentioned Devon Loch at least three times in press briefings during the run-in to that title charge, hoping it would make Blackburn's legs wobble (Devon Loch is the infamous horse who had a long lead at the Grand National, only to collapse mere yards from the finishing line). However, Kenny Dalglish's Blackburn weren't to be played by Alex's psychological ploy and would not indeed do 'a Devon Loch' as they went on to claim the Premier League trophy.

Alex would also attempt mind games with Real Madrid players as well as the referee before United entered a two-legged affair against the Spanish giants in a 2003 Champions League quarter-final.

Aware that Real players liked to dictate the pace of games by crying foul, Alex said in his pre-match press conference, 'We'll need a strong referee so they don't get away with their dirty tricks.'

Neither the referee — Anders Frisk — nor the Real players were affected by the attempted mind game, and, using their clever approach of dictating the pace of games, Real would demolish United 3-1 in Spain and would advance to the semi-final on aggregate two weeks later despite being beaten 4-3 at Old Trafford.

As the years went on, Alex began to learn who could and who couldn't be affected by his mind games.

Although he threw a lot of psychological warfare towards Wenger, for example, he realised the Frenchman to be too cool to his approach and so mind-games rarely, if ever, worked against his greatest rival. And when Jose Mourinho came into the mix, Alex didn't even attempt to wind up the Portuguese.

'He plays these games, too,' Alex would say of Mourinho. 'And he is brilliant at it. You are never quite sure what he is up to. So I don't go down that road with him. I just let him get on with it.'

It wasn't just at Manchester United where Alex attempted to win the psychological battle. After he had been taught his first lesson in this regard from Stein, Alex became relentless in his Scottish press briefings by routinely attempting to wind the opposition up.

'He was brilliant at it,' former Aberdeen coach Willie Garner admits. 'Every week he'd have a pop at something. I remember one in particular. Hearts lost the league title against Dundee the Saturday before we were due to face them in the Scottish Cup Final. The manager discovered Hearts had got a psychologist in to get them focused on the cup final and forget about the previous week at Dens Park. On the day, he made sure we arrived at Hampden first, ahead of Hearts. Sir Alex then said that when the Hearts' team bus comes "pick any player, walk up to them, shake their hand and say, 'Unlucky last week'." That just planted that defeat at Dundee right back into their heads. They had just spent money on a psychologist trying to get that out of their heads for a week. We put it right back in.'

Aberdeen would trash Hearts in that very one-sided final, 3-0.

The truth about mind games with the opposition is that if they worked, like this anecdote Garner tells, then they would look extremely clever—possibly gifting them a presence in the lore of Alex that is undeserving.

He himself would surmise in *Leading*: "Across my career people always assumed I had elaborate Machiavellian strategies. In reality, I didn't set out to master the dark arts. I did try the odd trick. Saying we always finished the campaign at a higher gallop and with heightened resolve could be classified as a mind game... I did it every year. And it always worked. It crept into the minds of our players and became a nagging fear for the opposition. Tapping my watch became another psychological ploy. I didn't keep track of the time in games. I kept a loose eye on it but it is too hard to work out how long might be added. Here's the key: it was the effect it had on the other team, not ours, that counted. Seeing me tap my watch and gesticulate, the opposition would be spooked... they would feel besieged.'

Fergie Time worked. It's the one mind game that is quantifiably measurable, given the records. Perhaps it would have been fitting for Philip Jackson to sculpt Alex tugging back the left sleeve of his sports jacket while eyeballing his watch after all. It was the late goals that won games. It was the winning of games that won titles. And it was the winning of titles that gifted the Govanman a stand named in his honour, as well as this ever-lasting bronze sculpture standing proud outside it. While a statue of Fergie Time would have been, no doubt, viewed in most quarters as humorous, it would have been a particularly fitting piece of artistry.

1998-1999

MANCHESTER UNITED WOULD WIN IT ALL IN 1999—JUST AS ALEX HAD brazenly predicted to his chairman, to his players and to his brand new assistant manager they would.

In the space of eleven days in May 1999 — between 16th and 26th — United would lift the Premier League trophy, then — seven days later — the FA Cup, followed — four days later — by the European Cup. A treble of this magnitude was unprecedented through football history, and it cemented Alex as the greatest club manager of all time. Yet, he was only half-way through his manage-rial career at Old Trafford at this point, with his most consistent run of titles yet to come.

Any time he is asked about a specific highlight of his career, his answer is always as swift as it is sincere: 'Barcelona in '99, ye cannae beat that!'

He is, of course, referring to United's dramatic late win in the Champions League showpiece that took place in Barcelona's Nou Camp stadium against German giants Bayern Munich. United trailed in that game from as early as the sixth minute thanks to a curling Mario Basler free-kick that left goalkeeper Peter Schmeichel flat-footed. But in the space of 101 seconds of injury-time, before which the game looked out of sight for a jaded-looking United, David

Beckham would deliver two corners — the first in the ninety-first minute, the second in the ninety-third — from which United would score two goals. The first arrived via a toe-poked effort from Teddy Sheringham who was luckily assisted by a Ryan Giggs mis-kick. And the second hit the top corner of the net thanks to a close-range volley from the right boot of Ole Gunnar Solskjaer after Sheringham had flicked on the Beckham corner. United were kings of Europe for the first time since 1968 and had stolen their seat back on that particular throne in the most dramatic fashion imaginable—two goals in injury time. Those surprised by quite how dramatic that final turned out to be had most likely not been paying attention during the entirety of the campaign, however, as dramatic late winners in injury time had become a staple of this Manchester United side.

The season had actually begun with Alex lambasting his players for allowing Arsenal to pip them to the previous campaign's title. He was at this stage concerned that Arsene Wenger was a serious threat. When Blackburn Rovers had pipped United to the title under Kenny Dalglish in 1995, Alex wasn't overly worried that they were in it for the long haul. But he firmly believed Wenger's Arsenal to be a major threat to United's domestic dominance. So, in the summer of 1998, before heading into what would turn out to be the treble-winning season, Alex read his players the riot act, telling them in no uncertain terms that if they wanted to win it all, then they had to give it their all.

The players weren't the only ones being read the riot act that summer. In August, just ten days before the season kicked-off, Alex was called to the office of Martin Edwards from where the United chairman would accuse his manager of taking his eye off the ball. Edwards was strangely accusatory in this meeting; suggesting that Alex's new-found passion for owning racehorses meant he was spending less time on the training pitch. Alex thought at first that Edwards was joking—even though he was well aware his chairman rarely joked. If ever.

'Hold on,' Alex replied, 'yer the one who told me tae get a new hobby.'

It was true. During a heart-to-heart talk some two years prior, Edwards suggested Alex was working too hard, and insisted he take at least one day off every week in which he could distance himself from the pressures of the game.

Alex was certain there was more to the accusation than his race horsing hobby in that meeting and felt the imminent signing of Dwight Yorke from Aston Villa — which Edwards was firmly opposed to, and in which ultimately ended the working relationship of Alex and his assistant Brian Kidd — was still very much a bone of contention. In that meeting, Alex was so riled by Edwards that he slapped both hands to his chairman's desk and snapped, 'Okay, shall we just call it a day, then?'

Alex, not for the first time, was calling Edwards' bluff. And Edwards, not for the first time, relented. He ended up apologising to Alex for bringing up his horse racing affairs and they both shook hands.

Then, having made up, they would fall out yet again just after the season had kicked off—about three weeks after the initial meeting. Edwards, unbeknownst to Alex, had been in negotiations with Rupert Murdoch's BSKYB about selling the club. The fact that these talks had gone on through the summer of 1998 — while Edwards was penny-pinching and determined not to sign Dwight Yorke — sent Alex into a rage. He was furious he hadn't been informed of these negotiations before a press release revealed to the world the likelihood of an imminent takeover of Manchester United. Quite why Alex was furious was beyond Edwards' comprehension. It wasn't the football manager's business to get involved in club ownership. Manchester United wasn't Alex Ferguson's club to sell. It was Martin Edwards'. And Edwards was genuinely willing to sell it to Murdoch until that press release went out and Manchester United fans reacted with strong vigour against their club being sold to the controversial Australian media mogul. Because of this outrage, Peter Mandelson, the then Trade Secretary of Tony Blair's Labour government — who had just taken power in the UK, and of whom Alex was a huge supporter — referred the proposed takeover to the Monopolies Commission. The tug of war took months to end, and it all occurred in the backdrop of United's greatest ever season. The controversy finally concluded when the Monopolies Commission deemed the takeover inappropriate, simply because BSKYB owning Manchester United could create a conflict of interest to any future broadcasting rights of Premier League matches.

Alex was chuffed with the finding. Edwards was seething. He had been hoping for a multi-million-pound pay-day that also would have seen him retain a title on the club's board of directors. As a result of this tug of war, the United manager and the United chairman's relationship was stretched as taut as it ever had been right through the entirety of the history-breaking treble campaign.

If, at boardroom level, spirits were somewhat low, then the opposite can be said of the atmosphere in the dressing-room. Alex's squad of defenders may not have read too hot on paper at the time, but he knew that his options at centre-back of Jaap Stam, Henning Berg, Ronnie Johnsen (who Alex is on record as labelling the most underappreciated player he has ever managed) and David May would prove strong enough for them to grapple the Premier League trophy back from Arsenal's grip, as well as prove so disciplined that they would hold off the attacks of the great European teams in the Champions League. In midfield, Beckham, Scholes and Butt had come of age, while Giggs was thrilling down the left-hand side as if he were still a teenager. New captain Roy Keane was arguably the greatest midfielder in Europe at the time and had grown in such stature over the previous two seasons that he was by now a main voice in the dressing-room. Up front, Alex could call on any combination of two from four top strikers that included new signing Dwight Yorke, Andy Cole, Teddy Sheringham, and his own personal favourite, Ole Gunnar Solskjaer. Solskjaer wasn't just Alex's favourite from that list of strikers, he was his favourite player from all the players he has ever managed. Solskjaer, like Alex, was a football geek, and would often lunch with his manager after training sessions in an effort to pick his brains on the coaching methods he had just endured, before he'd move on to asking about the tactics the team would employ for their next game. Solskjaer would bring a notepad and pen to his lunch meetings with Alex, and during training sessions would often run off the pitch to grab at this notepad just so he could jot down some notes. Sometimes Solskjaer would bring his notepad to the substitute bench with him during matches. He would study the opposition, ready to find a flaw in their defensive game and, should he be called on by his manager, he would challenge himself to expose the flaw he had noted. Alex had never known a player to be so obsessed with every facet of the game as Solskjaer. It wasn't as if Solskjaer reminded Alex of himself. The Norwegian's obsession with coaching and tactics went far beyond that. Solskjaer wasn't just moving around salt and pepper shakers as a footballer, he was building a coaching manual for himself—all too aware he was learning from the very best.

'Every game he played in and every training session he took part in, he wrote it all down,' Alex said of the Norwegian back in 2011. That was the year Solskjaer left Manchester United having spent fifteen years at the club; firstly as a player for nine seasons; then as first team striker coach for one season before being appointed by Alex as reserve team manager in 2008. Solskjaer would leave that role three years later, having been offered the job as Molde manager —a club equally close to his heart as Manchester United given that it was there he had made his debut as a full-time professional back in 1994. Solskjaer would win back-to-back titles as Molde manager in his first and second seasons—an incredible achievement given that the club had never been crowned champions over the course of their 100-year history before his appointment.

The Norwegian would find himself named as a substitute for much of the 1998-1999 season alongside Teddy Sheringham, given that Andy Cole and new recruit Dwight Yorke had hit it off as an ideal partnership as early as pre-season. Fans would be wowed by their new forward partnership in the early part of the campaign, after United had been drawn in a tough Champions League group alongside Barcelona, Bayern Munich and Danish outfit Brondby. It was during these European cup ties that Yorke and Cole would prove to be an impossible duo to deal with, even for the best defensive sides on the continent. United weren't favourites to get out of their tricky group, but they finished second—one point behind Bayern Munich who they would later meet in the final, and two points clear of Barcelona who were dumped from the competition.

But although it was Yorke and Cole grabbing all the glory, it was indeed Solskjaer who wrote the boldest headlines during that campaign. Not only did he come off the bench to score four goals (which had never been achieved in professional football history up until that point) during a resounding 8-1 victory over Nottingham Forest, but he would become the poster boy for United's dogged ability to win games late on from losing positions.

United looked like they were going to be dumped from the FA Cup as early as the third round when, having been pitted against bitter rivals Liverpool, they found themselves 1-0 down at Old Trafford with just two minutes left to play. A Dwight Yorke goal looked to have calmed United's fans' beating hearts, assuming the ex-Aston Villa man had earned them a replay at Anfield. But Solskjaer had other ideas. With the referee seconds from blowing the final whistle, he stole the ball from the foot of Paul Scholes inside the Liverpool box following a hopeful punt up field from Jaap Stam, before coolly sliding it though Jamie Carragher's legs (a finish the Norwegian practised over and over again in training). The strike bamboozled goalkeeper David James who was still diving the wrong way when the ball was nestling into the corner of his near post. It proved to be the last kick of that game and marked the first dramatic comeback of what proved to be a season of dramatic comebacks for United.

Perhaps the most dramatic of all the comebacks that season took place in Villa Park in April of 1999, just as a genuine question was beginning to circulate among football observers: 'Could United really win it all?'

By this stage they were in the FA Cup semi-final, the Champions League quarter-final and were leading Arsenal at the summit of the league table by a single point. Publicly, Alex would deny United could win all three competitions. He told one reporter who posed such a question ahead of their FA Cup semi-final clash against Arsenal that, 'The triple (that's what Alex called it, not 'the treble', but 'the triple'), has never bin done before, so no, it's nae possible.' However, behind closed doors, particularly in team talks, he would point and spit at his players, yelling, 'You can make history. If you believe in yaselves as much as I believe in ya, you can make history.'

There were plenty of hurdles still be jumped, of course. Six more games in the title race were yet to be played and — as is always the case in title run-ins — none of them looked easy. In between those six games was scheduled a Champions League quarter-final second-leg against Inter Milan, and an FA Cup semi-final against Arsenal.

It wasn't until after that semi-final against Arsenal that United fans started to believe they could win it all. They would go one-nil up in that game, played at Villa Park, thanks to a sublime David Beckham thirty-yard strike that mainly goes unmentioned in the history books given what followed. With twenty minutes to go, Arsenal would equalise through a deflected Dennis Bergkamp effort that he struck from pretty much the exact same spot Beckham had scored his goal from in the first half. And then, with just ten minutes left, Nicolas Anelka capitalised on a rare Peter Schmeichel error to slot into an empty net. The Frenchman would wheel himself away in celebration, only for a late flag to ruin his rush. Replays showed the Frenchman to be one stride behind the line of United defenders when the original shot came in from Bergkamp, a shot Schmeichel had spilled into the path of Anelka. The Frenchman was furious when, running down the touchline in celebration, he noticed the referee waving at him and signalling for a free-kick. Minutes later, with United on the ropes, their leader would see red. Roy Keane lunged into a tackle on Marc Overmars that was about two seconds too late, and David Ellery didn't hesitate in sending the Irishman for an early bath.

With the game inching towards the ninety minute mark United were on the back foot and holding out desperately for extra-time.

They were soaking up all kinds of pressure, coming at them from all kinds of angles—from Overmars making overlapping runs down United's right-hand side, Bergkamp and Anelka interchanging positions between the United defenders, and Patrick Vieira and Ray Parlour bossing the midfield. It was Parlour who ran at United full-back Phil Neville in the final minute of injury-time, backing him into his own box before jinking to his right, daring Neville into a tackle. The United full-back obliged, tripping Parlour up. Ellery didn't hesitate in pointing to the spot, and in doing so he all but ended United's dream of winning it all. Alex was already preparing his post-match interviews with the press in his head.

'I told ye we couldnae win all three.'

Bergkamp didn't miss penalties. He always struck the ball so cleanly that the net would rattle before the goalkeeper had landed his dive. But despite striking this penalty as cleanly as he struck any, Schmeichel would somehow make it all the way across to the left corner of his goal to slap two palms to the ball. United celebrated that penalty save as if they had won the game, and not the right to play on for another thirty minutes of extra-time with only ten men. It had been a long season for the Red Devils. They had made it far in every major competition. And so Arsenal, looking much more refreshed than United and with one extra player on the pitch, were strong favourites kicking off the extra thirty minutes. Somehow, United defended brilliantly, even though their players were collapsing with cramp and tired thighs. And then, as Arsenal chased a winner, Patrick Vieira's simple pass in United's half was intercepted by Ryan Giggs. The Welshman picked up the ball at full-speed and just kept on racing as fast as he could, the ball seemingly glued to his boot until he reached the Arsenal six-yard box. To get there, he would weave around Lee Dixon twice, send Martin Keown falling to his arse, and then round Tony Adams' sliding tackle before firing the ball into the roof of David Seaman's net.

Alex would, many years later, label it the greatest goal of his entire managerial career.

'Better than Rooney's overhead against Man City?'

'Oh aye,' he replied without hesitation.

'Better than van Persie's volley against Aston Villa?'

Alex paused on that question, then slowly nodded.

'Aye, it's better than that one. It's the perfect goal for me, really. Right player, right moment.'

That goal awarded United an FA Cup final at Wembley against mid-table Newcastle United, while the following week they would overcome Inter Milan with a disciplined second-leg display in Italy in which they ran out eventual 3-1 winners on aggregate.

Juventus awaited them in the semi-final of the European show-piece. It was a tough task. The Old Lady were an impressive outfit, boasting players such as Zinedine Zidane, Edgar Davids, Didier Deschamps, Alessandro Del Piero, Fillipo Inzaghi and Antonio Conte among other household names. A 1-1 draw at Old Trafford meant the Italians were favourites heading into their home leg, but a spirited United, led by captain Roy Keane and punctuated by an impeccable performance from Cole and Yorke up front, led United to their first European final since the 1991 European Cup Winners Cup victory. Keane's performance that night in Turin was hailed as particularly heroic given that he received an early yellow card for a foul on Zidane that ruled him out of the final. The Irishman's memory doesn't align to the history books, however.

'I don't think I did have a good game that day, far, far from my best,' he would admit years later.

Alex doesn't agree.

'That's what made Roy one of the greatest winners I ever had. He was never-say-die and was always in it for the team. He never played football for himself. He always played for the team. That night in Turin, he was unbelievable.'

Those two dramatic semi-final wins, coupled with a consistent run of victories as the Premier League raced towards its conclusion, all laid the perfect pathway towards those famous eleven days in May.

On the 16th, they would have to prove themselves comeback kings once again during the final clash of the league season in order to be crowned champions. Les Ferdinand had put Tottenham one up after twelve minutes, by cutely lobbing the ball over an advancing Schmeichel. However, given the precedence set that season by the players, nobody inside Old Trafford was panicking; not the manager, not the players, not the fans. It was as if the comeback was inevitable. David Beckham would equalise before half-time by thundering the ball into the far top corner from an improbable angle, likely in frustration after having missed a headed opportunity from just three yards out minutes prior. He would celebrate by thumping at his chest, still seething about the miss. Then, in the second half, with United in cruise control and roared on by a crowd chanting 'We want our trophy back', Andy Cole would trap a fantastic Denis Irwin pass just inside the Spurs penalty area before looping the ball over Ian Walker's head.

Forty minutes later, the players would lift the Premier League trophy for the fifth time in seven seasons, but they wouldn't celebrate. Not yet. They had an FA Cup final to plan for the following Saturday. Alex would pick a somewhat reserve side for the Wembley showpiece against Newcastle, given that the Champions League final was just four days away. Roy Keane did start, however, as he was suspended for the Champions League clash, but he would be stretchered off twelve minutes into the game having torn a thigh muscle. It was an injury that would've ruled him out of the Champions League final regardless of his suspension. Despite most of their main stars missing for the FA Cup final, United would make easy work of a very mediocre Newcastle, thanks to two neat finishes: firstly from Paul Scholes and then from Teddy Sheringham. The game ended 2-0, but United easily could have racked up more goals given their dominance on the day. When the final whistle blew, it confirmed United had won three domestic doubles in the space of six seasons. A double had only ever been won four times in one-hundred years before that. No manager had ever won a double twice, let alone three times. However, this astonishing milestone went largely unheralded given what was about to unfold.

United played Bayern Munich in the Champions League final in

Barcelona's Nou Camp on the 26th of May, 1999. It would have been Matt Busby's ninetieth birthday. And Alex certainly let the players know that during his team talk.

The most fascinating anecdote from that final occurred between the hecticness of United's dramatic equaliser in the 91st minute and their winner some 101 seconds later. As soon as Sheringham had swept home the equaliser, assistant manager Steve McClaren turned to an elated Alex to insist United immediately revert to their staple 4-4-1-1 formation, having thrown the kitchen sink into the Bayern box in search of a goal.

'No,' Alex said, shaking his head. 'They're on the ropes. We're gonnae win this before extra-time.'

It was a ludicrous suggestion. There was one and a half minutes of injury-time left to be played. McClaren was adamant United steady the ship and begin to plan for extra-time. Alex was certain extra-time wasn't needed. They hadn't long finished their conversation about not reverting to a conservative 4-4-1-1 formation when United were awarded the corner kick from which Solskjaer would volley home the most dramatic winner imaginable. The Norwegian skidded in celebration before his teammates, the whole squad of substitutes, and four coaches leapt on top of him. Alex raised his two fists aloft and jumped up and down on the spot like a motorised bunny. When the final whistle went some twenty-seconds later, Alex was herded, as he was contractually obliged, to an interview with ITV's Gary Newbon where he would slap his hand to his forehead, still soaking in what had occurred before him, when the microphone was pushed below his chin.

'Football, bloody hell,' he said.

His shock was warranted. United were extremely lucky to win that game. Bayern had twice hit the woodwork while United were throwing bodies forward in search of an equaliser. And Schmeichel had to pull off two fantastic saves to ensure the Germans didn't double their lead. In contrast, Oliver Khan in the Bayern goal had barely been tested up until the injury-time madness.

That wasn't the only accusation of 'luck' thrown at United

throughout that record-breaking campaign, though. There were plenty of late winners that some pundits decided were more owed to fortune than any level of genius, and then, of course, there was that penalty save from Schmeichel in the dying moments of the dramatic FA Cup semi-final clash against Arsenal—another match United easily could and perhaps should have lost.

Alex has always laughed off the suggestion United were lucky that year, though. He was convinced the squad of players he had assembled had such a strong never-say-die attitude that they never mentally felt beaten. He would admit he felt that Champions League final had got away from them, that Bayern were going to hold out. But he also believes that not one player on that pitch wearing red that night believed that game was over.

There was one slice of luck that occurred on the eve of the season kicking off, however, that Alex simply can't deny. During the turbulent summer previous, when Alex and Edwards were at logger heads — about horse racing interests, and then about Dwight Yorke being bought, and then about the BSKYB takeover — he would receive a phone call from then Tottenham manager David Pleat. Pleat would ask Alex if, given he had just signed Yorke, there was a possibility Solskjaer was purchasable. Alex dismissed the notion there and then. But would later that evening, in the comfort of his own home, reflect on the possible sale. He liked Solskjaer so much that he felt he owed it to him to be straight.

'Spurs have come in for you,' he told the Norwegian in a meeting the next day. 'I told them to get lost, but I think it could be a great move for you.'

Solskjaer agreed to mull it over and said he would speak to his wife Silje before deciding his destiny. It would be Silje who would ask her agonising husband later that night, 'Would you rather be a Manchester United substitute, or a Spurs starter?'

'A United substitute,' Solskjaer reportedly replied. And his decision was made.

If Silje hadn't used basic psychology to determine her husband's future on that night in mid-August 1999, it's most unlikely the treble would have ever been achieved given that the Norwegian scored dramatic and crucial late winners in all three competitions United would win.

The day after the Champions League Final, Cathy would ignite Alex's hangover by letting him know Alastair Campbell — the political strategist for the then Labour Government — had approached her the night before to extend the offer of a knighthood to her husband.

'I told 'im you wouldnae be interested in being called Sir,' Cathy said. Then she stared at her husband. 'You wouldnae be interested, would you?'

'Ach, no,' Alex said. 'It's no' for me.'

ALEX AND HIS POLITICS

ALEX WAS RELUCTANT TO ACCEPT THE OFFER OF A KNIGHTHOOD simply because it conflicted with his political ideology. He, like his father and mother before him, is a socialist. A *strong* socialist. Lizzie — Alex's mother — was particularly and consistently vocal about what humanity *should* be striving for. Her beliefs were cemented in concrete and had been since before she had even met and fallen in love with Alex Ferguson Snr—who happened to share her ideology, but with less fury. 'It's no' fair…' Lizzie Ferguson would often start conversations with before opening up a topic on the latest injustice that had riled her. She felt for people, was hugely empathetic and, despite being extremely well-read, could not comprehend why the political system didn't operate in a way that would ensure equality for all. Lizzie Ferguson, nee Hardie, was a feminist before her time. She was a liberal before her time. She was 'woke' before the word was even assumed as a political term. She and her husband were strong advocates for workers' rights—and steered both of their sons progressively in that regard. She could not stomach capitalism; that ideology was alien to her. To the Fergusons, it simply couldn't add up that anybody of working class could hold an ideology of capitalism. If they did, then surely they were only cheating themselves. Equality across the board was a mantra within the Ferguson household. The entire family were impenetrable socialists, and proudly so.

It was no surprise at all then, given the ideology of the household he grew up in, that Alex, by the time he was a teenager, was standing atop upturned crates inside the tool-making factory in which he worked, barking out instructions to men three times his age—yelling to inform them that they were being shafted in the workplace. The Govanman, or Goventeen as he was then, became a union representative and then the shop steward rather early in his apprenticeship at Remington Rand, proving not just a maturity beyond his years, but also a political and economic ideology that most of those senior colleagues he was barking at couldn't quite comprehend. An ideology of socialism was so ingrained in Alex, that by just eighteen years of age, upon hearing about the apprentices' strike in Glasgow, he found an empty tin can in the family kitchen, then ran around the multiple pubs and bars in the Govan area where he would stand up on a stool, shush the singsong that was going on, and begin to hold court.

'Ladies and gentleman,' he would say. 'Yiv all heard aboot the apprentices' strike, but let me fill y'in on some o' the details you may not yet knoo.' He would hold the attention of men and women many years his senior inside those bars and detail to them exactly why the apprentices needed their support. Then he'd persuade them to dig deep into their pockets to help out their community and, sure enough, his tin can would be rattling with loose coins by the time he was strolling out of the pub.

Having raised hundreds of pounds in loose change in a matter of days, Alex would then turn up front and centre at a march the apprentices would hold a few weeks later as they fought for better working conditions and fair pay. With his newly adopted Perry Como side-paring hairdo, Alex can be seen in video footage leading middle-aged men on the march.

Gordon Simpson, who took part in those protests, would recall many years later: 'There were seven of us who started at

Remington Rand at the same time and Alex quickly became the self-appointed leader of us, and was later made the shop steward. If there were any strikes happening, Alex would be right there and he'd tell us the ins and outs of what was happening and the reasons behind it. He was very political and incredibly intelligent. He was destined to be a leader.'

A leader is exactly how Alex prefers to label himself. Not a manager. A *leader*. Reflecting on his career, Alex said: 'Ma job was to make everyone understand that the impossible was possible. That's the difference between leadership and management.'

In his retirement, Alex would pen a book with his good pal Michael Moritz on leadership, simply titled: *Leading*. In it, he didn't write about his favourite players, or transfers, or tactics; the chapters were instead headed: Listening, Watching, Discipline, Drive, Conviction, Organisation, Preparation, Time-Keeping, Delegation and Frugality among others. Topics that could translate across any line of business leadership.

In 2012, Harvard Business School — one of the most respected universities in the world — would begin teaching a module called: Sir Alex Ferguson. It was Professor Anita Elberse who conceived the idea, so enamoured was she by Alex's evolving leadership qualities over the span of twenty-six years at Manchester United. Alex would fly to Boston on a number of occasions to not only witness the lectures in person, but to take part. The lessons he specifically lectured on might touch on football, and he would certainly use his personal experiences as reference, but the topics, as they were within his book *Leading*, were not specific to football, but to leaders from all walks of life.

The fact that the Govanman sees himself more of a leader than just a football manager has stoked a question that has been offered by plenty who know the real Alex Ferguson over the years.

Given that he is such a great leader, could he have been as successful in politics as he was in football?

'Ach,' Alex says, throwing his head back when posed with it, 'there's nae chance we'll ever know. I wouldnae went into politics whatever they were payin' me anyway.'

It's a disappointing answer to an interesting question, especially as he had shown keen interest in politics from such an early age. But the nearest truth is that Alex didn't much fancy a career in politics because he didn't like how the system operated. The playing field, as he saw it, wasn't level, and so he knew he would grow frustrated with such a career choice. He didn't much care for the establishment as it was. So, becoming a pawn within it was never on the cards.

If he had have become a political leader, however, there's no ambiguity over which team he would have led. It would be a red team. The Labour Party. He has been a supporter from as far back as the days he was standing on crates inside Remington Rand, barking at men three times his age.

'I'm a Labour man, aye, always,' he told regarded journalist John Snow in an interview for *Channel Four News*. 'I've always supported the leader of the party. No matter the criticism. Nothing would change it. Nothing. It's ma upbringing.'

He would write in *My Autobiography*, "My political convictions have remained largely unchanged from my time as a shop steward in the shipyards of Govan. People's opinions change overtime with success and wealth, but in my youth I acquired not so much a range of ideological views as a way of seeing life."

Despite his strong political allegiance, Alex has never lived inside a left-wing vacuum. Far from it, in fact. The sources of his news-consumption confirm a very balanced view on a number of political matters. Every weekday, Alex reads the *Daily Express*, even though it is undoubtedly a Conservative-supporting newspaper that delivers news slanted with right-sided spins. In contrast to that, at the weekends, Alex reads the *Scottish Sunday Mail* (seen as moderately left in its reporting), the *Sunday Express* (right-wing) and *The Independent* (left-wing).

It's also quite inaccurate, or lazy, to rubber-stamp Alex's political ideology as just a 'Labour man'. In truth, his political sweet spot is left of Labour, though nailing Labour to a sweet spot in political lineage through Alex's lifetime is akin to playing pin the tail on the donkey. Labour can sway from moderate to left-wing, depending on their leader at any given point. For instance, Alex's ideology would line up with former Labour leader Jeremy Corbyn, though Alex was never a huge fan of Corbyn given that the former Labour frontman never looked like a true leader in the Govanman's eyes. Corbyn's politics: perfect. Corbyn's leadership: rubbish. Alex would have loved Gordon Brown to get a proper crack at 10 Downing Street as he felt he could have been one of Britain's greatest prime ministers, but the Scot (born in Renfrewshire, ten miles from Govan, and ten years after Alex) would only hold such office for less than three years in a time when Labour had lost the will of much of the country following their sanctioning of the War on Terror in Iraq. Brown's rise to the summit of British politics arrived at the worst possible time, and Alex would not get to see a man he hugely admired and considered a friend, lead the country how they both saw fit. Instead, the Conservative party would win back power in 2010, much to Alex's irritation. He can't stand the Conservatives and more often than not, and rather dismissively, refers to the party as "them lot". If Alex hadn't despised the Conservatives enough through his mother's lifetime, then that hatred would be rubber stamped in her death.

Alex would write in *My Autobiography*: "As I stood outside in the corridor (of the Southern General hospital in which his mother was seeing out her final days in December, 1986), I became fully aware of just how disastrously a once-great hospital had deteriorated. It was appalling. The images of decay and neglect have remained with me, and I have never ceased to curse the Tory government for vandalising the National Health Service. Margaret Thatcher's aggressive efforts to privatise health care in this country were a betrayal of a service that has been one of the proudest achievements of our society."

Alex rising to prominence as a football manager in the mid-nineties just happened to coincide with the Labour Party rising in the polls too, finally putting an end to eighteen years of Conservative power. Labour turned a corner after leader Tony Blair would totally rebrand the party. Alex was a huge fan of New Labour and would contact Blair in the lead up to the 1997 general election to inform him of his support. After Blair's Labour thumped the Conservative party in that pre turn of the century election, Alex would become an unpaid consultant for the new Prime Minister. Unpaid and unofficial. Blair liked to pick Alex's brains on specific leadership matters.

'I thought he (Blair) was absolutely brilliant. Marvellous. Especially in Question Time. I loved watching him on Question Time,' Alex said of the former Prime Minister.

Alex truly appreciated how Blair would tackle his opposition in Parliament — then led by William Hague — by using very similar tactics to the ones adopted at Old Trafford. Blair liked to give Hague a false sense of security, then he would use that security to counter-punch him as they debated across the commons.

Alex was so enamoured by New Labour that he began to get intrinsically involved at the top tier of British politics via a mutual friend. Alastair Campbell had been appointed as Blair's Political Strategist (or spin doctor to give him his more apt title) through the 1997 general election and beyond. Campbell was a fan of Alex's (despite being a Burnley FC supporter) and the feeling was pretty mutual. Soon after Blair had been handed the keys to 10 Downing Street, Alex would begin to receive phone calls from the home of British political power.

It wasn't as if Campbell and Blair were seeking Alex's opinion on their foreign policy, or how they should tackle the ailing Health system. Blair was interested in picking Alex's thoughts on how he should lead his cabinet.

'I had dinner with Alastair, Tony and Cherie (the Prime Minister's wife) in the Midland Hotel in Manchester the week before the 1997 general election,' Alex admitted. 'I told Tony, "If you could keep your government in one room and lock the door yi'll have nae problems. The problem with government is that they all fly off on their own and they have their own allies, their own journalistic contacts. Controlling your government is gonnae be the hard part".'

Thereafter, Blair would seek Alex's opinion on how he could best lead his government to form unity from within. Unbeknownst to Alex, Blair would, one day in 2003, ask his opinion on how to deal with 'superstars who were getting above their station.' Blair didn't specify any names, but Alex became immediately aware that the Prime Minister was having trouble with a certain member of his cabinet.

'Tony,' Alex told him, 'the most important thing is control. The minute a superstar threatens your control, you have to get rid of them.' Alex had proven this theory many times. Superstars such as Paul McGrath, Paul Ince and later David Beckham and Roy Keane had been gotten rid of, despite being key players in Alex's teams after they dared question his authority.

Alex genuinely didn't know at the time, but the 'superstar' Blair was talking about was the one true Labour man Alex felt was the best of the lot: Gordon Brown. Blair would try, but ultimately fail, to get rid of Brown after heeding Alex's advice that troublemakers should be shown the door.

Alex would continue to give advice to Blair on how he could man-manage his cabinet. That was 'sacrosanct', Alex told him. 'You can't unite the country if you can't unite your own men.' On top of that, the United manager would also offer his two-pennies on Tony's media appearances. He told the Prime Minister that he looked jaded in recent interviews and insisted he take more naps during his manic schedule.

'Why don'tcha get a masseur on the bus with you?' Alex said to Blair when he was in the middle of campaigning. 'You need to keep in peak physical shape, otherwise y'ill git dragged down. The nation need to see you looking as healthy as y'can.'

Despite taking a lot of Alex's advice around health and well-being on board, Blair and Alastair stop short of hiring a masseur.

'If the people found out we were spending their money on massages...' Campbell said without feeling a need to finish his point.

Alex would ultimately be left heartbroken by Blair's insistence on Britain getting involved in America's War on Terror and their eventual invasion of Iraq in 2003—which he personally viewed as a slap in the face for true Labour supporters. But he would never fall out of love with the party and still supports them fervently today, despite the roller-coaster ride Labour have taken since they last handed the keys of 10 Downing Street to back to 'them lot' in 2010.

Alex did also fume at Labour's lack of will during the 2016 EU Referendum. Labour, Alex was insistent, should have done more to inform their supporters that leaving the European Union would be detrimental to Britain's standing in the world. He is adamant that countries need to come together for humanity to evolve. Splitting countries and drawing fresh borders is hugely regressive to him. He held the same views ahead of the 2014 Scottish Referendum, when the population of his home country went to the polls with a choice of either divorcing themselves from the United Kingdom or remaining a key cog in the union. Heading towards the referendum, the Scottish National Party — who advocated for the referendum and have been the driving force for Scottish independence — attempted to recruit Alex to their side.

'Jeez, can ye believe that?' Alex snorted. 'The SNP. Me? I told them were to go, nae doubt aboot it.'

The SNP had managed to persuade other Scottish icons such as Sean Connery and Robbie Coltrane to back their Yes vote for Scottish independence, but Alex thought the notion absurd and was quite relieved when the No campaign finally won the day.

It's rather ironic that Alex held such world views as equality for all when career-wise he led in an unmistakeable authoritative manner. The way he approached his leadership in football is in stark contrast to his strong socialist ideology. But as a wise one once said, "All great men are contradictions".

To establish some sort of legacy that would back up his ideology, Alex would become the UK Ambassador for UNICEF—a charity organisation he found real kinship with. UNICEF are a global charity whose aim is to raise money to provide humanitarian and developmental aid to poverty-stricken children worldwide. As part of his role at UNICEF, Alex has personally donated six-figure sums to the charity, witnessed their child protection work in Thailand, helped with children in both Africa and Geneva affected by HIV and AIDS, and was at the forefront of the Baby Friendly Initiative in his old home town of Glasgow in the midst of his retirement. Although Alex retired as a football manager in 2013, his work with UNICEF is still important to him and continues to pass many of his hours.

A lot of the other hours he has to himself in retirement can still involve politics in some guise. His fascination with American politics remains particularly strong. He has read countless books on John F. Kennedy and Abraham Lincoln and is fascinated by the evolution America went through throughout the twentieth century. As mentioned at the very beginning of this biography, if Alex appeared on Mastermind, his specialist subject would not be football. It would more likely be American Politics. More specifically, it would be the American Civil War. One of the best and most fascinating books Alex has ever read is *Team of Rivals*, which is an account of Abraham Lincoln's presidency, specifically delving deep into his leadership choices.

'What was fascinating about that book,' Alex would tell Alastair Campbell, who incidentally had sent Alex a copy for him to read, 'even though it was about slavery and the Civil War, was how he held together all these big personalities to make sure they all stayed on track (Lincoln famously made up a government of those who opposed his views, instead of 'Yes' men). Now, he was President of the United States in a totally different era. I am a manager of a football team. But I can learn about the art of team building and team management from all sorts of places. It's all about managing people and relationships in the end.'

Alex also spent many hours of his retirement listening to thirty-five hour long tapes of a professor called Gary W. Gallagher who lectures on the American Civil War.

'Every morning I got in my car, I'd play the tapes and just listen. They were fantastic. Absolutely fantastic.'

Such is his intrigue with the subject, Alex has visited Gettysburg, Manassas and Bull Run to walk the fields in which took place the biggest battles of the American Civil War.

What's most interesting about Alex's fascination with the Civil War and indeed President Lincoln, who Alex considers the greatest leader of them all, is that Lincoln played for the opposition. Lincoln was a right-wing Republican. Alex, no doubt if he were American, would be a Democrat supporter.

It was good friend Campbell — with whom Alex has had many a discussion about Lincoln through the years — who had been informed by Prime Minister Tony Blair ahead of Alex's best moment as a manager in 1999 that 'if United win the treble, we've got to knight Alex.'

So, after the final whistle in the Nou Camp, in which Campbell was one of the 90,000-capacity crowd, the Labour 'spin doctor' tried to find the Govanman to bestow such an honour on him. Alex was too busy, soaking in the surreality with his players and staff. Instead, Campbell approached Cathy.

'Cathy, can you ask Alex to ring me as soon as he can,' he said. 'The Labour government would like to offer him a knighthood.'

Cathy's face scrunched up.

'Ach aye, Alastair,' she said. 'D'yoo no' think he's won enough?'

The next day, while coming down from the high, Cathy and Alex would finally talk it out. Because of his social standings politically, Alex had never really been a fan the Order of the British Empire. He didn't care much for being knighted. But if his response was lukewarm to the honour, Cathy's was freezing cold.

'No, no,' Cathy said. 'Why'd anyone wannae be a Sir anyway? I think it's ridiculous.'

But it would be their three sons whose voices would ring loudest.

'Dad, c'mon, it's the greatest honour, why'd you turn that down?' Jason asked him. Darren and Mark would back Jason up. And Alex would go to bed that night contemplating the contrasting arguments raised by his wife and sons. But it wasn't any of their faces at the forefront of his thoughts as he tossed and turned in bed. Instead, he imagined his father.

'I kept thinking,' Alex would later admit, 'what would my father have done?'

The following week, Alex would ring Campbell to accept the honour. To this day, however, the Govanman doesn't like the title being used, and on the cover of the books he has published in his retirement, refused to have the title 'Sir' placed in front of his name. But his disinterest in the honour doesn't compare to his wife who officially became a Lady as soon as her husband was knighted.

'Don't call her Lady Cathy,' Alex once said. He may have laughed while saying it, but he was deadly serious. 'She hates it. Cathy cringes anytime someone calls me Sir or her Lady. She still says to this day, "A don't knoo why you accepted that in the first place".'

It could have been even worse for Cathy. In 2013 her husband turned down the title of Lord. He was offered a peerage through then Labour leader Ed Miliband, who Alex held total respect and regard for. But he was never interested in such a title. Lords were expected to turn up to Parliament on regular occasions and Alex had other things in mind for his retirement. He wanted to spend more time with his wife. And his wife certainly didn't want to be spending time with a man named Lord Alex Ferguson.

1999-2004

FOLLOWING THE EUPHORIA OF WINNING THE TREBLE, ALEX WOULD TELL Cathy during a heart-to-heart chat on their holiday to France in June of 1999 — just after he had accepted the offer of a knighthood — that he had decided upon a date for his retirement.

'Three more seasons,' he told her. 'Then I'll pack it in.'

He had settled on retiring at sixty, feeling it was an appropriate age to call it a day and would then announce to his sons following that holiday that he would be stepping down as United manager in May 2002.

Before that, he wanted to win the European Cup once again, and he certainly wanted at least another league title. In fact, he was adamant United could win the next two titles—insisting his side were capable of winning three in a row having come off the unprecedented treble-winning campaign. Only the great Liverpool side (1981-1983) had won three titles in a row in the post-war era, and it was a record Alex was convinced he could match.

After winning the Premier League title as part of the treble in 1999, United would go on to defend their status as champions in 2000 before winning it again in 2001. He would later go on to win three titles in a row once again, between 2007 and 2009—and remains the only manager to ever achieve the double treble.

Arsenal were United's only threat to that first triple of titles at the beginning of the millennium. Arsene Wenger was continuing to build an impressive squad, bringing in the likes of Robert Pires and Thierry Henry to add some Gallic flair to an already beautifully orchestrated continental side. To the eye, they looked a better outfit than United, but the league table wasn't judged by the eye. United raced to their next two title wins after the treble, until Arsenal properly clicked — storming to the title in 2002, eclipsing United by ten points in order to do so. United would reclaim the trophy the following year, but Arsenal would go on such a good run in the 2003-2004 campaign that they would end it unbeaten and as champions. 'The Invincibles' they were nicknamed, much to the annoyance of Alex. He hated that Wenger had got a record on him that he hadn't achieved himself, and ultimately never would. But Alex didn't view the invincible season as that impressive. Arsenal may have remained unbeaten in the league that season, but they did draw twelve of their thirty-eight games, finishing on ninety points. Alex's teams had reached the ninety-point mark to win championships, too, and he feels those league wins weren't given the same level of respect by pundits who were readily throwing flowers at the Gunners' feet. The bottom line of Alex's bitterness in this regard is rather simple: he was envious of what Arsenal achieved in the 2003-04 season mostly because he still held a high level of disdain towards Wenger. He remained irritated by the Frenchman's refusal to join in on the traditional post-match chit-chat and found his stance on this rather unforgivable. He also considered Wenger to be a somewhat cold character, rarely interested in opening any line of communication with his fellow managers even at League Manager Association dinners.

Cold, or lukewarm, or whatever temperature Wenger might have been during this period, he sure did light a hot fire under Alex. United and Arsenal were going at it hammer and tongs; fighting it out for eight league campaigns in a row and creating, arguably, the greatest rivalry the Premier League years have ever witnessed. Each time the two sides met, fireworks would go off. It was fascinating that both managers approached the game in much the same way—each opting to employ quick wingers who would counterattack at will. As a result, Manchester United versus Arsenal clashes at the very beginning of the millennium often played out like tennis matches, the ball quite literally shifting from end to end in a matter of split seconds.

Most of those games were tight and tense affairs. Between 1996 and 2005 — when Jose Mourinho arrived at Chelsea to put an end to the dominant duo of the Red Devils and the Gunners — Alex and Arsene pitted their wits against each other twenty-four times. Alex would come out on top in just eight of those clashes, Arsene would come out on top in ten, and there would be six draws. However, they were the individual battles. Alex tended to win the wars. In those eight seasons that the Red Devils and the Gunners went head-to-head for league titles, Alex would lift the Premier League trophy five times, to Wenger's three.

Despite the heated, end-to-end affairs, there were a large number of odd-goal wins either way and, for a period, it seemed as if every game United and Arsenal played in ended 2-1 to one team or the other, though Alex did mastermind an emphatic 6-1 win for United in 2001 to put a sudden halt to that run of close encounters. However, after that resounding defeat, Arsenal would go on to win their next three matches in a row against United as Wenger seemed to get the upper hand tactically.

Perhaps the most infamous clash between the two teams over this period occurred during Arsenal's penultimate season at Highbury Stadium. At the conclusion of the warm-up, as both players were shuffling down the narrow tunnel of the famous stadium, ready for their final team talk before kicking-off the much-anticipated televised clash, Arsenal captain Patrick Vieira pointed his finger in Gary Neville's face and snarled at him, telling him his constant moaning at the referee won't work today. Vieira had been incensed during the last meeting of the two teams that Neville seemed to get away with a lot of fouling on Arsenal winger Jose Antonio Reyes.

Neville didn't react to Vieira's snarling. He just retreated to his dressing-room, listened to Alex's team talk and then, as he was getting ready for the alarm to sound, he was informing his brother Phil what Vieira had been saying to him when Roy Keane overheard. The Irishman began to fume, just as the players were all making their way to the tunnel.

'You're some man,' Keane shouted in his thick Cork accent towards the Arsenal captain. 'Big fella like you picking on the smallest fella on our team. Why don't you pick on me? (ironically Keane and Neville are the same height!). Yeah… yeah… we'll see out there.'

Vieira squirted the Lucozade bottle he was gripping towards Keane and the Corkman lost it, pointing his finger towards the top of the tunnel and repeatedly shouting, 'We'll see out there, we'll see out there! You… shouting your mouth off every week. You think you're a nice guy. We'll see out there.' Referee Graham Poll had to hold a hand to Keane's chest before the Corkman eventually calmed down. Highbury was rocking.

Keane, as he said he would in the tunnel, got the better of Vieira that day, and United ran out resounding 4-2 winners.

The two sets of players really didn't like each other, and the clashes remained fiery, but the seed for such disdain was planted by the managers. Alex riled United every time Arsenal popped up in the fixture list, while Wenger, a lot cooler in the dressing-room than the Govanman, played his part in boiling the tensions between the two clubs, too. A year before Vieira and Keane's Highbury tunnel clash, United had beaten Arsenal 2-0 in a hotly contested affair at Old Trafford that put an end to The Invincibles' amazing streak of not having been beaten in the league for forty-nine matches. In contrast to the tunnel bust up at Highbury, this time the tunnel bust up happened at Old Trafford, and it happened post-match, not pre-match. The Arsenal players were livid after the final whistle as they — justifiably given the hindsight of slow-motion replays — felt Wayne Rooney had dived in order to win a penalty. Ruud van Nistelrooy would go on to coolly dispatch that spot-kick before Rooney celebrated over-exuberantly when wrapping the game up to score a second late on. In the tunnel afterwards, the United players, gloating in front of their counterparts, had to be separated from Arsenal players by referee Mike Riley and his assistants.

Alex, unusually, was trying to calm the waters and began separating players by holding out his two hands when, from the Arsenal dressing-room, a slice of pizza was flung at him, slapping on to his pale grey suit. He didn't react. He just took his suit jacket off, walked back into the dressing-room, then calmly and calculatedly set an investigation in motion. He wanted to know who threw that pizza. His investigation led him nowhere though, with the Arsenal camp remaining mute and all other eyewitnesses suggesting the pizza slice could've be thrown from any number of the many men inside the Arsenal dressing-room that day. Newspaper journalists would find out about the incident, but like Alex's investigation, they too couldn't convince anybody to name the culprit.

It was Cesc Fabregas. The truth is, the Spanish playmaker wasn't aiming the pizza at Alex, specifically. He just launched it into the melee of players and then got a shock, as did everybody else in the vicinity, when it slapped against the United manager's chest.

Alex would privately suggest to his closest confidants that Pizzagate would signal the end of the great rivalry. He felt the loss of discipline had gotten out of control at Arsenal following their tag of The Invincibles and that some egos inside their dressing-room were so overblown that Wenger would find it impossible to rein them in. It was a bold statement to make, even if he was making it privately. But Arsenal never did win another Premier League title after that.

The relationship between Alex and Wenger, that was cold to begin with, froze in the aftermath of Pizzagate, and the two would hardly even look at each other while shaking hands either pre or post-match. They would remain cold towards each other for nigh on a decade, right up until the day United battered Arsenal 8-2 in a league clash in August 2011. Alex was actually complimentary of the Frenchman in his post-match interviews following that game, suggesting his opposite number had taken such a heavy defeat with "fantastic grace" having congratulated the United manager at the final whistle.

Thereafter, they became close associates at League Manager Association meetings and would often seek each other out to share a cup of tea in the hotel's lobbies before meetings began. Then, upon Wenger's announcement of his retirement in 2018, and just before Alex would collapse at his home with his brain haemorrhaging, he insisted that when Arsenal visit Old Trafford that season the club award Wenger with a gift. It was Alex, who had by this stage retired five years prior, who would pass over that gift on the touchline of the Old Trafford pitch before that game kicked off. The seventy-five thousand spectators would reply in kind; applauding and lauding the Frenchman they had once despised.

'Arsene is without doubt one of the greatest Premier League managers and I am proud to have been a rival, colleague and a friend to such a great man,' Alex would say that day.

They weren't the only ones to form a new friendship in the post Arsenal-United rivalry era. Vieira and Keane made up too, and both took part in a short documentary film together where they looked back on the United-Arsenal rivalry many years later. They showered each other with praise during the filming and would then go on to join each other in broadcasting studios for punditry duties where they joked about their time playing against each other.

Upon hearing Vieira was joining him in the ITV studios for Euro 2021 punditry, Keane joked, 'Course he is. He's just been sacked, hasn't he? (referring to the Frenchman losing his job as Nice manager). That's why he's doing it, isn't it? Let's be honest, it's why we're all doing it.'

Keane also once admitted, with his trademark smirk etched on the top corner of his lips, that, 'Patrick was the toughest player I ever played against. He was so good, so strong. I have to say, though, I don't think he would have got in the United team back then.'

It was essentially in the very midst of this great Arsenal/United rivalry that Alex was due to retire, and it can certainly be argued that his lust for battle against Wenger was one of the reasons he ended up staying in his job. Well… there were three reasons, really. Firstly, the rivalry with Arsenal did have something to do with Alex's U-turn. He was relishing in the battle. Secondly, Cathy and her three sons walked into Alex while he was sprawled out on the sofa of their family home on Christmas Day in 2001, while he was taking a post-dinner nap.

Cathy would wake him by kicking at his foot.

'You cannae retire,' she said.

Alex was confused. He assumed Cathy was desperate for him to retire and had long since sold her the idea that when he calls it quits, they would finally go on the global trips she had often dreamed about. He had already been putting the plans in place for such holidays.

'I dinnae want you sulkin' round the house all day long. Ya need to be oot working. Yar too young to retire anyway.'

Mark, Jason and Darren would back their mother up, with the boys helping the penny drop inside their father's head that he was enjoying his job too much to give it all up now. Alex sat upright on the sofa, and told his wife and three sons that he would consider all they had just said. Then — and this is the third and final reason Alex U-turned on his initial retirement plans — he would find out that the Manchester United board, then led by Peter Kenyon (who had been hired by Martin Edwards to specifically deal with football affairs) had already lined up his replacement. It was Maurice Watkins — Manchester United's legal representative and on the board of directors — who would leave Alex's jaw on the floor by delivering the news, just as 2001 had turned into 2002.

'It's gonna be Sven,' Watkins told him.

'Goran Eriksson?' Alex said, as if there was another Sven who Watkins could possibly have been talking about. The Govanman was stunned. He couldn't believe all the work he had done at Manchester United over the years was going to be inherited by a man he was under no doubt was unworthy of such fortune.

Alex had got on reasonably well with the Swede who had just

become somewhat an infamous and intriguing tabloid figure having taken the England manager's job a year previous. But just because Alex liked his personality during the odd occasions they had met, that didn't mean he rated him as a manager. Alex was so flummoxed by the United board's decision that he went in search of answers. He approached Paul Scholes, a confidant he knew he could rely on for a straight answer.

'I must be missing somethin',' Alex said to his midfielder, 'what's so special about Sven?'

Scholes scoffed one of his deep laughs, then shrugged his shoulders. Scholes was just as dismayed as Alex was that the English FA had appointed the Swede in the first place. He would have been floored if Alex had have told him why he was inquiring about him now.

Alex would ring Maurice Watkins in mid-January to confirm he was U-turning on his decision to retire. Eriksson was heart-broken by this, though he did stay on with the English national team, leading them impressively, though not without controversy, to three major championships in a row before his career took somewhat of a nose dive and he ended up as manager of countries such as the Ivory Coast and the Philippines, as well as landing jobs at clubs like Notts County and little known Chinese outfit Shenzhen.

So, with his U finally turned, and Eriksson seething that the United job had slipped through his fingertips, Alex became hellbent on building a new team that he felt could take United to even greater heights. New players weren't all he needed at this stage, though. Steve McClaren, who he had appointed just before the treble win in 1999 and who was still Alex's assistant manager through the first three-in-a-row of titles, had announced he was leaving. It was no surprise. Whereas Alex had never seen his previous assistant manager Brian Kidd as managerial material, he had no doubt that McClaren had what it took to manage at an elite level. It was obvious to Alex that McClaren would one day be approached by another club and the subject had actually been an open conversation between the pair pretty much for the majority of the three years they worked together.

Alex would write in his second autobiography: "I always told Steve, 'Get the right club. With the right chairman. Essential. Always'."

Under that guidance, McClaren turned down approaches from both West Ham and Everton in 2000, before he knocked on Alex's door at the tail end of that next season, just after United had sealed their third title in a row.

'Had an offer from Middlesbrough,' he said.

'Take it,' Alex replied, without hesitation.

It was the right club. Right chairman. Alex had only heard great things about then Middlesbrough owner Steve Gibson. Bryan Robson — Alex's trusted captain for so many years — had been the previous Middlesbrough manager and, despite being sacked by Gibson to make way for McClaren, still couldn't say enough positive things about his former boss.

A week later, McClaren was named the new Boro manager and would eventually go on to manage the English national team—only for his dream job to turn into a nightmare as he was largely ridiculed by his own supporters who were coaxed on by the national press. After the ridicule, McClaren would move on to manage in Germany and Holland before coming back to England again. He had a reasonably good career as a football manager. But Alex can't help but wonder how much better it could have been had he not taken the poisoned chalice of a job known as the English national team manager.

'The England job. It's a fuckin' impossible job,' Alex would say.

He would think long and hard about who he could replace McClaren with. Given that his dressing-room was now multi-lingual, as well as multi-cultural, he wanted a man who could speak several languages and who also had vast experience of coaching in an array of different countries. The name that flew to the top of his list every time he made different calculations was Carlos Queiroz. The Portuguese coach had been in charge of his home nation underaged teams through the late eighties before he took the job at Sporting Lisbon. From there he moved to the United States to manage the New York Metro Stars, simply because he'd always fancied living in the Big Apple. But less than one year later, he would be on the move again, this time to China because the money on offer from Grampus Eight was way too ridiculous to turn down. Two years later he would become manager of the United Arab Emirates before being appointed manager of South Africa. No wonder he kept coming out top of Alex's lists. The man spoke five different languages and had, over the past fifteen years, experience of managing in five different countries on four different continents.

Alex was wooed by the then forty-eight-year-old when they would first meet. He thought him outrageously handsome and as about astute a football man as he had ever conversed with. So he hired him on the spot.

Queiroz would arrive at United's training ground to run a pre-season camp in July 2002 that would shock the players. They couldn't get to grips with the cultural reboot, though they did eventually all fall into line before the season kicked-off. They had surrendered the title the year previous to Wenger's Arsenal, but with the help of Queiroz's coaching methods the players lifted their game to wrestle that trophy back. After they were crowned 2003 champions (Alex's eighth title win in eleven seasons) he and Cathy would go on holiday to the south of France for a well-deserved break. It was while lying on a sun-lounger during that holiday that a waiter would tap Alex on the shoulder.

'Telephone call, Sir.'

Alex lifted up the receiver in the hotel lobby to hear Queiroz's voice.

'I'm gonna fly out to your hotel. I need to speak with you.'

By the time Queiroz had flown to France twenty-four hours later, Alex had already guessed what was going on. The Portuguese tactician had been offered a job too good to turn down.

'Real Madrid want me as first team manager,' Queiroz would tell him.

Alex tried to talk him out of it. He didn't think it was a good move.

'You will be Real Madrid manager for one year, Carlos,' he said, 'whereas you could be at Manchester United for a very long time.'

Queiroz told Alex that the offer was just too good to turn down, and that he'd surely regret it if he didn't accept.

Alex was on the money, though. Queiroz did only last one year in the Real Madrid hot seat. But as soon as he was sacked the following May, because Real had only finished second in La Liga, Alex was on the phone.

'Yer job's still here if ya want it.'

In fact Alex purposely hadn't appointed a new assistant over the course of the 2003-04 season because he was certain Queiroz wouldn't last at Madrid. Not because he felt the Portuguese lacked the skills to manage at such an elite level, but because of the reputation of the club itself. They chewed managers up and spat them out readily. There was a point in September 2003 where Alex almost hired Dutchman Martin Jol as his assistant, but ultimately decided against it, trusting his gut that Queiroz would return the following summer. He did. Queiroz was back at Manchester United in time for 2004 pre-season training and would stay at the club, as Alex's assistant, for another four years, helping United to another Champions League win in 2008 before taking his real dream job—managing the Portuguese national team.

Despite wrestling the title back from Arsenal in 2002, the Gunners would win it again in 2003. Alex would put the inconsistency of title wins (winning it and then losing it again) down to the fact that he felt his players slacked off after he had pre-announced his retirement. He was certain that his squad needed an overhaul, and that, once again, he would have to make some bold decisions. One of the first decisions he made was that he would never pre-announce his retirement again. When it was time for him to call it a day, whenever that would be in the future, he would literally do it on the day he was retiring. He would not put up with his players slacking again, knowing the manager wouldn't be around for long.

And so, from 2002 up until his retirement in 2013, Alex only ever signed rolling one-year contracts with United.

During his refreshing of the squad, Alex would once again sell a lot of players who were already considered club legends. Denis Irwin, Alex's greatest ever signing, was among them—leaving for Wolves. So too was Dwight Yorke, who signed for Blackburn Rovers while Ronnie Johnsen, another Alex favourite, transferred to Aston Villa. But the biggest surprise was that Alex decided to sell superstar David Beckham. At this stage, the right-winger was the most celebrated footballer on the planet. Nobody in their right mind could make sense of Alex wanting to cast him off. Not only was he a marketing dream for the club, but he was still performing to a high level, for both club and country.

A lot of fans were up in arms over the decision, but they weren't to know the full extent of how much the manager and player's relationship had strained. They also weren't to know that the greasy, spotty teenager Alex would replace Beckham with would go on to become, as far as Alex is concerned, the greatest player the game has ever seen.

A rather tired and lazy debate has been going on in football circles for fifteen years: *Ronaldo or Messi?* For Alex, the answer is as clear as day.

'Ronaldo. He's ma boy.'

The truth is, Alex is equally as wowed by the diminutive Argentine as the rest of the footballing world, but he's not as fixated on him as he is Ronaldo. Ronaldo, for him, has attributes that Messi simply doesn't possess. He's stronger, quicker and is better in the air. Also, Ronaldo, Alex feels, could play in any team and be equally outstanding. Whereas he's not quite certain Messi could.

'Ronaldo could play for Millwall, Queens Park Rangers, Doncaster Rovers... anyone, and score a hat-trick in a game. I'm not sure Messi could do that,' Alex has said.

He has also suggested to close associates that he thinks Ronaldo could have equalled Messi's career—in that he could have played at Barcelona for the majority of his career and then on to

PSG and been just as influential and free-scoring as the Argentine was. Whereas he is certain Messi could not have equalled Ronaldo's goalscoring feats were he the one to play at Sporting Lisbon, then in the Premier League with Manchester United, then at Real Madrid, at Juventus and then back to Manchester United.

However, despite capturing the signature of the most exciting teenager he had ever signed — who arrived in a new shake-up over the course of two summers along with the likes of Klebersen and Eric Djemba Djemba — Manchester United would have to wait for further success.

After United had surrendered the Premier League trophy to Arsenal's Invincibles in 2004, they wouldn't hold it again for three more years. It was the most barren spell Alex would suffer at United since he had won his first title. However, it wasn't Arsene Wenger who was bettering him this time. It was a new continental rival. A Portuguese one.

Chelsea, following FC Porto's amazing Champions League win in 2004 against all the odds (in which they had beaten United in the quarter-finals), opted to appoint their handsome, charismatic manager as they went in search of their first ever Premier League win.

Jose Mourinho would come in, anointing himself as 'The Special One', and then go on to prove such an audacious claim was accurate by winning two Premier League titles in a row straight off the bat (2005 & 2006). It was during those two league championships that pundits and journalists, as well as a small faction of Manchester United fans, began whispering out loud that Alex may be past it.

Given how fresh-faced and dripping with charisma Mourinho appeared to be — certainly when compared to the United manager who was, by now, in his mid-sixties and greying by the day — that question could have been viewed in some quarters as rather legitimate. Except, those who were beginning to whisper such notions would end up embarrassed yet again, as Alex's most successful run of trophy wins was yet to come.

ALEX AND THE MEDIA

Alex sniggered while watching Mourinho's debut press conference as the new Chelsea manager in which the Portuguese proclaimed himself 'The Special One', but he wasn't surprised one little bit.

He'd been around the Mourinho block before; had asked plenty of his contacts plenty of questions about him, as he did about all young up-and-coming coaches. And, as a result, he had been made privy to the many anecdotes about the Portuguese tactician's unapologetic arrogance. Plenty of football people were fans of Mourinho, Alex would learn, but nobody was a bigger fan of Mourinho than Mourinho himself.

It wasn't as if Alex was a stranger to turning on the arrogance while sat at a desk in front of the world's press. He had been the king of it in England up until Mourinho arrived and turned the dial up several notches. But whereas Alex's arrogance was control-driven, Mourinho's was unmistakably ego-driven.

Alex didn't much like the press. Or he certainly didn't like how the press evolved over his years as a manager. And when press conferences and pre and post-match interviews were beginning to be written into his contract (as it was for all Premier League managers as soon as the rebrand began in 1992) he began to resent dealing with the media even more. He simply couldn't quite compute the level of importance he was expected to place on journalists—most of whom, Alex was certain, wouldn't be able to pass the initiation test for coaching badges in the sport they would readily preach about.

That's not to suggest he detested the individual journalists. He actually got on with most of them, and certainly struck up lifelong friendships with quite a number of hacks, most of whom he had come across in his early days of management. The likes of David Meek, Bob Cass, Paul Hayward and Hugh McIlvanney (who Alex considers the best football writer he came across through all his years) were all close associates of the Govanman. It was more the editors who placed such enormous pressure on these journalists who Alex couldn't quite find a level of respect for.

'The newspapers are a nightmare,' Alex would candidly admit in an interview with the *NewStatesman* in 2009. 'They have all this space to fill under pressure from TV and the internet and the journalists are on short-term contracts and worried for their future, but so much of what they write is just rubbish. I tell you, the press in our country are a real problem. They do real damage. Not just in football. In politics, too. Government needs to do something about it, because the press has got worse, not better.'

Alex learned his first lesson about how to deal with the media from a relatively young age. To explain a lengthy ban he received while playing for St Johnstone, Alex was interviewed on national Scottish television.

'Aye, that's the Star Chamber justice they operate in Scotland,' Alex snarled into the microphone. He thought his answer, pre-planned, sounded intellectual, descriptive, strong.

Two days later, a letter would arrive at St Johnstone from the SFA, instructing Alex to explain his comments. His manager at the time was as miffed as the SFA were.

'Where the hell did you get this Star Chamber nonsense from?' he asked

Alex shrugged.

'Eh, I just saw it in a book I'm reading at the moment.'

In trying to sound intellectual through the media, Alex ended up coming across as pretentious. From then on, he made a mental note to be as straight as an arrow in all future relations with the press. There was no need for him to prove he was well-read. He wasn't pleasing anybody. That's not what the media were interested in. It certainly wasn't what the fans were interested in, and that, Alex came to realise, is who the media exist for.

The word "media" derives from the Latin word translated to mean *middle*. The media is quite literally the middleman between the person or organisation of public interest and the public themselves. All Alex had to do when speaking into a microphone was address the fans. It should have been that simple. He realised it was that simple. Yet, on occasions, he couldn't quite help himself.

After his *faux pas* about 'Star Chambers', Alex would go on to form decent relationships with a number of Scottish reporters as they went in search of stories. But as time went on, especially when he moved to England to manage Manchester United, he would eventually feel exasperated by the amount of spin journalists were placing on the words he spoke, especially as the tabloids, in particular, were beginning to learn that sensationalist headlines on the back pages worked just as lucratively as they did on the front.

In *My Autobiography*, released after his retirement, Alex would write: "There was an intensity and volatility about the modern media that I found difficult. I felt by the end it was hard to have relationships with the press. They were under so much pressure it was not easy to confide in them. When I first came to Manchester, I was wary of some but I wasn't as guarded as I was in my final years."

To deal with the sensationalisms printed about him or the club in his early days at Old Trafford, Alex often took legal action. But he soon found it to be a redundant exercise. At best, after receiving a warning letter from the Manchester United solicitor, the newspaper would agree to retract their lie. But instead of retracting it in the same manner in which they had printed the original lie, the retraction was hidden away in the small print.

"As for an apology," Alex would continue in *My Autobiography*, "Forty words tucked away on page eleven was a long way from a story with banner headlines on the back page. So, what was the point?"

Instead of getting the club's lawyer to act, Alex decided to start banning journalists from his press conferences anytime they stepped over the line. Hacks on the Manchester beat used to joke that they wore their banning from Carrington press conferences as a badge of honour, such was the frequency in which suspensions were handed out.

John Bean, a well-respected freelance sportswriter, was said to have been banned on three separate occasions by Alex even though he and the journalist were known to have a friendly relationship. It has been suggested that Bean was used a little like Giggs in the United dressing-room in that he often got it in the neck as an example to others. After all, if Alex could ban Bean, that meant everybody's place inside those press conferences was on the line. Bean's three bans may have been used as a lesson to every journalist, but there certainly were suspensions handed down to some that were issued under heavy ire of the Govanman.

Once, when journalist Rob Harris posed a question to Alex about Ryan Giggs's private life (at a time when Giggs had been reported in national newspapers of having multiple affairs), Alex leaned over to his press officer, Karen Shotbolt, and whispered, 'Who's the guy who asked about Giggs?'

Karen, who was conscious the press conference was still ongoing, mouthed: 'I'll tell you later.'

Still fuming while the questions continued, Alex leaned back towards Karen.

'Is he coming Friday (to the follow up post-match press conference)?'

Karen nodded.

'Aye, well then we'll get him. Ban him on Friday!'

They may have been whispering to each other, but there were so many microphones in front of the pair that their conversation was recorded. It didn't matter to Alex that it was recorded. Rob was still shown the red card.

This anecdote is mild in comparison to some bannings, but from 2007 Alex's press conferences were filmed for *MUTV* and other broadcast channels and that meant he had to curtail his 'hairdryer' treatment of press members. In his earlier days, without the cameras turned on, Alex would berate the hacks much like he could his players in the dressing-room.

'It would make News at Ten if he did the hairdryer to the press these days,' regarded journalist Daniel Taylor said. 'Seriously, I'd seen it many times. Everything you've heard, it's worse. Believe me.'

Still, hairdryers remained in vogue for Alex when the cameras were off. Journalist Mark Ogden has never forgotten the treatment he received from the United manager in 2012, even if he still laughs about it today and actually has a framed piss-take article hung on his wall at home, offered to him by his colleagues at *The Telegraph* to mark the occasion. In the lead-up to the incident, Ogden had utilised his sources to find out that Rio Ferdinand would likely be out of the Manchester United team to face Everton in a Premier League clash due to a thigh injury picked up in training earlier that week. Alex had hoped to keep the news in-house, so that Everton manager David Moyes would be surprised by Ferdinand's omission and couldn't capitalise on United's centre-half being out. But Ogden broke the story two days before kick-off and, armed with the news of Ferdinand's absence, Moyes picked Marouane Fellaini to play up front against make-shift defender Michael Carrick. Fellaini would outjump Carrick to score a late winner in that game to gift Everton the victory. The next time Alex came across Ogden, he was fuming. His finger was pointing and his face was purple.

'You cost us those three points!' Alex fumed.

Ogden would receive a three-month ban from United press conferences for essentially reporting the truth.

Alex acknowledges that it was through his evolution into a managerial great that helped him to control the media. He is well aware that without the successes he had achieved, his control over who could and who couldn't attend his press conferences would have proven slippery.

'In banning reporters I was saying: "I'm not accepting your version of events", Alex said. 'I was in a strong position because I had been at Man United for a long time and been successful. If I had been some poor guy struggling on a bad run of results, the scenario would have been different. In most cases, I felt an under-lying sense of sympathy because I knew the extrapolation or exaggeration was a product of the competitive nature of the media business. And now we have it every day. For twenty-four hours, Sky Sports News is rolling. A story will be repeated over and over again.'

To ensure he wasn't as riled up as he could have been heading into what he considered redundant press conferences, Alex developed a tic. He would brush his hand over his face before heading up the stairs that led to the press room at Carrington, ensuring his ire with the contractual obligations to face these journalists wasn't plastered across his features. Before that tic, he would mentally prepare himself to face the press, discussing what questions may or may not arise with his press secretary Karen Shotbolt so he was ready to tackle them head on. He also held his press conferences as early as possible—mostly at nine a.m. in Carrington.

'I always held my press conferences before training. Most managers do them after training. I don't see sense in that. After training, I'm still thinking aboot training. But for the press, I need full focus. So I held them as early as possible before training, to get them oot of the way.'

His biggest frustration with the press was that they just

assumed knowledge based on very little information. In 2006 Oliver Holt, who was the chief football writer with the *Daily Mirror,* would write about Alex's upcoming twenty year anniversary at Old Trafford: "Fergie's anniversary amounts to nothing more than a lazy and meaningless ballyhoo for a man who has stayed on too long. Whatever United go on to achieve this season or in seasons to come, nothing changes the fact that Ferguson should have quit in 2002 when he said he was going to quit."

Two years later, after United had won the Premier League and Champions League in the space of a week, Holt would write, "If there's one thing Ferguson doesn't need to worry about anymore, it's the applause. It'll never die out. Not for him. Not now. Because he erased the last quibble about his greatness as a manager by winning the Champions League for a second time. There weren't many doubts anyway."

That was the sort of hypocrisy journalists could brazenly get away with. Alex once wrote that the main objective of the press is "to help irate the fans" but he could never quite comprehend why fans put so much faith in those who had never played the game anywhere close to the level they would readily preach about, especially when these writers were often contradicting themselves.

Yet even those who did play the game at an elite standard could still rise the ire of the Govanman. For example, he has been equally miffed by modern TV pundits and how they preach sensational overreactions as he has been by old-school press reporters over his years.

'Some of the ex-player, ex-manager pundits are the worst,' he told the *NewStatesman*. 'It's a disgrace the way they sit there criticising guys they used to play with, just to make a bit of an impact. I couldnae do that.'

His main problem with modern commentary on football was the short-termism and reactionary nature of it all, but that was mainly because Alex couldn't adopt anything other than a long-term view of any situation. Pundits and journalists would form such strong opinions based on such little information, often focusing on one tiny phase of play over and over again. Alex could never understand that. Pundits would watch a phase of play in slow-motion and on repeat up to ten times, decided there and then that one player — or perhaps even a manager — made a wrong decision. Their broadcast opinion on that one phase of play would then help form a fan's viewpoint of that player or manager that would stick around—possibly forever. This made such little sense to Alex as there was no way those pundits or journalists showed any understanding of the bigger picture in football. They simply weren't privy to the bigger picture. If repeated slow-motion replays and twenty-four news existed in the late 1980s while Alex was taking his time to build his empire at Old Trafford, there is little or no chance he would have stayed in situ. The demand for instant success, brought about by constant slow-motion replays and twenty-four-hour rolling news is the reason, Alex is certain, that the turnover of managers at the elite level is at an all-time high, and getting worse. Managers in the Premier League now last an average of two years and seven months in their positions. This is all the modern media's fault, Alex is certain. The media dictates the mood of the fans. And the fans pressure the board members at clubs.

That's not to say that Alex's issue with pundits was born out of frustration with the evolution of the media. As far back as the late eighties, he would fume at one of Britain's most loved football icons. Ahead of what was billed as Alex's make-or-break game against Nottingham Forest in the 1989 FA Cup, Jimmy Hill — who was punditing for the BBC at the time — would remark during the warm-up, 'The United players already look beaten.'

Alex wouldn't forget the remark and was still holding it against legend Hill some five years later when the pundit made a scathing remark about Eric Cantona's aggressive style of play. Upon hearing Hill's remark, Alex would scoff to the press, 'Jimmy Hill is verbal when it suits him. If there's a prat going about in this world, he is the prat. He once wrote us off in a warm-up, that's how much he knows aboot the game.'

The spat wouldn't last long. After contemplating his comments, Alex would send Hill an apologetic letter in the post along with an expensive bottle of his favourite wine. Hill was so taken aback by the gesture that he would ring Alex to accept his apology, and they both remained friendly up until the legend's passing in December 2015.

But there was one spat with the media that Alex didn't resolve straight away. In fact, it once took him seven years to end a stand-off with not just one journalist, but a whole broadcasting network. It just happened to be the biggest network in Britain, and arguably the most respected news broadcaster in the entire world: the BBC.

A short documentary film entitled *Fergie and Son* appeared in the listings for BBC Three on May 27, 2004. The film pointed a finger at Jason Ferguson and the role he may or may not have played as a football agent for two Manchester United transfers. In truth, the documentary film was a poor production and very cheap in budget, what with paper mâché heads used to depict Jason, cartoons drawn to recreate what may have happened, and fake actor voices used to speculate on quotes from different sources. Nonetheless, Jason had indeed played some role in different guises for two Manchester United player sales. The first was for a company called L'Attitude—a football agency that mostly represented players in the lower leagues. Jason had become a director at this agency which happened to be involved in the sale of goalkeeper Massimo Taibi from Manchester United to Reggina in 2000 for £2.5m, and then again one year later — while Jason was working with Elite Sports Agency — when Jaap Stam was sold to Lazio for £16m. Jason may have just had a bit-part role in both player transfers, but given that the deals involved his father's club, a conflict of interests could and should have been duly noted with Jason taking a step away from the deals. On top of those specific deals, former United academy graduate David Healy would say, rather innocently some years after he left United to join Preston North End for £1.3m in early 2001, 'When I was moving, he (Alex) just asked, "Do you have an agent?" And I said "Yeah." And he said, "Because if you don't, my son Jason will sort you out with your stuff".'

No other Manchester United player has ever come forward publicly to say Jason was offered to them as an agent, but Alex's offer to David Healy, even though the player didn't take him up on it, certainly crosses the boundary of what is and isn't acceptable from a man in his position.

However, Manchester United had cleared Alex, Jason and indeed Elite Sports Agency of any wrongdoing even before the documentary had been aired through an internal investigation, but a decision was agreed by all that Jason would no longer take part in any Manchester United dealings.

So irked was he by the documentary, Alex simply refused to have anything to do with the BBC, including his contractually obliged post-match interviews with the broadcaster for their renowned *Match of the Day* highlights programme. His boycott would last from April 2004 until August 2011 when the broadcaster's Director General, Mark Thompson and their northern England BBC director Peter Salmon approached Alex to broker a peace deal. The BBC didn't offer any apology for airing the documentary, something Alex had insisted on to end the feud, but the trio still talked it out until the United manager agreed to put an end to his stand-off. Although the Fergusons were cleared of any wrongdoing, no matter how minimal Jason's involvements in Taibi and Stam's transfers were, he should have stepped away given the conflict of interest, and his father should not have been offering the services of his son to a player contractually under his management.

The reason Alex got so riled by how the media in the UK operates can somewhat be explained by his political beliefs (he has always viewed the BBC as a rather conservative institution and his boycott in 2004 wasn't his first run-in with the broadcaster) but it really has more to do with the fact that he has no control over them. Yes, he could dictate who could and couldn't attend his press conferences, but outside of that, the media had free rein to paint portraits of him as they saw fit. And that irked him. Massively so. But quite why he transfixed on the negatives remains a mystery even to those closest to him. For example, Sky Sports' broadcast of live Premier League games around the world happened to coincide with Alex leading Manchester United to unprecedented glory. So, rather than United's achievements being witnessed solely in the UK, the team were watched around the globe, turning the club into a commercial giant that, by the time of his retirement in 2013, was bringing in revenues to rival the likes of mega brands such as *Apple* and *Toyota*. As much as the media could irk the Govanman, they sure did play a huge part in cementing his legacy. He just never saw it that way.

2004-2008

FOLLOWING HIS U-TURN ON HIS EXPECTED RETIREMENT AT AGED SIXTY BACK
in 2002, Alex privately suggested that he would hold off leaving football until the expected retirement age of sixty-five. But as his years
began to tick upwards to that number, the Govanman was feeling so
excited about the squad he was building that he approached Cathy
in the kitchen of their three-storey Cheshire mansion in the summer
of 2004 to tell her, 'I'm gonnae keep goin' till am seventy.'

She genuinely didn't mind.

That would take him up until the end of the 2012 season—the
summer in which he finally planned to take his patient wife on all of
the adventures he had been, for so many years, promising her he
would take her on. Cathy had always been excited about their
loosely planned trips around the world as well as Alex's long-held
proposal of taking her on a date to the Oscars. But, despite that, she
wasn't exactly itching for her husband to call it quits. She was
enjoying her life in Manchester with him out of the house. In fact,
she was enjoying life in Manchester so much that she told Alex
during this same conversation that when he did eventually call it
quits that they wouldn't be returning to Scotland; not to Aberdeen
where she had once settled and loved, nor to Glasgow where many
roots of their family trees were still growing. They would remain in

Manchester, where their social circle had grown to a level that ensured Cathy was more than content, and more than comfortable. His wife's insistence that they would remain in Manchester was music to Alex's ears, for even at this stage he knew that when he stood down as Manchester United manager that he didn't want to say goodbye to the club for good. He was eyeing a role on the board of directors and held an assumption that such a role would be offered to him regardless of who would own the club come his intended retirement date of May 2012. By this stage — round about the time he and his wife were having this conversation about the extension of his retirement plans — an American family called Glazer were snapping up more and more shares of Manchester United and a full takeover began to look like a real possibility.

Alex was initially perturbed by these reports and — as he did when he was trying to find information on players and coaches — did some digging around. Yet despite his thirst for knowledge and natural skills for research, he would find out very little about the family who were looking likely to be his new bosses. Malcolm Glazer and his two sons, Joel and Avram, despite owning the NFL franchise Tampa Bay Buccaneers, were an extremely private family—and those closest to them never opened up. Alex tried to penetrate their inner circle in America, but he was fed little or no information. His closest confidant at the club — by now the chief executive, former finance director, David Gill — was equally intrigued. Whereas Alex made zero public statements on the Glazers while their takeover pursuit persisted, Gill did go on record to say, 'The level of debt, coupled with their business plans means theirs is an unattractive proposal. We've seen many examples of debt in football over the years and know the difficulties it causes. We think it (debt) is inappropriate for this business.'

Gill would backtrack on that sentiment once the Glazers finally purchased the club in June of 2005—mounting the club with a staggering debt totalling £525m. But, astonishingly, both he and Alex would end up enjoying working under the Americans' reign while leading the club to their greatest ever era of success. The story of

Alex's relationship with the Glazer family is so intrinsic to his final years at the club, however, that it deserves its own chapter (one which you can read straight after this one), but the truth is, while he was hugely sceptical at first, Alex genuinely thought the Glazer family to be ideal owners for the modern day. The fans, however, would view it *very* differently.

Off-field battles weren't the only thing Alex couldn't quite get to grips with during this period. He was also facing his biggest task on it. Jose Mourinho was doing what Arsene Wenger had managed eight years prior. He was evolving the culture of English football. And Alex, enamoured as he was by the Portuguese, had to scramble to keep up.

Alex would, at first, try to pinch at the balloon that was Jose Mourinho's ego by suggesting, 'We have the best Portuguese coach in world football here,' (referring to his assistant manager Carlos Queiroz), but the Chelsea boss wasn't to be put off his stride as the Blues steamrolled to two Premier League titles in a row—both impressively built on stunning home form that was backboned by strong pragmatic tactics. Chelsea would surpass the ninety-point mark in both seasons—while United flailed eighteen and then eight points behind. United finished third in Mourinho's first year in the Premier League, and that is what sparked the whispers of Fergie being 'past it', just as he was telling Cathy that he wanted to keep going until he was seventy. United finished the Premier League in third position three times under Alex; second five times and as champions thirteen times in all twenty-one years the Govanman managed United in that competition. It's undoubtedly such an impressive record that it's ever likely to be beaten. But his most difficult period over the course of those twenty-one-years happens to coincide with Mourinho's arrival. However, he was positive that he was building for the future and that he would get the better of the Portuguese in the long run.

Alex had decided, after his initial retirement U-turn, that he wanted to rebuild from the very bottom once again; a brand new team filled with youngsters who would be hungry for success. As the English game had moved on — made much more continental thanks to the influx of foreign coaches — Alex felt he needed to add different types of players to the core of homegrown talents he had been promoting into the first team. While the likes of John O'Shea, Wes Brown and Darren Fletcher would go on to win thirty-one major titles between them in the first team of United, other academy grad-uates that Alex had placed high hopes on such as Chris Eagles and Kieran Richardson couldn't quite bridge the gap from the academy to being Premier League title contenders. And so Alex decided that in order for United to win back their status as top dogs in England, he would have to bring in young stars from elsewhere. Having snapped up Cristiano Ronaldo, whom he was certain would go on to prove himself to be the best player in the world, Alex would then turn his attentions to a homegrown English teenager he had been scouting since he was fourteen years of age. It was no secret Wayne Rooney was going to be something special. When he was turning out for the Everton academy at fifteen years of age, he already looked like an established pro. And although the boy Rooney was no hidden secret and every club across the continent was keeping tabs on him, it seemed somewhat inevitable that he would end up playing for Manchester United. Alex had long earmarked Rooney as a transfer he had planned to conclude in the summer of 2005. But after the Liverpudlian striker had made such an impact while staring for England in the 2004 European Championships in Portugal, the United manager was forced to act twelve-months prior, especially so after Newcastle United had made a massive bid of £30m for his services. Once that Newcastle bid was accepted by Everton, Alex persuaded David Gill to match it, knowing full well that Rooney would choose Old Trafford over St James' Park.

Although the United squad was beginning to look as pretty as it ever did on paper, it would take a couple of seasons for the new kids to develop as a fully functioning unit. What's interesting is that United's re-climb back to the summit — which they reached in 2007 by topping Chelsea by six points and ensuring Mourinho didn't equal Alex's three-in-a-row record — was achieved over the backdrop of two major storms. In late 2005 — as Mourinho's Chelsea were storming it in the Premier League — United would be rocked twice. Firstly, captain Roy Keane — who had been a stalwart of the club's success and current club captain — was surprisingly turfed out the club (a move *nobody* but Alex and his coaching staff saw coming) and secondly, the Glazer family would confirm their purchase of Manchester United to the absolute disdain of the club's supporters.

Although Keane's departure, which happened on November 18 in 2005, dropped the jaws of the football world, Alex had actually been stewing on the thought of letting his talismanic captain go for quite some time. The truth is that although Alex had adapted to the continental game becoming more dominant in England, Keane simply hadn't. Alex had to alter his man-management approach to get the best out of these modern players. Whereas he used to shout and rollick players such as Gordon Strachan, Bryan Robson, Ryan Giggs and even Keane himself over the decades, he knew that his latest recruits, such as Cristiano Ronaldo, Klebersen, Eric Djemba-Djemba and even Ruud Van Nistelrooy were much more sensitive in their nature than those who had experienced a traditional British/Irish upbringing.

Keane, Alex felt, hadn't adapted to the Premier League's conti-nental evolution. The Irishman was still shouting and berating players in training and giving them ultimatums in the dressing-room; ultimatums they simply couldn't compute given their heritage. It was Carlos Queiroz who first raised such an issue with Alex. He felt Keane — although arguably still United's best performer on the pitch — was ultimately holding the team back from winning the Premier League and competing at the tail end of the Champions League. Queiroz told Alex in the summer of 2005 that it would be best for the team overall if Keane was sold, but at that time the manager hadn't fully comprehended how bad the situation would become. Though there certainly were warning signs that summer.

Queiroz had hand-picked United's pre-season training camp in Portugal at a vast venue called Vale do Lobo. It was as stunning as any training camp Alex had ever seen, with a dozen training pitches, a swimming-pool, a gym and multiple villas which he felt were perfect for the players to stay in as he looked to harmonise a camaraderie amongst the new-look squad. Except Keane had other ideas. He didn't like the villas at Vale do Lobo and insisted on staying a fifteen-minute drive away with his family at a much larger villa that had its own private pool.

By the time Alex had arrived in Portugal — flying in straight from a family holiday with Cathy in France — Queiroz and Keane were already at loggerheads over the accommodation. When Alex confronted his team captain over the argument, Keane ranted and raved about the training facilities even though Alex had genuinely never seen such an ideal base for a pre-season gathering. Everything Keane was saying to Alex came across as negative. There wasn't one positive thing the Irishman had to offer and it was becoming clear he held a lot of resentment towards Queiroz specifically. Alex patted Keane on the shoulder and tried to speak in hushed tones in an attempt to dilute the tension.

Keane tutted.

'You've changed,' he said to his manager.

'Of course, I've changed, Roy,' Alex replied. 'You have tae change. Because today is not yesterday. It's a different world we're in now. We have players of twenty different nationalities here these days. You say I've changed. I hope I have. I've had tae. I wudda never have survived this long if I didnae change.'

Alex tried to persuade Keane to apologise to Queiroz, but the Irishman refused and so United entered the 2005-06 season with the manager unsure of his captain for a plethora of different reasons. He was no longer sure his captain was a team player as the penny began to drop that Keane wasn't evolving with the times.

Then, one-third of the way through that season — in November 2005, with United trailing six points behind Chelsea in the Premier League table — Keane appeared on Manchester United's in-house TV channel, MUTV, to analyse United's dire 4-1 defeat to Middlesbrough. During that pre-recorded analysis, Keane would lay into his teammates.

'Just because you get paid a hundred-and-twenty grand a week and play well against Spurs for twenty minutes, doesn't mean you're a superstar,' he had said of Rio Ferdinand. Of utility player Kieran Richardson, Keane scoffed, 'He's a lazy defender.' And of Darren Fletcher, he questioned why 'people in Scotland rave about this player?'

Alex had always appreciated that Keane had been his lieutenant —his second in command on the pitch. He loved that the Irishman passionately revved up his teammates in his own unique way. But hanging them out to dry on the fans' TV channel was way out of order. Alex was fuming—feeling that this was the last thing any captain should ever do. And there would be major consequences. He immediately rang United's director of communications to ensure the recorded interview would not go out on the network that evening, then asked that a tape of the show be left on his desk for him to view first thing the next morning when he arrived for work.

Alex would write in *My Autobiography*: "Jesus. It was unbelievable. He slaughtered everybody. Darren Fletcher got it. Alan Smith. Van Der Sar. Roy was taking them all down."

During a fiery one-to-one meeting after training that morning, Alex blew his lid and tossed it towards Keane. Keane would catch the lid and throw it back. Both of them were snarling at each other and voices were well and truly raised. The meeting ended with Keane suggesting they leave the argument up to the players—by showing them the tape and letting them decide for themselves if he had hung them out to dry.

What happened next was excruciating. One unnamed player who attended the viewing of the Roy Keane analysis tape, said, 'That half-hour or whatever it was was the most squirmish half an hour of my life. It's fair to say we were all cringing in that meeting.'

In a dark room, the entire squad and coaching staff sat and watched Keane analyse his teammates' performance in the shocking defeat to Boro. When the analysis ended, Keane immediately stood up and asked if anybody had a problem with what they had just watched. Edwin van Der Sar didn't hesitate in coming forward and let his team captain know he was way out of line. Keane's blood boiled. He let the Dutch keeper have it, telling him his opinion wasn't particularly worthy. Ruud van Nistelrooy interjected, letting Keane know that he agreed with Edwin. Keane pointed at and lashed out at the striker. Without barely breathing, the Irishman then turned to Carlos Queiroz who was sitting with his legs crossed on the far side of the room in silence. Keane began to question the Portuguese's coaching methods and dragged up the pre-season trip to Portugal all over again. Some players were already stunned into a silence, but Keane had one more line to leave them with. He swivelled to his manager and without context snarled, 'And you brought your private life into the club with your argument with Magnier (which you can read all about in the next chapter).' And that was it. Alex would write in *My Autobiography*, "(as soon as the meeting finished) Carlos saw that I was quite upset... 'He needs to go, Carlos,' I said. 'One hundred percent,' he said. 'Get rid of him'."

In a meeting the following week, in which Keane was joined by his lawyer Michael Kennedy as they sat across from Alex and David Gill, the Corkman would be riled further by the fact that Alex had got wrong the fact that the Irishman could immediately sign for another club upon termination of his contract as he'd have to wait until January when the transfer window reopened. Then Alex further riled him by giving the secretary who wrote up the minutes of the meeting the wrong dates of when Keane first joined the club. It had all fallen rather petty, but that meeting well and truly signalled not only the end of Keane's time as a United player, but the relationship between the manager and his captain. They would have a few conversations after this meeting; firstly when Keane would surprise his old boss by calling in to speak with him at the Carrington Training centre. Keane apologised to Alex that day, but has gone on record since to suggest he regrets offering up that apology. Then they would speak, albeit rather frostily and uncomfortably, at Keane's Manchester United testimonial which took place the following summer after Alex ensured a testimonial was stipulated in the termination of the Irish-man's contract. They also pitted their wits against each other in the Premier League where they shook hands for the cameras. But their rift has never healed. And they both remain rather bitter and petty about Keane's departure from the club.

The newspapers buzzed on this story for months, but the loudest buzz would sound whenever the gossip would turn to the player Alex would delve into the transfer market to buy to replace his bullish captain. Most would be underwhelmed by his choice. Alex was under no doubt that he wanted Michael Carrick in his midfield. He had never seen a player dictate the pace of the game from such a deep-lying midfield position and was already in love with the idea of bringing the Spurs player to Old Trafford. Carrick was the epitome of the player Alex had tried to turn Keane into in his elder years. After Keane's hip injury in 2002, Alex had drawn up plans for his captain to be employed in a more deep-lying role. So in truth, Carrick turned out to be a ready-made replacement, given that he ticked all the boxes Alex wanted in his new No.16.

Carrick's discipline would allow United to be more adventurous in the final third and, despite having been headlocked to two league titles in a row by Jose Mourinho's super-strength Chelsea, Alex felt confident heading into the 2006-07 season, determined that he would stop the Portuguese boss from equalling his record of winning three Premier League titles in a row. The pundits and the fans didn't share Alex's optimism, however. Neither did the bookies. United were 10/1 to be crowned champions that summer—the largest price they'd ever been since the Premier League began. The whispers that Alex was 'losing it' were at their loudest at this stage. And replacing Keane with Carrick only offered those whispering a megaphone.

The megaphones would be tossed into the bin by Christmas 2006 however, as United headed towards the new year ahead of Chelsea at the summit of the division, leaving bookies rueing their pre-season miscalculation. With Cristiano Ronaldo evolving into the world-class player Alex insisted he would become when he initially signed him, United were looking a mirror of the team that had set the Premier League alight in the mid-nineties. They would counterattack at such pace that most Premier League teams refused to open up, for fear of leaving gaps in behind which Ronaldo and Rooney could take advantage of. Carrick was also proving to be a shrewd purchase and his shielding of the defensive unit allowed United more numbers in forward positions to penetrate the low block teams were adopting against them. They would go on to win the title by six points ahead of Mourinho who would be ruthlessly sacked by unforgiving owner Roman Abramovich the following September—four weeks into the 2007-08 season when United were proving too strong for them once again. This time, United — who had added Portuguese pair Anderson and Nani to their ranks as Alex decided to blend more continental youth to his side — won the title at a canter, topping nearest rivals Chelsea by fifteen points in the end. The Premier League wasn't the only trophy they'd be lifting at the expense of Chelsea that season. Alex's rejuvenated United were about to write themselves a fresh chapter in the history books.

Since their magnificent treble of 1999, Alex would be frustrated as he went in search of a fourth European trophy. They would make it to two semi-finals and three quarter-finals in that time, but ultimately they wouldn't prove good enough, even if Alex still maintains they were unlucky along the way.

When they were drawn against Pep Guardiola's Barcelona in the semi-final in 2008, it was thought they would come up short again as, despite United bossing it in England, Barca were being regarded as one of the greatest club sides ever with Lionel Messi weaving his way around La Liga defences with relative ease and Andres Iniesta and Xavi pulling the strings in midfield.

But Alex would get the better of Guardiola over the two tense legs, with Paul Scholes scoring the only goal of the entire 180 minutes by blasting home a twenty-five-yard screamer into the far top corner.

It set United up for a Champions League final against their biggest domestic rivals at the time, Chelsea—now managed by

Israeli coach Avram Grant. The clash would take place in Moscow, on a rainy May night, and would prove to be so tense and tight that the contest wouldn't conclude until midnight had passed in the Russian capital.

Alex made one swift change to his line-up that seemed to raise the eyebrows of pundits and fans alike. Cristiano Ronaldo would begin the game on the left-wing, not on the right as he had done all through his career. Alex had noted a weakness in the Chelsea team at right back — where they had to deploy midfielder Michael Essien due to an imbalance in their squad — and knew there was no better player on the planet than Ronaldo to take advantage of such a weakness. Essien was a great player, of that Alex was in no doubt. But he was no right full and he certainly wasn't a man who could control a back post. So, Alex worked with his players on delivering deep balls from the right across to Ronaldo at the back post. The plan came to fruition with almost perfect synchronicity when — half-way through the first half — right back Wes Brown (who, according to Alex had his best ever game for United on this very night) pitched the type of high cross he had been practising all week towards the back post where Ronaldo rose almost twice as high as a flat-footed Essien to head United into the lead. From there, they would almost bask in the fact that they were in total control and began to play like a team convinced the trophy was coming home with them. In truth, they could, and should, have been more than one goal up as time ticked towards half-time. But then, with time running out, Essien tried a rather audacious thirty-yard shot that pinged off the backs of two United players — firstly Nemanja Vidic and then Rio Ferdinand — before bouncing on the penalty spot. Edwin van der Sar should have easily swept the danger up into his hands, but as he was advancing for the ball he slipped on the wet grass and Frank Lampard — a player Alex always admired, specifically because of his timing — nicked the ball home to equalise.

If United had it all their own way in the first half, they were to look second best for the second forty-five minutes. Though in truth, Chelsea never really looked like scoring either. And although the game was an interesting spectacle due to the growing intensity, a highlights reel for that second-half wouldn't last long. Extra-time, however, created a whole heap of drama. Didier Drogba thundered the post with a twenty-yard effort before he was sent off for slapping Nemanja Vidic across the face. Then Ryan Giggs missed a sitter in what was his 759th game for the club—breaking Sir Bobby Charlton's all-time appearance record. Either team could have clinched the game in the thirty minutes of overtime as counterattack after counterattack took place, albeit through players who were now tiring, yet giving it their all. But this contest — the first ever Champions League final played between two English teams — would ultimately be decided on penalties.

While John Terry was walking up to take his penalty, which would have won Chelsea the trophy had he scored from it, Alex was already contemplating what he would say to his players in the dressing-room to console them. He was convinced the Chelsea skipper would score. But as Terry was about to strike the ball, his left foot gave way on the soaked surface and he was sliding to his arse as his penalty clipped the outside of the van der Sar's left-hand post. Alex didn't react. He remained seated on the bench while all the coaches and substitutes stood nervously along the touchline. Not even Anderson rattling the net with the next penalty kick could lift Alex from that seat; neither could Giggs when he slotted a neat penalty into the corner of the net. In fact, the Govanman didn't even move when Nicolas Anelka stepped forward for Chelsea only for van der Sar to guess right, diving to his right to slap two palms at the ball and in doing so confirming Manchester United as European champions for the third time in the club's history. While all of the staff and players rushed towards van der Sar to celebrate, Alex remained seated on the bench, staring at the race track beneath his feet. He was in shock. He couldn't believe the drama that had unfolded in front of him that very night. Twenty minutes later he was beaming and soaked head to toe with rain while gripping both ears of the big old European Cup so he could thrust it up and down in front of the cheering United supporters.

ALEX AND THE GLAZER FAMILY

ALEX FERGUSON SNR WAS, LIKE MANY OF HIS CONTEMPORARIES, A fan of a frequent flutter. He would often stand inside a bookies or prop himself up against the bar of one of the many pubs Govan had to offer, while clenching a betting docket and shouting support for his horse as he listened in to radio commentary. Both of his sons inherited this pastime, but Alex more so than Martin became particularly intrigued by the strategy of horse racing. Unlike his father, though, Alex would get to love horse racing from inside the arena, as opposed to clutching dockets while listening to crackling commentary in a packed pub. And he would instantly fall in love with the atmosphere of a roaring racetrack. As his stature grew in football, the company in which he kept at racing venues evolved. One spring day, in 1996, he was sitting with famed Irish trainer John Mulhern in the lounge room at Cheltenham alongside Cathy when he turned to his wife and asked, 'Do ya fancy buying a horse?'

Cathy scowled at him, but when he explained that the responsibility of owning a horse might offer him some light relief from the rigours of his day job, his wife decided a new hobby would indeed be beneficial.

The first horse Alex bought, he named Queensland Star—after the great ship his father was helping build in the docks of Govan while Alex and Martin were growing up. Since then, Alex has purchased or owned shares in as many as fifty different racehorses and has won, among others, The Lexus Chase and the Aintree Bowl with WhatAFriend, the Betway Bowl with Clan Des Obeaux and claimed victory in the lucrative Irish 2000 Guineas, the St James's Palace Stakes and the Prix du Moulin de Longchamp with a horse called Rock of Gibraltar—equally famous as he is infamous. That horse's name has made it in print not just on the inside pages of race cards within the centre spreads of newspapers, but also on the back pages for achieving unprecedented success in his field, before becoming a fixture on the front pages of newspapers when Alex would entangle himself into a legal spat with lead owner John Magnier.

Magnier, who held twenty-seven percent of the PLC shares in Manchester United with his long-time friend and fellow horse racing mogul JP McManus at the time, had offered Alex a fifty percent share in Rock of Gibraltar during a private conversation in 2001 as a gift. Exactly what was said during that conversation remains a mystery—but that chat can arguably be pinpointed as the main reason the Glazer family were able to take full control of Manchester United in 2005.

By 2002, while Rock of Gibraltar was stealing all the headlines in the back pages of the newspapers having won seven consecutive Group One races to set a new record, his estimated total value was reported to be a cool £50m. At this stage, Alex thought it opportune to cash in. It was only when he contacted Magnier to see how he could sell his fifty percent share that the Irish magnet informed him he didn't own fifty percent of the entire horse, just fifty percent of any the prize money accumulated by the horse.

Two years later, the matter would be settled out of court, though the details of such an agreement remain elusive to all but those directly involved.

"It was resolved," Alex would write in *My Autobiography*, "The matter was closed when we reached a settlement agreeing that there had been a misunderstanding on both sides."

But before the matter of who owned how much of Rock of Gibraltar was resolved, Magnier and McManus — having fallen out with the United manager over the debacle — would sell their shares in Manchester United to the Glazer family (who had, beforehand, owned a similar number of shares as the Coolmore racing magnates). Having also purchased minor shares from a number of small percentage shareholders, the Glazers suddenly owned over sixty percent of the world's most supported football club. Little by little, they began to assume more and more shares. By May 2005, they owned ninety-eight percent of the club, before the final two percent was forced into their hands from those who were desperately hanging on.

As the Glazers were buying up, Alex began to conduct due diligence on his future owners. He was concerned not so much by the manner in which the Glazers raised the money to purchase Manchester United (they leveraged up to £700m of debt against the club's assets), but more so about how far they would stick their oar into the running of football affairs. Two years prior, Russian oligarch Roman Abramovich had purchased Chelsea and it had already become apparent that he was leaning heavily on his managers to make specific player purchases. Abramovich had made tentative moves to sign Ukraine international Andriy Shevchenko for huge money from AC Milan, not because the manager at the time Jose Mourinho wanted the striker, but because the owner himself did. Alex wasn't going to put up with such interference in his dressing-room and was largely sceptical of the new owners from the outset. But try as he might to get a lowdown on the American family, Alex could garner little information. The Glazers, by this point, had already owned NFL franchise The Tampa Bay Bucca-neers and Alex attempted to ask questions about how they oper-ated the American Football club. All he could find out was that the entire family were hugely secretive and liked to remain in the shadows.

Great, he thought. *They're the type of owners I've always wanted.*

Still, he was apprehensive and became aware early on of the animosity their ownership would create amongst the supporters. United fans were furious, not because they felt the new owners might jeopardise their manager's control in the dressing-room, but because of the manner in which the club had been purchased. They also feared from the outset that the Glazers would be much more interested in the commercial revenue a brand like United could bring in, rather than results in football games on Saturday afternoons. The fan protests would evolve into the Green and Gold campaign, whereby supporters inside Old Trafford opted to wear the colours of founding club Newton Heath, from which was originally born Manchester United in 1902, than the red commercial jerseys that would now line the pockets of the Glazer family.

Alex sympathised with the Green and Gold campaign, but by the time it had caught fire to the extent that Old Trafford was more green and gold than it was red, and those fans were constantly chanting "We want Glazers out", he had met with Joel Glazer twice and been assured that the running of the football side of the business would not be meddled with at all. Alex and his chief executive David Gill would be left to look after football affairs, while the Glazers would shift around personnel in the commercial arm of the club to capitalise on what they considered untouched revenue streams. Yet despite feeling relieved by the new ownership model, Alex didn't dare back the Glazers publicly for fear of upsetting the club's most loyal supporters, and so he instead adopted the same stance the Glazer family had taken by staying absolutely silent on the subject of ownership publicly.

Privately, however, he was buoyed. For the first time in all his years of management, Alex had total autonomy over the football club he was managing. While the Glazers — thanks mainly to a balding, smiling Englishman named Ed Woodward, who helped broker their takeover and was then offered the title of the club's executive vice chairman — were busy growing annual revenues from £170m in the year before they took over to £480m in 2013, the year Alex retired, Alex and Gill retained total control over football matters and were met with no meddling at all by their bosses. It pains a large segment of supporters that Alex never spoke out against the Glazer ownership model, but the fact is he liked the club being owned by a family who preferred to stay in the background, allowing him to do what he did best. Some supporters insist Alex must've been angered by their ownership but chose not to speak out because he simply wouldn't have put his job in jeopardy. But given that Alex had very public spats with Willie Muirhead at his first job at East Stirlingshire, fall-outs with Willie Todd at St Mirren, with Dick Donald at Aberdeen and also with Martin Edwards at Manchester United, it's highly unlikely he wouldn't have let the Glazers know what was best for the football arm of the business had they tried to muscle in. But they simply didn't need to be told that, because they were happy for Gill and Alex to keep doing what they were doing; which was competing for major honours in English and European football year on year.

'When Manchester United became a PLC, without doubt it was always going to be sold,' Alex finally went on record as saying in 2010. 'Somebody was going to buy it. That was inevitable. It's unfair that because a particular family like the Glazers have bought it, that they should come under criticism when anybody could have bought it. I have tae say, they've done their job well. They support maself, the manager, and they've supported the players. I've never been refused when I've asked for money for a player. So what can I do other than carry on the way we're doing it? I've nae complaints.'

On the fans' main issue of the Glazers saddling the club with debt, Alex would say, 'The debt has come through the club being bought out by an owner. You know very well that no matter what business is bought nowadays, it's usually bought with debt. But because it's a football club, it seems to attract a different type of negative reporting through the media.'

The truth is, there is only a certain type of owner who could have bought United without debt, and that was the type of owner Alex would have hated at Manchester United: an owner who would turn the football club into a reality version of the console game *Football Manager*. For perspective, for Abramovich to buy Chelsea in 2003, the Russian billionaire had to part with just £60m. Two years after United were bought by the Glazers, their greatest rivals Liverpool Football Club would be bought out for £218m. Sandwiched in the middle of those two takeovers, in 2005, the Glazers had to raise £796m to take control of Manchester United. The club was so much more valuable than their rivals that it was nigh on impossible for anybody to purchase such an asset without having to service a large level of debt. If anybody could have afforded to purchase United without debt, which amounts to pretty much a handful of the nearly eight billion people alive, then they were likely purchasing United as a plaything; owners who almost certainly would have wanted a say in football matters. Alex would have been so irked by such meddling that it's likely he wouldn't have taken it; he certainly wouldn't have taken owners buying players for his dressing-room. He had fallen out with owners before for their meddling in minuscule matters such as player fines and kit colours, and no doubt wouldn't have settled for ever diluting control of his dressing room—most certainly not in the pomp of his career when he felt he deserved that control more than ever before. Of all the options open to those who could have bought Manchester United Football Club while it was a PLC and valued up to £800m, the Glazers model, Alex felt, was as good as it could have got for him. He didn't want an oligarch or an oil billionaire or the ruler of a state taking over his football club and poking their nose into the transfer market on his behalf. It also must be addressed that one of the reasons the Glazers endeared themselves to the Govanman was their agreement to increase Alex's wages considerably to ensure the manager was paid more than any player in his dressing-room—a deal Alex had been pushing for long before the American family took control. But the real reason he was fond of the Glazers owning the club was that the alternative likely would have meant he'd have to resign. Not only would Alex have been so riled by owners having a say in his team, but he also wouldn't have given credence to such a football philosophy, and in fact *doesn't* give credence to such a philosophy. Alex finds it difficult to praise PSG, or Manchester City or Chelsea for their title wins, given the manner in which the clubs are financed. He is certain those clubs breach financial fair play, though agrees that curtailing such a ruling is an impossible task for governing bodies to control. What is most interesting is that when Claudio Ranieri won the Premier League with Leicester City in 2016 and when Jurgen Klopp did the same at Liverpool to end a thirty-year wait in 2020, Alex was straight on the phone to both managers to congratulate them for their feats. He has never telephoned a Chelsea or Man City manager for winning such a title. Not due to bitterness (if he was bitter, the last club he would congratulate would have been his biggest rivals Liverpool), but due to his strong footballing beliefs. Football clubs are supposed to be football *clubs*, not just football teams. If clubs aren't producing their own players from within, or they aren't operating in the transfer market from within the means of the club, then they aren't really a football club. Just a football team. This went totally against Alex's footballing philosophy. It certainly went against what Manchester United had stood for. Although United are the most popular football club in the world, they truly only ever have been successful over two periods in their lifespan. It's just those two periods happened to last for long stretches (for fifteen years under Matt Busby and for twenty years under Alex Ferguson). But those two dominating eras lasted so long because the club

continuously recycled their first-team squad from within the football club. Busby's success was achieved by promoting players
from the club's academy into the first team, so too was Alex's.
That was the Manchester United way. United becoming a billionaire's plaything wouldn't have sat right. Not with Alex. He
would have loathed it had United taken that route and rendered
the academy and his strong football philosophy as redundant.
Despite Alex's preference for the Glazer model over the alternative, the supporters of Manchester United simply couldn't see
how Alex was viewing matters from within. And although he
was assuming as much control as he ever had at Manchester
United and was feeling positive the club were set to for loftier
heights under the Glazer regime (which did occur given that
Alex went on his best run of title wins and Champions League
finals in his final years), he could empathise with the fan frustration.

The supporters remained outraged that the Glazers had
mounted the club with serious debt even though they were
growing revenues at such a rapid rate that they were taking in up
to ten times more than was being spent repaying the loans per
annum. On top of the debt, the supporters were apocalyptic that
the Glazers were taking money out of the club for their own
private gains. Yet because of the freedom in which Alex was
allowed to run the football side of the club (his transfer targets
were never rejected by the Glazers and they genuinely stayed
away from football affairs), he viewed the level of debt and
Glazer payments as passable given the alternative. Under the
Glazers, Alex would purchase Michael Carrick for £18m (a price
tag that raised eyebrows at the time) without the Glazers holding
back in any way until the player was finally released by Tottenham's Daniel Levy. The following year they would then sign two
of the most-coveted young players in Europe in Nani and
Anderson for hefty price tags of £23.5 and £28.3m respectively—
fees that got football clubs in Europe hot under the collar. They
would also spend £22.5m on Owen Hargreaves from Bayern

Munich and pay £11.5m to loan Carlos Tevez for two seasons—an innovative arrangement that also raised eyebrows around the football world. The year after, they would spend £30.75m on Dimitar Berbatov who offered very little resale value given that he was almost twenty-eight years old, and then do the same with Robin van Persie ahead of Alex's final season in charge. What Alex wanted, he seemed to get under the Glazer regime, and the owners had even green lit moves for Gareth Bale and the return of Cristiano Ronaldo only for the players to opt to stay at Real Madrid instead. Despite the spending and indeed the trophies that were being collated regularly, the supporters remained insistent that more could have been spent on the squad had the club not being paying back so much to service their debts. Yet after Alex retired, and in a desperate attempt to regain their place at the summit of English football, the Glazers would spend over £1bn in transfer fees for players over a span of seven summers. Fans arguing that the debt repayments impacted on Manchester United's transfer activity in a negative way has proven a difficult stance to take, given the evidence.

Although the Glazers didn't poke their noses into Alex's running of the football side of their business, he would, as was his inquisitive mind, poke his nose into theirs. He was intrigued to know how they were amassing such massive turnovers since they first took control of the club in 2005. He would find out that the brains behind the operation was the balding, smiling, executive vice chairman Ed Woodward.

Woodward was offered his title by the Glazers who had eyeballed the untouched commercial markets as gold mines before deciding to buy the club outright. Once in situ, Woodward would hire a research marketing company called *Kantar* to find out how many Manchester United fans existed in the world. The number *Kantar* came back with would prove astonishing. 650 million. Literally, *Kantar* revealed, one in ten people in the world at the time followed Manchester United. Though "followed" is the key word in their findings. What Woodward had done through *Kantar* was to find out how many people in the world showed interested in Manchester United by 'following' their progress, regardless of whether or not they considered themselves supporters of the club. What Woodward had realised was that fans of all other clubs also followed the fortunes of United, mostly because they wanted United to lose. And United were missing a trick by not capitalising on such an obsession. It didn't matter to commercial assets how many prying eyes wanted United to win or lose, what mattered was that one in ten people in the world were watching. Armed with such an astonishing number (which has risen since according to *Kantar* who later revealed in 2012 that United had by then 1.1bn "followers"—one in eight people in the world), Woodward would enter negotiations for commercial opportunities telling these businesses that one in ten, or one in eight as it turned into, people on the planet would be eyeballing their brands. To be associated with United was to open up a whole new world of opportunity. That's why Woodward could secure a record-breaking and rather head-scratching £410m from *Chevrolet* for their logo to be emblazoned across the team's jerseys for seven years in 2012. It's how he persuaded *Adidas* to offer United a further record-breaking £750m in 2014 just to manufacture their kits for a ten-year stretch. Woodward's commercial savvy meant that those people worldwide who were "following" United because they wanted the club to lose were actually helping the club to ludicrous numbers in revenue. It was an extraordinary and innovative commercial approach, which made Woodward even more popular with the Glazers. Alex was hugely impressed, too—and continued to be stunned as the former JP Morgan investment banker hooked in commercial deal after commercial deal, finding all manner of avenues in and around the football club that could be deemed lucrative. Woodward pioneered training jersey sponsorship at United which all major clubs have since adopted as a high-income revenue stream, and pushed hard for commercial space to be used on the sleeves of Premier League team kits. Due to such innovation, commercially, United's revenue grew year on year right through a global recession, meaning the repayments on the debt (which were approximately £45m per year at their highest) were easily manageable. Yet fans were still wrangled by these loan repayments and were even more livid that the Glazer family were taking money out of the club for their own personal gains. It was estimated by *90 Minutes* magazine in 2021 that the Glazers had taken up to £1.1 billion sterling out of the club. Alex has never made any comment on this element of the family's dealings and notably skipped the subject in *My Autobiography*. The taking of money by owners for personal advantage, while normally the fundamental objective of owning any business, has been the main platform from which fans have shown their ire at the Glazer ownership, and it is certainly a legitimate stance for them to take given the traditions of ownership throughout British footballing history specifically. However, given that Alex went through his most successful period as a manager at the tail end of his career under the ownership of the Glazers, by the time he was retiring in 2013, the green and gold had practically faded back to commercial red inside Old Trafford.

That was until a rather astonishing period in the midst of the global pandemic in 2021 when — out of the blue — the Glazers, along with the owners of eleven other major clubs around Europe (Arsenal, Chelsea, Liverpool, Manchester City, Tottenham, AC Milan, Inter Milan, Atletico Madrid, Barcelona and Real Madrid) announced they were forgoing the Champions League to join a newly established competition called the Super League. The green and gold T-shirts and scarfs came back out, and United supporters would protest at Old Trafford during nation-wide lockdown that concluded with their vital Premier league game, due to be broadcast worldwide, against Liverpool being called off at the eleventh hour. This time, Alex was totally on the side of the supporters, but was by now eight years into retirement. He couldn't understand the Super League, feeling football holds much less value to supporters if small clubs can't dream about the big time. Alex, after all, had achieved an impossible dream by leading a small club in Aberdeen to European glory. The notion that dreams like that could no longer happen was unfathomable to him.

'Talk of a Super League is a move away from seventy years of European club football,' Alex moved to tell news agency *Reuters* in the wake of the announcement. 'I dreamed the dream in Europe—both as a player for a provincial team, Dunfermline, in the sixties and then as a manager at Aberdeen winning the European Cup Winners' Cup. For a small provincial club in Scotland it was like climbing Mount Everest. Everton are spending £500m to build a new stadium with the ambition to play in Champions League…'

Under the Super League proposals, Everton would never get to the summit of European football as the clubs already on board were locked into the competition. No promotion. No relegation. The idea, backed by the Glazers and Liverpool owners FSG more than most initially, bombed within twenty-four hours of its paltry launch, with pundits, players and managers alike readily ridiculing the concept and fans out protesting at many of the clubs involved, particularly in England. When United fans returned to Old Trafford as lockdowns eased for the start of the 2021-22 season, some of the commercial red in the stands had notably turned back into green and gold.

The wake of the Super League was the first time in which Alex had ever spoken negatively about a decision made by the Glazer family. But it wasn't the first time he would be dismayed by one of their decisions.

In February of 2013 Alex was preparing to leave his office at Carrington when Ed Woodward's knuckles rattled against his door. It was the week after United had been dumped out of the Champions League by Real Madrid and two weeks after David Gill had informed the Glazer family that he would be stepping down from his role as chief executive at the end of the season (all of which you can read more about in a later chapter).

'Hi Alex,' the commercial genius said. 'Don't want to disturb you, but thought I should see you face-to-face to deliver the news. I've been appointed as David's successor and just wanted to let you know that I'm really looking forward to working with you.'

2008-2011

HAVING WON THE CHAMPIONS LEAGUE IN 2008 UNITED WOULD GET TO two more finals over the next three seasons, but the big old trophy would ultimately elude Alex forevermore thanks, in the main, to Pep Guardiola's FC Barcelona renaissance. Although Alex had got the better of the Spaniard over two intense legs en route to winning his second Champions League in April of 2008, Guardiola's Barcelona would evolve into such a cohesive unit that they would arguably etch themselves into the history books as the greatest club side of all time.

'They were the best team to ever line up against my Manchester United,' Alex said. 'Easily the best. I think during that period (2009-2011) they may have been unplayable.'

Unplayable would certainly prove to be the case for Alex anyway. Manchester United would face Barcelona in both the 2009 and 2011 Champions League finals and United would be, by far, the second-best team on the pitch on each occasion.

United, as far as Alex was concerned, were as good as they had ever been throughout his reign. They were dominating English football and collecting more points than they had done in previous years in order to see off the threats of rival clubs such as Chelsea and Manchester City who were being funded by billionaire owners. But despite such envious domestic form, United had to settle for being the bridesmaids in Europe. After winning the title alongside the 2008 Champions League final, they would retain their crown as England's champions the following season—holding nearest challengers Liverpool at arm's length by the conclusion of the campaign. It was halfway through this season that Rafa Benitez, the then Liverpool coach, tried to rattle Alex with his 'facts' rant. Alex instantly knew from watching that press conference on TV that the Spanish coach had done the opposite of what he had intended to do. The 'facts' rant backfired dramatically, as detailed in a previous chapter, and United would go on to win their eleventh Premier League title in the space of seventeen seasons with relative ease. The players would lift the trophy and collect their medals on the final day of that season —one week before they were due in the Eternal City of Rome to face Barcelona in the 2009 Champions League final.

Within two hours of arriving in the Italian capital they were feeling deflated. The hotel they had booked to stay in wasn't up to the standard they were used to in England, and players were complaining about the noise outside their echoey and dated high-ceilinged bedrooms. Some were even arguing that their mattresses were too stiff to sleep on. Alex held a meeting in which he instructed his players to rein it in. They were forty-eight hours away from playing in a Champions League Final. 'So shut up moaning,' he told them. But within two hours of that meeting, he would prove to be the one moaning the loudest. He had just been informed that the chef Manchester United took with them to all away games had been turned away at the hotel's kitchen and wouldn't be allowed to cook the squad's dinner that evening. Instead, they would be fed by the hotel's in-house chefs.

Alex demanded a showdown with the hotel manager, but he ultimately wouldn't get his way, and the United staff and players would sit down to eat a meal made by the hotel's chefs. The following morning, Ryan Giggs was sitting on the toilet with his stomach growling. He wasn't the only player, but he was the one most affected by a bug that had unearthed itself overnight.

Alex is reluctant to speak about conspiracy theories, and to this day still scoffs at the thoughts of foul play. Despite the fact that the hotel in Rome wasn't good enough, and the club's own chef not being able to cook meals for the players, Alex blames himself. He should have looked into that pre-match schedule with more rigour than he actually had.

However, the fact that it was Giggs who was handicapped by the mystery stomach bug more than anyone else proved most unfortunate. United had trained and planned all week on the Welshman using his extensive energy levels to get about the Barcelona midfield diamond. His job was to hunt down Iniesta and Xavi and stop them dictating play at their own pace. Except, on the night, Giggs could barely run from one of those Spanish stars to the other without heaving for breath.

Another reason Alex feels United were bettered in the 2009 final is because his central defenders didn't have the game to defend against Barcelona. Although Rio Ferdinand and Nemanja Vidic were considered amongst the best defensive partnerships on the continent at that time, Alex thought them too traditional in their approach to the art of defending to go toe-to-toe with the evolutionary manner in which Barcelona attacked.

On reflection of that specific final, Alex would write in *My Autobiography*: "To beat Barcelona during that cycle you needed centre backs who were really positive. Rio and Vidic were at an age where their preference was to defend the space. Nothing wrong with that. But against this Barcelona that's a limited approach. You need centre-backs who are prepared to drop right on top of Messi and not worry about what is happening in behind them."

No matter the excuse, be it stiff mattresses on hotel beds, club chefs not being allowed access to the hotel kitchen, Giggs not being able to carry out United's plan, or centre-halves who were proving to be too old-school, the fact remains that United were beaten in that final because they simply came up against a better side. An early goal from Samuel Eto'o and a late header from Lionel Messi would clinch that final for Barcelona. The fact that they were simply too

good a side for United, and ensuring all the above excuses are
redundant, would be rubber-stamped twenty-four months later when
the two sides would go toe-to-toe again in Europe's biggest
showpiece.

The 2009 Champions League final was the first European final
Alex had ever lost. And he took it bad. Despite proving to be kings
of England again — and in the process winning another trio of titles
on the trot — Alex holidayed with Cathy in the United States that
summer, still bulling from the defeat in Rome. His mood wouldn't
improve much over the next nine months as United encountered a
tough title battle with Carlo Ancelotti's Chelsea in which the London
team would come out on top by a single point. He would also have a
frustrating time in Europe that season— dumped from the Champions League at the quarter-final stage on away goals following two
frantic legs against Bayern Munich.

2009 was also the summer in which he lost Cristiano Ronaldo.
The Portuguese wonder had always dreamed of playing for Real
Madrid, having grown up a fan of the Spanish giants in Madeira.
Real had come in for Ronaldo following United's 2008 Champions
League win, but Alex had to have a heart-to-heart with the player, to
tell him he needed him to stay for one more year.

'One more season,' he told Ronaldo, 'and you can join Real. But
only if we get a world record fee for you.'

The following summer, Real would part with £89.9m to capture
the services of the attacker. The main reason Alex wanted Ronaldo
to stay for one more year was not simply because he was proving
himself to be the best player in the world, but more so because Alex
knew it would take two summers for United to adjust to losing such
a unique talent. Ronaldo couldn't simply be replaced like-for-like.
That was nigh on impossible. Which makes it inaccurate to say that
Alex replaced Ronaldo with Wigan right-winger Antonio Valencia in
the summer of 2009. Ronaldo was replaced by a combination of
Dimitar Berbatov *and* Antonio Valencia. Alex was changing up his
attacking approach to replace Ronaldo. He opted to replace the
Portuguese star with a more traditional right-winger who could make

ten to twelve crosses every game *and* by introducing the silkiest receiver of crosses in the Premier League into the opposition's penalty box—Berbatov, who would be signed six weeks after Alex and Ronaldo held that meeting in which they both agreed the player could leave for Madrid in twelve months' time. And a week after Ronaldo would finally leave one year later, Valencia was signed. United fans felt underwhelmed, but they knew by now not to question the manager's instinct for evolving his teams. And despite losing the league title on the final day of the season to Chelsea in 2010, United would wrestle their trophy back the following year, with Valencia proving to be a shrewd purchase by providing old-school assists for Berbatov and Wayne Rooney who were both on fire in front of goal.

United strolled to that title, and while they were strolling, they strutted their stuff in Europe too, seeing off domestic rivals Chelsea, German side Schalke and French giants Marseille in the knock-out stages to book themselves another final against Guardiola's Barcelona—this time, on the more familiar turf of Wembley Stadium.

Despite being overrun by the Spanish giants two season prior, United players were optimistic they could pull off a win. They believed their manager had learned from his mistakes in the 2009 final. But after they had lifted the Premier League title in May 2011 and settled down to a team meeting to discuss the tactics for the Champions League final, they immediately began to lose such positivity. It became evident, to many of them, that Alex *hadn't* learned from his mistakes in 2009.

He was intent on attacking Barcelona, attempting to win the Champions League in style by going toe-to-toe with the side most observers were already categorising as the greatest of all time.

As mentioned in a previous chapter, Wayne Rooney would label Alex's approach to this final as "suicidal". Rio Ferdinand would admit five years later that Alex simply "got the tactics wrong".

Alex would, in time, justify his attacking approach by writing, "We were trying to strengthen our philosophy by winning in the right manner." What's difficult to fathom is that Alex had taken a more

pragmatic and defensive approach against Guardiola's Barca over
two legs in 2008—en route to winning the Champions League. So
quite why he wasn't willing to adapt a similar approach was baffling
his players in the lead up to the 2011 final. The truth is, Alex was
pained by those two legs in 2008. He felt them torturous as United
tried to hold on to their 1-0 lead by camping two sets of four players
on the edge of his own box. And despite winning that clash, he still
felt somewhat hallow about how United approached those games.
He would go on to label the victory in 2008 over Barcelona in *My
Autobiography* as "agony on the touchline". That agony may have
swayed his tactical approach for the two finals that were to follow
against Guardiola's side.

United would practise their attacking tactics for five training
sessions leading up to the Wembley showpiece. Their whole idea
centred around Javier Hernandez (a young Mexican international
who Alex adored and chose to play in this game ahead of Dimitar
Berbatov for this specific reason), who was charged with running
across the line of the Barcelona defence, stretching them away from
each other so that Rooney could threaten the spaces between them.
The plan worked somewhat in that Rooney scored from this manner
of play to equalise on the night, but overall, the approach came off
as rather lacklustre and even pretty redundant. Alex would complain
that Rooney had a poor game that evening, failing to carry out his
boss's orders. Rooney would argue the boss's orders weren't good
enough.

Barca went ahead through winger Pedro who scored because
the United defenders, as Alex had feared, weren't proactive enough
in defending the space in front of them. He had trained Vidic and
Ferdinand all week on being on the front foot, but it wasn't their
natural game and neither were particularly world class at it; certainly
not world class enough to deal with Messi or David Villa who would
run them riot that night. Despite Rooney equalising seven minutes
after Barca took the lead and the teams going into the break level,
Alex wasn't for changing his tactics, even if he did have to shuffle a
couple of players around. Right-back Fabio Da Silva got injured and

had to be replaced with winger Nani, which meant Antonio Valencia was forced to drop into the right back position. It unbalanced all United had planned for over the previous five days, and in the second-half Barca were dominant; holding on to the ball and almost teasing their counterparts with it. Messi would score his second Champions League final goal against Manchester United nine minutes into the second half, and then Villa would go on to round out a comfortable 3-1 victory with twenty minutes left to play. By the end, United were flat out, and proving to be far from a match for Barcelona—even further so than they had been in 2009. Although he doesn't regret how he tackled those two European finals, Alex does consider himself somewhat unlucky that the best team he ever assembled at United happened to coincide with that Barcelona powerhouse of a side. He, personally, would have loved to have won three European Cups. It wasn't to be.

On Barcelona of that period, Alex firmly believes that Johan Cruyff is as responsible for their successes as then-manager Pep Guardiola. It was Cruyff who constructed the foundations for the shape of the team, which was built to dominate as much possession of the ball as possible. Guardiola continued the tradition that had been carried by Dutchmen Louis van Gaal and Frank Rijkaard since Cruyff had set the system in place, but ingeniously added an extra dimension to it. Not only were his Barcelona side fluid in possession and as a result rarely losing the ball, they would have to be dogged-like on the rare occasion that they didn't have possession, creating a counter-press that Alex thought was near outrageous. When he inquired as to how Guardiola was implementing such tactics, Alex would mutter, 'Bloody hell,' upon hearing that the Barcelona manager would drill his players for an hour during each training session whereby an attacking team would surrender possession of the ball and as soon as they did, Guardiola's coaches would begin to count to six. If the attacking side hadn't won the ball back within those six seconds, they failed their mission. Alex studied tape after tape of Barcelona's games under Guardiola and realised how they had so much energy to hunt the ball down after they had lost it.

Barca players simply reserved all their energy for when they *didn't* have the ball. When they were in possession — which was usually sixty-to-sixty-five percent of the time — they let the ball do the work. Players rarely carried the ball forward or ran with possession (aside from Messi). They stood still in possession. And played the ball. All their hard work was done when they didn't have the ball. Alex was wowed.

He would go on holiday disappointed again in 2011, despite having won a twelfth Premier League title (United's nineteenth championship since they were founded in 1878). The most title wins in English history now stood at Manchester United 19, Liverpool 18. The enormity of what he had achieved was so outstanding that anybody who predicted such a turnaround in fortunes for the two greatest football clubs England has ever produced in the mid-eighties could only have been an alien out of touch with earth's reality.

Alex's legacy was well and truly set in stone. In fact, it was *literally* about to be set in stone.

In the November of 2011, United were due to play at home against Sunderland in a Premier League game that would coincide with the twenty-fifth anniversary of when the Govanman had first become manager of the football club. It was quite appropriate that they were playing Sunderland that day in the sense that the Black Cats had three players in it who had graduated under Alex's academy at Manchester United: John O'Shea, Wes Brown and Kieran Richardson. Both sets of players were lined up outside the tunnel as Alex walked out, applauding him through a guard of honour. All he was told before walking down the tunnel was that David Gill was waiting for him in the centre circle. He noted, as he walked towards the half-way line that there was something lying by the chief executive's feet. Perhaps they had a crystal made for him to mark his twenty-fifth anniversary and were about to reward him with it in front of the home supporters. Gill slung his arm over Alex's shoulder, then gripped the microphone tight.

'Alex, twenty-five years—what a magnificent achievement. On

behalf of Manchester United fans and the football world generally, many congratulations. The club wanted to celebrate this occasion in an historic way, a unique way never, ever done before in our 133-year history.'

At this stage, Alex was beginning to think there were gold bars at David Gill's feet, and not just crystal glass.

'So I'm delighted to say that from today,' Gill continued, 'the North Stand, the biggest stand in this magnificent stadium, is to be called the Sir Alex Ferguson Stand.'

Alex would bend over in disbelief, before looking up at Gill and muttering the words he always muttered when he was momentarily stuck for something meaningful to say, 'Bloody hell.'

Gill grinned at the manager, then spun him around to face the old North stand where a team of ten construction workers, standing atop the roof, curled up a cover to reveal the new name of the stand emblazoned in red capital letters across the top.

Alex was so overwhelmed that he immediately whispered to Gill, 'I don't deserve this.' What he was saying wasn't making much sense. If he didn't deserve a football stand named after him, nobody in the game past or present did. It was quite clearly Alex's successes on the pitch that enabled the North Stand to be extended into the biggest stand in British football club history.

A week later, Alex would be bowled over once again when it was confirmed to him by the club in private that they had commissioned renowned artist Philip Jackson to sculpt a bronze statue of the Govanman—a statue that would be set in stone forevermore directly outside the newly named Sir Alex Ferguson Stand.

ALEX THE FAMILY MAN

ALEX SAT NEXT TO CATHY ON THE FRONT ROW OF THE LARGE gathering (a gathering that included the entire Ferguson family; a selection of current and former Manchester United players; current and former members of the club's staff; the club's board of directors and a crowd of chanting, local fans) and quizzed her on who she thinks the club had invited to unveil the large sculpture that was covered under heavy tarpaulin on the stage in front of them.

Initially, Cathy thought Alex's good friend, TV personality Eamonn Holmes, had been chosen to unveil the statue. After all, he was now standing on the makeshift stage in front of them that spread across the exterior of the Sir Alex Ferguson Stand.

'Nah, it's not Eamonn, he's just here tae host the unveiling,' Alex said. 'It's gonnae be someone special. Has tae be.'

Cathy looked about herself, trying to locate the clues that would lead her to the mystery guest.

'Perhaps it's some movie star, y'know,' she said, knowing well her husband's penchant for Hollywood. 'Or a politician. Ye think they'd have asked the prime minister?'

Given that the Prime Minister at the time was Conservative leader David Cameron, Alex's eyebrows raised.

'I bloody hoop not,' he said.

It was the first time in quite a while all five Fergusons had been seated together. And around them, Alex's daughters-in-law were joined by the freshest branches of the Ferguson family tree —his and Cathy's grandchildren. All eleven of them. Jake, Ella, Sophie, Harvey, Hannah, Grace, Ruby, Freddie, Murray, Callum and Frankie. Their upbringing is stark in contrast to that of their famous grandfather's. The one message Alex has always tried to instil in his grandchildren, as he did their fathers before them, was to simply have pride in whatever they choose to do. That's the continuous and consistent message Alex delivers to young people he comes into contact with; it's the one message he wrote on a note to his grandchildren while sitting up in his hospital bed recovering from his brain surgery in 2018. In truth, his grandchildren aren't lacking much for pride, certainly not when it comes to him. But they are filled with pride more because of the story of his upbringing than for the trophies he collected along the way. Alex and Cathy had quite literally evolved from low working-class families whose parents were earning .12p per hour, into a Lady and a Knight of the Realm who were enjoying a luxurious lifestyle of fine company and even finer wines. Alex has often muttered to himself in later life, wondering what his father would make of it all. Alex Snr had died in February 1979 — having never witnessed his son reach the great heights he could have only ever dreamed of for him. Alex's mother, Lizzie, passed away some seven years later, in late 1986—mere weeks after her son had been appointed manager of Manchester United. Alex grieved for both in different ways. But he has never felt anything but blessed to be the son of parents who possessed the willpower and confidence he was fortunate enough to inherit in abundance.

There are multiple people who could arguably boast that Alex Ferguson is their best friend—from his very close brother-in-law through marriage John Robertson who he spends a lot of time with, to his oldest pals from his school days such as Duncan Peterson, Tommy Hendry and Jim McMillan, to football friends like Archie Knox, Albert Morgan, Sam Allardyce and David Gill. Or celebrity pals that include Eamonn Holmes, Mick Hucknall, Michael Moritz and Alastair Campbell. But there is no argument over who *he* considers to be *his* best friend. That's Martin. His brother. By a long stretch. They've travelled many a road together, through rain and shine, and yet, despite growing up in environments that could be described as hostile back in Govan, they were always by each other's side. They never fell out. Not really. They were always united, just as they were raised to believe brothers should unite. That's not to say there weren't disagreements along the way, but they never ablazed in argument all though their years. They'd shout and gesticulate at each other in the worst of times, but those arguments would inevitably be resolved the next day when they would talk it out over the phone. The Ferguson brothers have never been oblivious to the chemistries that bond them tightly. But those chemistries are interwoven simply because they are two apples that have hung along the same branch, from the same tree, inside the same orchard for pretty much the entirety of their eight decades. There is only fifty weeks between Alex and Martin, so it is no surprise that they have often been mistaken for twins. In their younger days, Alex did appear older than just one year over his brother due to his presence. But in the middle of their life, there was hardly any telling Alex and Martin apart. They were still clinging on to their Perry Como-inspired hairdos, and by this stage were mirroring each other in not just body language but in tonal delivery. If you squinted your eyes in the company of the Ferguson brothers throughout the 1980s and 1990s, there would be hardly any telling them apart. In later life, they have evolved to be physically dissimilar, but their character has never parted ways. They are both upbeat in personality and can each spin a tale or two with relative ease. Both remain eager anecdotalists.

Although Martin's name stayed out of the newspapers throughout the years, Alex is certain he couldn't have achieved all he had without his brother by his side. Martin's voice throughout Alex's managerial career was constant and almost always sought-after—especially when it came to analysing players. Martin is simply the best scout Alex ever worked with. He trusted his brother's eye more than he trusted anyone else's. Even his own, sometimes.

Growing up, Martin would prove to be just as good a footballer as Alex, though he never quite caught the same breaks his older brother did, and as a result mostly played as a professional in the lowly paid, lower divisions. Though he did play in three separate countries, having appeared for Patrick Thistle and Greenock Morton in Scotland, Doncaster Rovers and Barnsley in England and then on to Waterford United in Ireland. He was actually player-manager of Waterford United for one season (in which he managed to win the league title) before going on to manage East Stirlingshire and then Albion Rovers. The latter two managerial jobs can be best described as mediocre, certainly so when compared to the record of the greatest British manager of all time.

When Alex began re-building a network of scouts at Manchester United and knew he wanted a voice in his ear that he could trust, the first voice that sprung to his ear was his brother's. And so Martin was appointed one of Manchester United's lead scouts, where his role would evolve over the years from looking internally in Britain for young players that he could introduce to the academy, to a position of chief European scout where he would unearth gems for his brother to sign in the shape of Diego Forlan, Ruud van Nistelrooy, Anderson, Nani and one of Alex's all-time favourite signings, Ji Sung-Park.

A claim of nepotism has periodically been flung at Alex, over not just his brother's role in the scouting department at Manchester United, but also because Darren became a player at the club during his father's reign. Those claims never really held up, though, as to argue that Darren got chosen to play for United ignores the fact that Alex also has two other sons who never turned out for the club. On top of that, Martin's role at

Manchester United turned out to be inspirational throughout two decades of unprecedented success. It was impossible to argue Martin wasn't worthy of his position.

When Alex's sons were coming of age, it's true to say Darren was Alex's favourite, or at least he was the one he shared most of his time with. It helped, of course, that they were both involved heavily in the professional game and were never short on anecdotes to share. In later life, Alex has grown closer to Jason, with whom he worked with on a documentary film about his father's life following his brain haemorrhage in 2018. In preparation for the production, they watched hundreds of hours of old footage together as well as rifled through a mini mountain of paperwork. During research for the film, Jason would hook Alex up to a microphone to probe him on the finest details of his life. His father would describe taking part in the documentary as a highly rewarding experience during his retirement. After the film's release, they took part in a press tour together in the midst of the global pandemic where they further deepened their bond. But it is son Mark who has been the one consistent ally of Alex's through the years. He was the most mature, disciplined and single-minded out of the three boys, and Alex could effortlessly relate. They share the same dry humour, too. Though it must be said, Mark's more relaxed approach to life is in stark contrast to that of his old man's. In that regard, Darren is most like his father, and indeed followed his footsteps into football management to relatively modest success with clubs such as Preston North End, Doncaster Rovers and in particular Peterborough United where his name will be forever etched in the history books having managed the club across three separate spells. Darren is also the son who looks most like his father, though in different ways each son can mirror their old man, depending on which angle they are observed from.

Jason would go on to achieve global critical acclaim for the documentary film which he entitled *Never Give In*, having already proven to possess the goods as a broadcast producer. Despite playing football at a decent level during his teenage years — as all Ferguson boys did — Jason never saw a future for himself as a footballer, nor did he seek it. Though it did take him some time to figure out exactly what he wanted to achieve in life. Jason studied media through a Granada TV scheme and because he adored the sport in which his father was building a legacy in, sought work within broadcast sports media. He has had a split career since graduating college. He would work his way up from junior producer to senior football director at Sky Sports while the network was launching the new Premier League brand throughout the nineties and would later entangle himself further into the game as a footballer's agent where his presence at Manchester United would become a speculative part of the infamous BBC documentary that ignited Alex's earlier written about seven-year blackout. Jason would then return to his first love, broadcast production, and now works in film making. Mark, who had appeared as a teenager in Aberdeen's reserve team before bowing out of the game to study, ended up being promoted into high positions within the finance sectors in London city where he still works today. His career has seen him involved in multi-million-pound deals with companies such as Schroders and Goldman Sachs.

Financially, all three Ferguson sons have done well and each can be considered high-achievers in their respective professional fields. The only blot that can be found in the family's history, however — aside from the controversial BBC fallout — can be considered quite a dark blot. Darren pleaded guilty to an assault charge brought about him by his wife, Nadine, in 2007. Nadine claimed Darren kicked her in the abdomen during a row about childcare that happened to occur in the driveway of Alex and Cathy's home. Darren would later plead guilty to common assault in a court of law, but on the basis that Nadine ran into his raised leg more so than he physically swung a leg at her. The judge accepted his guilty plea and fined the then Peterborough United manager £1,500. Alex would privately chastise Darren for the incident that he considered "disgusting". Cathy had been present when the row between Darren and Nadine initially ignited and considers all that followed needlessly dramatic and hyperbolic.

They all get on well though, the five Fergusons. And their family bond has remained rock solid, so strong is Alex's insistence on 'loyalty'. The bond, however, is strongest between Alex and Cathy. The only time Alex felt he truly let his wife down during their half a century plus years of marriage was on the day he signed for Rangers, and a club director approached to quiz him over Cathy's Catholic faith.

'I really felt I let her down that day. I shudda just told him to fuck off, I really should,' he would say many decades later.

If Cathy Holding wasn't sure what she was getting into when she married Alex Ferguson in the spring of 1966, then she would certainly find out within an hour of becoming his wife. Alex would lead Cathy back out of the registry office after they had been confirmed as a married couple, then across the street where they would pose for photographs before he, alone, got into Martin's car to be chauffeured to East End Park where he would play up front for Dunfermline against Hamilton (a game in which Dunfermline won 1-0, but Alex didn't play well in).

There can be no argument that Cathy made many sacrifices for the sake of Alex's career and those sacrifices can perhaps best be summed up by the fact that the first time Alex ever had breakfast in his home with his wife wasn't until *after* he had retired in 2013.

'She is the bedrock, no doubt aboot that,' Alex said of his wife. 'Without her, none of this is possible. She sacrificed everything.'

Those sacrifices though, it must be said, led Cathy to a luxurious lifestyle. Aside from their Tudor mansion in Wilmslow, the Fergusons own a luxury apartment in New York City (Alex's favourite place to visit), holiday each summer in Cote d'Azur in France (Cathy's favourite place to visit) and own a stunning apartment on the grounds of a five-star hotel at Loch Lomond.

Despite their Tudor home being more than grand, Cathy would still not allow her husband to display any football memorabilia in any of the sixteen rooms, not even one of the four bathrooms. Talk of football was often hushed inside the home. Cathy didn't care much for the game when she met Alex for the very first time in 1964 and that ambivalence hasn't receded in all the decades since. She very rarely went to a game, and if she did, it was normally a cup final where she could be found sitting inside the director's box sipping on a cup of tea rather than take her seat in the stand.

'She didn't go to many games, no,' Alex said. 'Mabee the odd cup final or something like that in Wembley, but she never enjoyed it, even if we won.'

In Alex's retirement, and with the need for him having an office space within their home from where he reads and writes, Cathy finally gave him the green-light to display his football honours and so, since 2014, a couple of Alex's medals have been dusted off and placed on a shelf inside the house for the very first time. Though most of his honours can actually be found inside the Old Trafford museum.

'If you're gonna display 'em,' he said. 'Display 'em for the fans.'

Despite Cathy's lack of interest in her husband's career, she has always been the first person Alex pined to share his biggest victories with. After he had learned United were crowned champions of England for the first time under his reign, while he was on a golf course in 1993, he went straight to the pay phone at the golf club and rang his wife to deliver the news. And straight after the historic victory at Camp Nou which confirmed United as treble winners in 1999, Alex stood on the sideline as his players celebrated behind him with his hands up to his eyes to shield them from the glow of the floodlights so he could seek out Cathy in the stands. When he spotted her, he grinned like a Cheshire Cat, then raised his fist at her in celebration.

Cathy and Alex were an ideal fit from their earliest days, and friends would describe them as a typical double act in the traditional sense of a British double act. A Morecombe and Wise marriage, if you will. One straight one. And one goofy one. Alex is the goofy one, always singing to his wife, or cracking a joke at her expense (he particularly likes to wind her up). Cathy is straight as a dye. And could cut him down with a one-liner that would be delivered with the fatalist of blows and in the thickest tones of her Glasgow accent.

Like with Martin, Alex never fell out with Cathy, and their marriage has continued to evolve since his retirement. The only spat they had that has stayed with them through the years was from the time Alex sold Darren to Wolverhampton Wanderers back in 1994.

'She never let me live that down,' Alex admits. '"You sold ya oon son." She still says that to me. Anytime a conversation comes up about loyalty, she'll turn to me and say, "Aye, and you sold ya oon son."'

It sounds like a catchphrase from their Morecombe and Wise double act, but in truth, Cathy is not messing, nor never has been, when she accosts Alex for sanctioning the sale of Darren, even though she never once watched a full game of football in which he played.

As part of their double act however, Cathy would always try to play down the lack of time she spent with her husband while he was away working, insisting she was happy being an independent housewife.

'When he's here, he gets under ma feet,' she said in the mid-nineties, in the midst of Alex's success at Old Trafford.

The fact that Cathy dissuaded Alex from retiring in 2002 suggests this opinion wasn't produced for the sake of saving face. During Alex's career, Cathy was happy to keep their nest intact, and was more than content to engage in her own social circle without the company of her other half. The guilt in that regard all lies within Alex's head.

'She raised the kids, aye. No doubt aboot that. She did everything,' he would confess when interviewed on national television in America during a face-to-face chat with controversial quizzer Charlie Rose. 'She got them dressed every morning, going to school, doing the homework, putting them to bed. She was fantastic. There's nae question.'

He also once said, in 2001, just before he was supposed to retire, aged sixty, 'I did not see my boys grow up. I saw an entire generation of young footballers grow up. That is why they (his sons) see me more as a friend than a father. That is perhaps one of the reasons I am retiring. I hope I can make up for lost time. Cathy raised our boys. She did a great job.'

He always took an opportunity to praise Cathy when the subject of his home life arose in interviews.

He once told Channel Four's Claire Balding, 'She's a good wife. A good mother. A great grandmother.'

When interviewed by his son Jason, Alex would tell him. 'She really is the catalyst for it all. She sacrificed tae support me one hundred percent. Fifty-three years married. That tells you a lot.'

Given Alex's progressive political ideology, it still eats at him that he and his wife adopted such traditional values throughout their marriage, traditional values that meant the husband went out to earn a crust while the wife nested the home. Despite accumulating a British record number of winner's medals, there is a pinch of regret inside Alex that ignites when he thinks of the sacrifices Cathy had to make in order for his legacy to be formed.

In fact, it was that pinch of regret that was at the forefront of his mind when Eamonn Holmes stepped forward on the stage to a warm round of applause from the large gathering.

'Now Alex, do you have anybody in mind... anybody from the world of showbiz or any pin ups you would like to unveil your statue?'

'Not really, no,' Alex replied, sniggering. 'Mabee Elvis, but I hear he can't make it.'

When the laughing shushed, Eamonn continued: 'It had to be

somebody very, very special. And somebody who would be perfect for this occasion.'

Cathy was still sat in the front row, her head swaying from side-to-side in search of the mystery guest.

Then David Gill took a step forward on stage to join Eamonn and Alex.

'When we thought about who would be perfect to unveil this statue, there was only person,' Gill announced. 'Based on my experience, I know Alex wouldn't have had the success he has had without the support of this wonderful woman. While he was concentrating on the successes of his career, she was busy raising their three sons—all of who went on to have very successful careers in their own right. Even to this day, she brings a sanity and normality to counterbalance this mad world of football. And I do believe, genuinely, that he's scared of her. Ladies and gentle-men, please welcome... Lady Cathy Ferguson...'

2011-2013

As if to coincide with the celebrations around the North Stand being named in his honour, as well as the public announcement of the statue, Manchester United would get off to a perfect start in the 2011-12 campaign by winning all five of their opening Premier League fixtures. Alex was beginning to feel smug, as this was to be his final year in management and he was determined to bow out in style. He was about to turn seventy at the turn of the year, and would be calling it a day the following May just as he had promised Cathy. He had even gone so far as to enquire about their holiday plans the following summer, determined to fulfil all of the dreams he had been, for years, scheming with his wife.

His smugness, however, would erode within a matter of weeks. In mid-December, United would be unceremoniously dumped from the Champions League at the group stage. Alex was furious. But only with himself. While he is still adamant he called the two Barcelona finals in previous campaigns as well as he could have, he readily takes the blame for the shock early exit from the competition in 2011. United were paired in a group alongside Benfica, FC Basel and little-known Romanian outfit Otelu Galati. They were easily favourites to top the group having established themselves top seeds following a run of five Champions League campaigns in which they managed to appear in three finals, one semi-final and one quarter-final. The problem that arose in 2011 was that Alex believed the group was too easy. And he took his eye off the ball. United would finish that group in third place, dumped from the Champions League, after they were beaten 2-1 in the final game away to Basel. They had been in total control of the group up until that point and were top, seemingly a dead cert to enter the first knock-out stage, but a 2-2 draw with Benfica in their penultimate game, followed up by that final shock defeat in Switzerland saw them dumped from the competition.

"It was my fault," he would write in *My Autobiography*. "I took the competition for granted. We had come through previous group stages comfortably and looking at this one I thought it would be straightforward, though of course I never said that publicly."

He was so upset with himself that he was storming around the house, clenching his fists. Then he calmed himself down and went to talk to Cathy.

'I'm gonnae give it another go.'

He was reneging on his retirement plans. It wasn't that he didn't want his legacy blemished by being dumped from the Champions League so embarrassingly in his final season that was causing such a U-turn. It was because Alex *genuinely* believed United would win the Champions League that season.

This was the first time Cathy felt disappointed by her husband's retirement U-turn. After all, it was she who had coaxed him out of retiring ten years prior. But by this stage, she was ready for them to spend their older age together, fulfilling all they had been talking about over many years. Besides, they had already made tentative plans for the following summer and had been discussing their first trip overseas just weeks before United were dumped from the Champions League. And now here he was, making yet another retirement U-turn, drawing comparisons in his own family with his favourite crooner, Frank Sinatra. Yet, despite her disappointment, Cathy didn't try to talk Alex out of it.

The only person aware of Alex's retirement plans outside of the immediate family was David Gill. Alex had long considered United's chief executive much more than just his boss. Gill was a close friend, a dear friend. It was by far the most comfortable working relationship Alex had ever experienced in all his years in football.

'David is the best chief executive I ever worked with. No doubt aboot that at all,' Alex admitted.

Gill wasn't surprised about Alex's U-turn. He knew how hurt he had been by the Champions League exit, especially so after the two had talked extensively about United winning it in his final season. That wasn't the only secret they held, though. By this stage, the pair of them had also agreed who Alex's successor would be. That appointment, however, would now have to be delayed for another twelve months.

Despite the Champions League shock, United were still performing at their best in the Premier League. They were heading for, it seemed, a toe-to-toe battle with nearest rivals Manchester City who had, by now, amassed a squad so rich in ability thanks to the investment of the deputy prime minister of the United Arab Emirates, Sheikh Mansour, that they could compete with United at the summit of English football.

The city rivals were pretty much neck and neck heading into the turn of 2012 after an erratic half to a season that produced a number of bizarre results. Firstly, United trashed Arsenal 8-2 at Old Trafford, before being trashed themselves, 6-1, at the same venue just two weeks later, by title rivals City. But the main talking point around the club that season occurred at Anfield where Liverpool and Manchester United were playing out a tense 1-1 draw. During the game, Patrice Evra was racially abused by Liverpool striker Luis Suarez. According to the FA findings — which were released a year after the incident — Evra, frustrated with a hard tackle Suarez had put in on him, asked, in Spanish, why he felt a need to be so vicious with his challenge.

Suarez replied: 'Porque tu eres negro.' Translated to English, that means, 'Because you are black.'

The shameful incident would blow up even further when the two teams faced each other at Old Trafford later that season. Suarez refused to shake Evra's hand as was customary in the pre-match ceremony. United would go on to beat Liverpool 2-1 that day thanks to a Wayne Rooney brace, and Evra would be reprimanded by Alex for over-celebrating next to Suarez after the final whistle. But the whole affair left a sour taste in Alex's mouth. Fuming that Suarez didn't shake Evra's hand in the pre-match build-up, Alex would spit in a post-match interview that the Uruguayan international was 'a disgrace to Liverpool,' and that they should 'get rid.'

What caused his blood to boil wasn't the blatant racism alone, it was more to do with how Liverpool handled the situation as a club. Rather than take seriously Evra's version of events, which were later ratified in the FA investigation, Liverpool chose to publicly defend Suarez. Before a game against Wigan, the playing squad wore training T-shirts emblazoned with an image of Suarez celebrating, and his name and number on the back. It was a tedious response to a very serious claim. Years later, Jamie Carragher would publicly apologise on behalf of Liverpool Football Club for wearing those T-shirts to Evra on live TV. But it wasn't just the T-shirts that annoyed Alex. It was the fact that his old friend and sparring partner Kenny Dalglish — who was managing Liverpool for a second spell during this whole debacle — seemed to be the ringleader in steadfastly ignoring Evra's racism claim.

Alex would write in *My Autobiography*: "I thought the T-shirts supporting Suarez was the most ridiculous thing for a club of Liverpool's stature. I felt we handled it well, mainly because we knew we were in the right. The FA asked us several times not to publicly talk about the incident. But Liverpool couldn't leave it alone. David Gill would not have allowed any manager to handle it that way. Nor would Bobby Charlton. They are experienced people who know about life. There seemed nobody at Liverpool willing to pull Kenny's horns in."

Liverpool, Alex felt, had a fresh board of directors at this period, and he thought Kenny's status, rightfully so, as a club legend somewhat hampered the running of the entire club.

"I think Kenny was falling back on the chip on the old shoulder," Alex would continue to write. "The problem, I felt, was there was no Peter Robinson at Anfield anymore. Peter Robinson would never have allowed the Suarez situation to be handled the way it was. The young directors there idolised Kenny and there was no one to say, 'Hey, behave yourself, this is out of order, this is Liverpool Football Club'."

Alex and Kenny have had a roller-coaster of a relationship ever since they first met in Glasgow. Even though they both showed huge promise as footballers — though Alex was almost a decade older than Kenny — nobody could have predicted the heights they would go on to reach as sporting legends. They tussled as players north of the border, then as managers south of the border while both despising and being in awe of each other at the same time. They were close associates in that their careers paralleled, but not so close given that they would, for some reason only known to them, tense up when they were in each other's company socially. But their relationship would shift when the football world was rocked by the most tragic of circumstances in April 1989.

Alex was at home, watching the match on television. Liverpool were playing in an FA Cup semi-final against Nottingham Forest at the neutral venue of Hillsborough when the game was abandoned shortly after kick off. Firstly, it appeared to Alex that some Liverpool fans were making their way on to the pitch to make some sort of protest. However, after a still and eerie few seconds, it finally became apparent what was going on. Too many Liverpool supporters had been allowed to enter the Leppings Lane end of Hillsborough stadium and a number of them were being crushed into the fencing that separated the supporters from the pitch. Ninety-seven Liverpool supporters would eventually lose their lives in the most tragic of circumstances. Two days later, Alex was on to phone to his old rival Kenny, attempting to console him and letting him know both he and the Manchester United family would do all they could to help Liverpool FC through the tragedy. Alex and a number of his players would attend the funeral of one of the victims,

Colin Ashcroft, some two weeks later. And then Alex would write a letter to United fans, letting them know they and Liverpool fans were now united in their grief. Some weeks later, a still shocked Kenny Dalglish would write to Alex, letting him know he was grateful for all he had done in the wake of the Hillsborough disaster, and from that moment on, the two legendary Glaswegians never tensed up in each other's company again, instead exchanging joke after joke with each other as they turned into the best of friends during social gatherings. But it is because they had become so close in the intervening years that Alex was both dismayed and disappointed over Dalglish's handling of the Suarez affair. Racism, Alex was absolute, was the wrong topic to ignore.

Despite the drama with Liverpool, United remained focused on the task in hand, and by the time the season had reached Easter they looked like they were going to be crowned champions once again having amassed a six-point lead over City with just six games left to play. But they were somehow beaten away to Wigan despite being the more dominant side, before playing out an outrageous 4-4 draw with Everton at Old Trafford—a game they seemingly were in full control of until the final few minutes in which they conceded two goals that ultimately reduced their lead at the summit to just one point—with a tough encounter away to Manchester City yet to come. City would win that game thanks to a Vincent Kompany headed goal, but the title race would go right down to the wire. Quite literally to the final kick of the season.

On the last day, City were ahead on goal difference and only had to match United's result to be crowned champions for the first time since 1968. However, they found themselves 2-1 down to QPR in front of their own nervy fans while United were comfortably winning away at Sunderland. When the United result was confirmed, their players walked towards their travelling fans to applaud them, not knowing what was going on at the Etihad Stadium. But they were beginning to get a sense that they may be crowned champions given that the United fans were in full voice. Alex was applauding the fans himself, but tentatively so. He had been told by a young member of the Sky TV staff that City were 2-1 down. But he was hesitant to celebrate given that there was still injury time to be played at the Etihad Stadium. Then the United fans would fall silent. City had equalised through Edin Dzeko. And then sixty seconds later, just before the final whistle, Sergio Aguero scored the most dramatic goal in Premier League history—winning City their very first ever Premier League title in style with the last strike of the entire season. Two goals in injury time, to edge a thirty-eight game campaign. It was an astonishing finale.

The United players would continue to applaud the travelling fans as they walked off the pitch, not reacting to the dip in atmosphere, especially as the Sunderland supporters began to celebrate. But they were extremely sombre by the time they got to the dressing-room. Alex had already decided to U-turn on his decision to retire, but given what had just occurred, he likely would have U-turned on this day itself. It is highly unlikely he would have retired from football on the back of such a heart-breaking sucker punch.

He would tell his players in the tiny away dressing-room at Sunderland: 'Firstly, y'see those Sunderland fans celebrating? I want you all to remember that. Remember that moment. And let it drive you next season. Secondly, you have nothing to be ashamed of. Walk out that door with ya heads held high. I certainly will.'

The players were all positive in their post-match interviews and Alex congratulated City on such a dramatic victory. Yet despite smiling his way through those interviews, all Alex could think about was throwing those two goals away at home to Everton in the 4-4 draw three weeks prior. That game was still eating at him.

He was certain, however, that Manchester United would win the title in his last ever season; though it was still only close family and David Gill who knew that to be the case. David Moyes was soon to learn his faith, however. The official story goes that Moyes only found out he was the chosen one twenty-four hours after Alex confirmed his retirement publicly on May 8, 2013. But that's not how it went down at all. Moyes was already in on the act and had in fact turned down three contract proposals from Everton over the course of the 2012-13 campaign already aware he was heading to Old Trafford. Alex had approached him in the summer of 2012 to anoint him. In fact, that wasn't the first time they had spoken about such a plan. Alex had hinted or nudged at Moyes over the years that he would be his eventual successor. Alex and David Gill had spoken for at least three years about Moyes succeeding him before he actually did. From every angle of Alex Ferguson's philosophy and for continuing to evolve from the foundations set at the club, Moyes wasn't just the chosen one in Alex's eyes. He was the only one.

Alex has announced publicly that he hadn't planned his retirement and that he didn't make up his mind until his final season. But that's not a true reflection of how his final years played out. The reason he suggested he only decided to retire after Cathy's sister Bridget (the woman whose living room it was Alex had agreed to become Manchester United manager in twenty-six-years previously) sadly passed away in late 2012 was to protect the fact that he had promised newest signings Robin van Persie and Shinji Kagawa that he wasn't planning his retirement imminently when they agreed to join the club. That's not to say Bridget's tragic passing didn't play a part. It did. When she died, that cemented Alex's retirement plans. There was no turning back after that. Bridget had not only been Cathy's sister, but undoubtedly her best friend. Alex wasn't going to leave Cathy without a best friend for the rest of her life. So, in November of 2012 it was set in stone that he would be stepping down regardless of what played out that season. But in truth, his retirement had been planned well before his final season had kicked-off.

To ensure United wouldn't be beaten on goal difference in his final season, like they had been by City on that dramatic final day of the 2011/12 campaign, Alex insisted on buying a new striker. His top choice was Arsenal's Robin van Persie, but it also seemed like a redundant choice given that it would be nigh on impossible to prise him away from such rivals. However, after doing his due diligence, Alex became aware of the player's desire to join United, and when he heard that contract negotiations with Arsenal chief executive Ivan Gazidis had stalled, he prompted David Gill to pounce.

It would be a tricky negotiation to handle, but United would prise van Persie away for £22.5m, only made possible because he had one year remaining on his contract and was having a tough time renegotiating with the Gunners.

Alex will admit that he took time to realise the genius of van Persie. He says he wasn't overly impressed by the Dutchman during his early days as an Arsenal forward. He was certainly silky in possession and held all the trademarks Alex looked for in his back-to-goal striker, but he made too many wayward runs that Alex was convinced the player was wasting too much energy during the wrong moments in games. But, after studying the player as much as he could, Alex began to appreciate that it wasn't van Persie's wrong-doing in making those runs. It was his teammates. The runs were perfectly justified and superbly timed. The fact that no team-mate was picking them out was the flaw. Alex would work heavily with Paul Scholes, Wayne Rooney and Michael Carrick on spotting van Persie's off-the-ball movement and United would strut their way to a comfortable league title in Alex's final season. They would win the title over City with four games left to play, meaning Alex had won thirteen Premier Leagues in the space of twenty seasons. It was a glorious way to end his reign as Manchester United's longest-serving manager. But that season wasn't to go all to plan. Alex would be heartbroken once again by Manchester United's Champions League exit.

There wouldn't be the same complacent repeat of the year previous in the group stages, however. Despite being drawn in a tricky group alongside Galatasaray, CFR Cluj and FC Braga, United would storm to the first knock-out round as group winners where Alex would come up against his old Premier League rival, Jose Mourinho—now managing the might of Real Madrid. Alex wasn't worried, however, despite the draw looking tough on paper. United were a much more cohesive side than Mourinho had inherited in the Spanish capital and Alex felt that if they got through that test, then they would surely be on their way to winning another Champions League title. He genuinely had that much belief in his final United team.

They would prove to be the best team over those two legs against Real, but the best teams don't always advance given the Champions League knock-out format. They would dominate proceedings in Madrid, despite only coming away with a 1-1 draw. Alex had attempted to nullify the threat of his former star Cristiano Ronaldo by employing Phil Jones to man-mark him. The Govanman held Jones in such high regard that he never had any qualms about him carrying out his orders—even if it was to keep the best player in the world quiet. Jones and Chris Smalling had been bought as long-term replacements for Rio Ferdinand and Nemanja Vidic, but for Alex's successor more so than for himself as both players were yet to fully mature. Jones did a sterling job on Ronaldo, keeping him starved of any playmaking influence and United would take the lead through Danny Welbeck. Yet, despite not having much influence in Real Madrid's attacking play, Ronaldo would produce one of his trademark outrageous leaps to head in an equaliser for the home side against the run of play. It was a stunning goal that is still jaw-dropping to watch to this day. The Portuguese's leap seemed almost unnatural. He met that ball with the centre of his forehead while it was eleven feet in the air. Alex would say after that game that no other player in the world, past or present, could have scored such a goal.

The 1-1 away result ensured United were still favourites heading to the Old Trafford clash two weeks later. United seemed in total control for much of the second leg, and Welbeck should have put them ahead on the half-way mark when he was one-on-one with Real keeper Diego Lopez. United would eventually take the lead on the night five minutes into the second half when Real centre-half Sergio Ramos stabbed the ball into his own net while trying to cut out a driving Nani cross. The Portuguese winger wheeled off in celebration, but he'd have his head in his hands, almost crying, some five minutes later when Turkish referee Cuneyt Cakir showed him a red card for dangerous play. It was an extremely harsh sending off. Nani was stretching his leg upwards after the ball had floated over his head to try to control it with one touch when Real defender Alvaro Arbelo stuck his head towards the ball. Nani's boot caught his shoulder. Alex was sat back on his bench, seemingly content with how everything was going. At first, his brow knitted together because he saw the referee shovel his hand into his pocket as he approached Nani. No way, Alex felt, did that deserve a yellow card. It was an obvious accident. But when Alex saw that it was indeed a red card the official had reached for, he was incredulous. He slapped his hands downwards to the chair in front of him, pushed assistant coach Rene Meulensteen out of this way and raced down the six steps of Old Trafford's unique benches to the edge of his technical area. He ranted and raved at Cakir, but it was clearly a redundant argument as Nani was already strolling down the pitch towards the dressing-rooms in the far corner of the stadium. Some Real Madrid players would tell their United counterparts that the sending off was harsh in the time it took Nani to get to the dressing-room. Old Trafford would deflate into an atmosphere of nervous agitation. Real reacted so positively that they would equalise through Luka Modric within minutes, before Cristiano Ronaldo of all players struck home a winner from close range. He would celebrate the goal by holding his hand up in apology to the United fans. Real boss Mourinho would apologise, too. He knew his team had got out of jail. The two legs produced intense, exciting battles, but there only ever looked like one winner up until Nani was sent-off.

'I doubt eleven against eleven we would win that match,' Mourinho said straight after the game. 'Manchester United were playing very well. They were compact. They were very aggressive. Tactically they were very well organised. The tie was very difficult for us.' When asked about the red card, Mourinho said, 'Independent of the decision, the best team lost. We didn't deserve to win. But this is football.'

Although Old Trafford was stunned into The Theatre of Silence, not one of the seventy-six thousand fans inside the great old stadium that night was more upset than Alex Ferguson. He was devastated. He knew that was his last chance of European glory gone. He had never cried after a game. It wasn't part of his make-up, not as a player, and certainly not as a manager. But he was as close to tears as he ever has been after a game that night. He was so upset that he, for the first time ever, felt unfit to conduct his post-match interviews and so asked assistant manager Mike Phelan to stand in front of the cameras instead. Mike would later admit he was so shook by how upset Alex appeared after that game that he guessed, correctly, the reason why.

Two weeks later, Alex would let Joel Glazer know, on a phone call and as per his contract, that he was calling it quits come the end of the season. His contract stipulated he had to let the owners know two months in advance of his standing down. Both he and Gill filled Glazer in on the steps that should be taken next. David Moyes would be appointed United manager to continue the great work laid out by his predecessor. But it was imperative, Alex insisted to Glazer, that Moyes be given time. Glazer had always left the decision to Gill and Alex and their minds had been made up at least two, maybe even three years, prior to this phone call. Alex, of course, wasn't the only void the Glazer family had to fill as Gill had announced his departure from the club some four months prior. The coincidence of both men leaving at the same time can largely be attributed to Alex holding his retirement off by a year. Gill had been approached by FIFA numerous times over the years for a full-time role within the organisation, given his success at United coupled with the great work he had carried out in his part-time role as vice chairman of the FA. Yet, despite turning down multiple approaches between 2009 and 2012, Gill began to reconsider the trajectory of his career during Alex's final season as manager. He was beginning to feel as if he could have more influence over the sport as a whole at a higher level and began to open up a line of dialogue through email with FIFA's biggest wigs about him assuming a role on the UEFA Executive Committee that eventually evolved into him becoming the UK's Vice President of FIFA. FIFA were so blown away by a proposal Gill laid out in a meeting just before Christmas 2012 that they offered him the position there and then. He accepted, telling them he would assume his new job at the end of the current English football season. He knew it would look bad, that the Glazers would find it doubly tough having to continue the dominance of the club with two large voids to fill, and he knew the fans would suggest the coincidence was no coincidence at all. So Gill made public his departure in February of 2013, long before Alex would release his news.

After United had romped to the title, Old Trafford turned out in celebration of the Govanman for his final bow at the famous stadium. With the red-ribboned Premier League trophy on display, the fans chanted Alex's name for the entire ninety-minutes of their 2-1 win over Swansea City. The Swansea players and their United counterparts would form a guard of honour for Alex as he walked onto the pitch for a final time to the score of Andy Williams singing *The Impossible Dream*.

That same song would sound after the game, just before the Govanman was walked to the centre-circle of the Old Trafford pitch. Once there, the stadium announcer, Alan Keegan, would, to a roaring crowd, introduce the manager by saying, "One man who had been part of the tapestry of the history of this football club, who won five FA Cups, four League Cups, ten Charity Shields, one European Cup Winners Cup, one European Super Cup, two Champions Leagues, the International Continental Cup, The World Club Cup and… *thirteen* Premier League titles. The impossible dream, made possible, by the greatest British manager ever… Sir Alex Ferguson.'

But despite being humbled by the celebratory atmosphere to his retirement, Alex wasn't for joining in. He only had one message he truly wanted to get across to the Manchester United fans that day.

'I'd like to remind you that when we had bad times here, the club stood by me, my staff stood by me, the players stood by me. Your job noo,' he said, pointing dots around the stadium, 'is to stand by our new manager.'

ALEX AND THE AFTERMATH

WHEN ED WOODWARD RATTLED HIS KNUCKLES AGAINST ALEX'S office door to tell the manager he was looking forward to working with him, the Govanman had to sit the balding, smiling commercial genius down to confess that he would in fact be retiring come the end of the season.

Woodward was gutted to miss out on the opportunity of working alongside the legendary manager, and Alex felt bad that the commercial genius's excitement had been instantly doused. But Alex's overriding feeling, when Woodward shared the news that he had been chosen to replace David Gill, was one of intrigue. Alex was a huge fan of Woodward, had thought it quite astonishing how he had transitioned into a power broker and innovator who was leading the way in commercialism throughout the sporting world. But Alex also understood that success in commercial business doesn't fully translate to football business, even if managing a squad has evolved into a headache for even the savviest of accountants given the ludicrous explosion in scale of transfer fees and player contracts in recent years. Alex could see where the Glazers were coming from in promoting Woodward to such a position and his name had even come up in conversation when he and Gill were speculating on who may replace the outgoing chief executive. But while Alex couldn't be sure if the appointment was the right call exactly, he was nevertheless intrigued. He would fill Woodward in during that meeting that David Moyes would be the man he would be working with and told him that he hoped they would be equally as successful a duo as he and David Gill had been in running the football arm of the club. Alex also reiterated during this meeting that Moyes must be given time. He spoke about how the club had been patient with Matt Busby in his early days, and how they had stayed patient with him—and that it was in United's best and long-term interests that the new manager be given time to put his stamp on the dressing-room. Alex lectured Woodward that although a perception exists that United had been a hugely successful club through their lifetime, they had, in truth, only been successful during two periods over their 140-year history. Those two periods just happened to be long periods of success, but they were built specifically with the goal of long-term success in mind. The successes lasted, firstly, for fifteen years in Matt Busby's case. And for twenty years under Alex. Both managers experienced dominant trophy-laden periods because they had been given the time to build from within. This was the Manchester United way. As far as Alex was concerned, Woodward showed complete understanding of the need for patience in the new manager during this meeting.

When the batons were finally handed over, from Alex to Moyes and from Gill to Woodward, four months later on the last day of May in 2013, the first act the Govanman undertook was a long-schemed boating expedition around the islands of Scotland known as the Hebrides. He invited most of his male friends and family members for a lads' trip that had been over a quarter of a century in the waiting for some on board.

'I'd always wanted to do it,' Alex said when recalling the holiday, 'And it was one of the best things I've ever done. I was brought up in Glasgow, twenty minutes from Loch Lomond, which is really the start of the Highlands on the west side. But the nearest I'd ever got tae the islands was summer camp, at the southern end. But you'd only ever see documentaries of the islands, the Inner Hebrides, and they were fantastic. Absolutely fantastic.'

During this holiday, while Alex and his 'lads' (which included some of his earliest friends from Govan, friends from the football world, his three sons, his eldest grandsons, his brother and his brother-in-law) were taking in the sight of sea eagles and whales and sharks, he would tell them that he felt confident Manchester United would continue to be successful given the structures in place at the club even if it would take time for Moyes to cycle into his first round of success. Not only was the conveyor belt of an academy as strong as it had ever been, but the club had grown to such commercial envy that they could match any club's spending power when they needed to—even the clubs who were owned by entire states. It was later during this holiday that he would learn the big-named signings he had teed up for Moyes, which included Toni Kroos and Gareth Bale, had decided to stay put at their clubs and not sign for the new-era United. Alex was deflated by this, as he thought Moyes needed to nail one big-name signing that summer to help put his first stamp down on the dressing-room. He had thought Bale in particular was destined to sign for United that summer. Instead, Moyes would fail in pursuit of his own personal target — Cesc Fabregas — before he ended up landing only Marouane Fellaini from Everton on the eve of his debut season kicking off. It became apparent to Alex through his sources that Moyes had dithered on the proposals of transfers left behind by his predecessor (if he had acted sooner, he certainly could have landed Kroos before Real Madrid turned his head) and that Woodward was trying to approach his transfer business too nonchalantly which, in fairness, was an approach that had worked wonders for him in the commercial world.

Alex decided not to attend games for the first three months of Moyes' reign for fear of intimidating the new manager—as if the looming shadow of Britain's biggest ever club stand, named in his predecessor's honour that casted over Moyes every time he sat in the dug-out, wasn't intimidating enough. Results would be mediocre, certainly by the standards set at Old Trafford, three months in and, as Alex expected, the media were starting to turn the heat up under his replacement. Alex remained calm, however, certain that the Glazers and Woodward fully understood the need for Moyes to be given time. The former Everton manager had been tied down to a six-year contract on Alex's instruction, and there was no way the club were going to cave into media pressure. Alex was also confident the fans would act as he instructed them to act: supportive 'of our new manager.' To their credit, the supporters at Old Trafford backed Moyes in full voice; gifting him his own banner at the ground (space usually reserved for established club legends only) and creating a chant about their new manager that they would sing regularly. Even when a minor group of fans hired a small aeroplane to fly over Old Trafford during a home game with a banner that read: "Wrong One - Moyes Out", the majority of United fans inside the stadium stood up to support their manager with a round of applause.

As the onerous season was playing out, Alex began to live the dream life he had always promised his wife they would. They visited France, as was usual, New York City, also usual, and Alex even took in trips to American Civil War battlegrounds to add to his already vast knowledge of his favourite subject. He would be approached by Paul McGinley, who had been announced as Europe's next Ryder Cup captain and asked, one year in advance, if he fancied playing a role in helping players with the mental side of the team format. Alex agreed to become an unofficial member of the coaching set up, a little because he was a huge fan of the Ryder Cup, but mostly because he was blown away by the meticulous level of detail in McGinley's pitch.

At the half-way point in the football season, Alex began to hear stories that the senior players were starting to undermine

Moyes and his coaching staff during training. He was furious. But mostly with himself. He had made a point of telling the fans that Moyes needed time, of telling the owners that Moyes needed time, of lecturing Woodward on why Moyes needed time. But he had never sat down with his players and explained to them that they needed to be patient with the new manager, too. It became blatantly clear to Alex that Moyes needed to cut these players from his dressing-room the following summer, but he certainly didn't offer such a strong opinion to his successor. As far as Alex was concerned, he had retired and wasn't going to go meddling in affairs—certainly as he wouldn't have accepted such interference from any ex-manager of Manchester United while he was the one in the hot seat. Alex was conscious of not getting involved, but he believed that the mid-aged players in the United squad such as David De Gea, Nani, Anderson, Jonny Evans, Chris Smalling, Phil Jones, Darren Fletcher, Shinji Kagawa, Javier Hernandez and Robin van Persie could cycle into more mature roles if more experienced players had to be let go. The established pros such as Rio Ferdinand, Nemanja Vidic, Wayne Rooney and Ryan Giggs perhaps needed moving on as they had played for so long under Alex that they were inevitably comparing Moyes' tenure to his. On top of the mid-aged players stepping up, Alex had left a host of youth talent at the club for Moyes to invite into the first team if and when he saw fit in the shape of Danny Welbeck, Jesse Lingard, Sam Johnstone, Tom Cleverley, Michael Keane and Adnan Januzaj—as well as Wilfried Zaha who Alex had purchased the January before he retired, so enamoured was he by the winger's confidence when running at defenders. The age and attributes of the squad Alex had left behind were as diverse as any squad he had at any point during his career at the club. So too were the contract end dates among certain players. All Moyes had to do was turn the cog on the older players who had been conditioned in the Alex Ferguson way and then start promoting academy graduates and — when and where needed — sprinkle the squad with fresh blood in the transfer market. Alex felt that once Moyes had a dressing-room that respected and accepted him as Manchester United manager, then the cycle and recycling of the first team could continue to be successful. Next summer, Alex thought, Moyes should take the big decision of letting some of the established players go and then begin to cycle from there, much like he had done a quarter of a century prior. Except David Moyes wouldn't get to next summer.

Alex was at home reading a book when he answered a phone call from Gill.

'They're letting David go,' Gill told him.

'Fuckin' hell,' Alex opted for, over his usual 'bloody hell.'

He was furious. Moyes had failed to finish in the top four of the Premier League and therefore United wouldn't enter the Champions League the following season. It meant that under the terms of the contract Moyes had signed, he could be let go. Although Alex was aware of the stipulation in his successor's contract, he never believed in a million years that it would be invoked. Moyes was supposed to be there for the long-term. Sacking him after ten months made very little sense.

Alex would learn that Ryan Giggs would be offered the managerial role until the end of the season but that Woodward himself would then make the decision on who would become Manchester United's next full-time manager. Even though Alex had taken conscious steps to not get involved in football decisions, regardless of his new title of director and club ambassador, he was beginning to feel totally cut off. He would learn that Woodward had opted to appoint Louis van Gaal from the following season and while Alex was still furious with the shocking sacking of Moyes, he took heart in the fact that the executive vice chairman had chosen a man known for developing players and not just buying them. To suit traditionalists such as Alex and Bobby Charlton, and their insistence on the long-term strategy of competing for multiple titles over multiple years, Giggs would be offered the role of van Gaal's assistant manager

—with the long-term plan being that the Welshman would take over the main role full-time when van Gaal's contract came to an end in three seasons' time.

Despite his scepticism about this decision, and his feeling of being cut off, Alex began to calm down in the wake of Moyes's sacking, noting that the club were still keen to continue a long-term strategy. In truth, he blamed himself somewhat for not having a heart-to-heart with the players about Moyes' reign and he also blamed the replacement himself for insisting on bringing in his own coaches to Old Trafford. Alex still feels that had Moyes retained one of his assistant coaches — either Mike Phelan or Rene Meulensteen, or, preferably, both — as part of his staff, then he would unlikely have been met by the level of undermining that occurred within the dressing-room.

While Alex was meeting with Paul McGinley to discuss Ryder Cup plans in the summer of 2014, he would learn that United had sanctioned the signing of Angel di Maria. Then, a month later, they would announce the loan signing of Radamel Falcao. He couldn't believe it. He admired both individuals' ability, but thought them far from Manchester United players, certainly not at this point in their respective careers where it seemed they were both desperately chasing their next big contract. What irked Alex most of all was the scattergun approach in which Woodward was snapping these players up. Neither Di Maria, nor Falcao's names were on a list of potential transfers offered up by van Gaal to Woodward. Instead, they were names actually brought *to* van Gaal *by* Woodward. When Alex learned this, he realised for the first time, if he hadn't already when Moyes was sacked, that United were under the control of a runaway vice executive chairman. The successful duo of Alex and Gill had not indeed been replaced by another duo in Moyes and Woodward, but by Woodward alone. The former JP Morgan banker now had complete control over all football matters at Manchester United. Most observers wrongly assume Alex Ferguson was replaced by David Moyes. In truth, he was replaced by Woodward, for it was he alone who inherited control of the world's biggest football club in May 2013. Alex, to this day, feels as if Manchester United lost their identity and all that he had built, not when he retired in 2013, but specifically on April 22, 2014—the day on which David Moyes was sacked. For it is that decision that turned the entire ship he had spent twenty-six years sailing — a ship that could cycle through great team after great team while consistently competing for titles — into a club with a completely contrasting philosophy of hiring and firing short-term, big name managers and the constant transfers of even bigger-name Galactico-type players.

As Alex was assisting Europe to beat America in the 2014 Ryder Cup, he observed van Gaal's first season kicking-off with one eyebrow raised and his mood as intrigued as it was irked. He came around to accepting the notion of van Gaal training Giggs into the hot seat as a long-term project, but the short-termism of the player transfers made by Woodward blemished such content-ment. The new-look United would frustrate fans as they limped to a fourth-placed finish that season, and the following summer Woodward would oversee the purchase of Bastian Schwein-steiger who was just about to turn thirty-two. Although Alex had been impressed by van Gaal's insistence on buying young promise in the shape of Anthony Martial and Memphis Depay, as well as promoting Adnan Januzaj from the academy, he was baffled by Woodward's wild forays into the transfer market for former world-class players who were clearly on the decline, not to mention chasing the biggest final contracts they could land. Alex's frustration would be compounded by a quote Woodward would give to the press that summer.

'We can do things in the transfer market that other clubs can only dream of. Watch this space.'

It had become abundantly clear to Alex that United were *desperately* trying to win their next league title and had forgone the idea of competing for multiple titles over multiple years. That's the one word Alex has privately used to describe Woodward's running of the club: *Desperate*. Not desperate as in terrible, but desperate as in having *way* too much desire. Ed Woodward simply couldn't wait for Manchester United to win their next major title. The idea of playing the long game preached to him by Alex had truly deserted him in favour of such desperation. It would be no surprise to the Govanman that when Woodward eventually stood down as United's executive vice chairman in the final quarter of 2021, he would write in his farewell statement: "I desperately wanted the club to win the Premier League during my tenure and I am certain the foundations are in place for us to win it back for our passionate fans." From that statement one word said it all. "I desperately wanted to win the Premier League." *Desperately*.

To cement that desperation during his time as United's vice executive chairman, the commercial genius would spend £1.1bn of the club's revenues in the space of seven summers to buy players such as the aforementioned di Maria, Falcao and Schweinsteiger as well as Zlatan Ibrahimovic, Paul Pogba, Romelu Lukaku, Henrikh Mkhitaryan and Alexis Sanchez among others. He would also hire four managers and fire three. United couldn't have been operating further from the Manchester United way. Gone was the diversity of ages in the playing squad; gone was the consciously structured contract end-dates; gone were the four players of multi-use within the balanced squad; gone was the pressure of young players nipping at the heels of senior stars. Everything Alex had built had been dismantled by Woodward's desperation to win a league title as quickly as he possibly could.

Despite his stature at the club, Alex would hold his tongue, knowing all too well that he would come across as hypocritical had he tried to stick his oar in given that it was common knowledge he wouldn't have put up with such interference himself. But while his club were turning 360 degrees from his and Matt Busby's footballing philosophy, Alex's personal life was bringing him unbridled joy.

During the two-season period in which van Gaal finished

fourth and then sixth while managing to win the FA Cup, Alex
was living out many of his dreams. He and Cathy would be
guests at the Oscars where they would attend a party with Daniel
Day Lewis (Alex's favourite actor) and also rub shoulders, albeit
from a distance, with Meryl Streep, Leonardo DiCaprio and Brad
Pitt. He would be walked as a special guest around the White
House—a building that holds genuine intrigue for the Govanman. He would attend the US Masters at Augusta the magical
year Danny Willet — a complete outsider — claimed the green
jacket. Alex also ticked off another dream sports experience from
his bucket list by being in amongst the roaring crowd during the
Kentucky Derby. And he would also sit proudly in Wimbledon
centre court's Royal Box next to a special date that day—his
daughter-in-law Fiona, the wife of Mark who is a keen tennis fan.

While living through those surreal experiences, around about
half-way through van Gaal's second season at United, Alex
would catch wind of what Woodward had planned next in his
desperation to win a league title. He had already made moves to
replace the Dutchman with what he considered a sure bet—a
man who had won a league title with every club he had ever
managed. Alex had considered Jose Mourinho — who he
admired and got on well with — the antithesis of a Manchester
United manager.

'He's good looking — he has that George Clooney look — can
speak five languages or whatever he can and most of all, he wins.
He is a winner. I think it's unfair really,' Alex once joked when
asked about the Portuguese.

He rated Mourinho's managerial skills above any other in the
world at the time, but he never saw him as a fit for the conveyor-
belt, long-term philosophy at Old Trafford. Mourinho would
once complain on live TV as Chelsea for once since Abramovich
had taken over, looked like they were adopting a long-term
strategy by hiring a young manager in Frank Lampard who
promoted young players from their academy into his squad, that
those young players simply weren't good enough. The players

Mourinho was talking about were Mason Mount and Tammy Abraham. Mourinho proclaimed Lampard shouldn't be thinking of the future, just the present. It confirmed publicly and on record that the Portuguese's philosophy does not include the nurturing of young talent. For his managerial genius to work, he needs a settled squad filled with physically big and experienced pros who will, over the course of three seasons, give their all under his dogged and pragmatic approach. Of course he had proven before he came to United that his methods worked in the short term, but after that three year cycle, those teams were left overaged and overworked with no continuity plan of what would happen once that one cycle had run its course. Mourinho — as brilliant as he had proven to be at collating trophies — was simply the antithesis of Alex Ferguson because his vision was short-term. If it hadn't been obvious to everyone over the preceding two years, it would become transparent that United were no longer thinking long-term with Woodward's hiring of Mourinho. Alex held nothing personal against the Portuguese. The two men get on very well in each other's company which used to consist of an after-match glass of wine, or on the odd occasion in a hotel lobby before an LMA meeting. But those catch-ups became a lot more frequent once Mourinho was working at Manchester United. They share the same winding-up sense of humour and have massively complementary pragmatic football mindsets. But they rarely talked about football in truth. The peripherals around the game, yes. But the game itself, no. Alex was adamant with all managers who succeeded him at Old Trafford that he wouldn't get involved in their affairs. Mourinho once claimed while filmed for Tottenham Hotspur's Amazon Prime documentary that Alex told him he should go out and buy Dele Ali. Alex is certain no such conversation took place. Although they got on perfectly well during Jose's tenure, one thing that irked Alex was the fact that the Portuguese refused to settle in Manchester. While Mourinho's family remained living in London, he took extended rentals at the Lowry Hotel on the outskirts of Manchester city centre, choosing to base himself in a suite on the top floor. As far as Alex was concerned, that life-choice accentuated Mourinho's short-term planning.

If there was a hopeful notion that Mourinho might settle in Manchester and look at making the United job his long-term project, that hope would be dashed by his dealings in his first transfer window. Woodward would splash cash on players such as Paul Pogba, who Alex had let go for free, as well as Zlatan Ibrahimovic and Henrikh Mkhitaryan. It was a monumental outlay in transfer fees and on contracts for players who were at the peak of their game, yet United wouldn't improve much on previous campaigns and would finish sixth, with a League Cup victory and the club's first ever Europa League win pocketed as very welcome accessories.

While Mourinho promoted Scott McTominay — a player Alex highly rates — into the first team for the following campaign, it proved little to support any notion he may be thinking long-term as in that summer the Portuguese would also sign Nemanja Matic and Romelu Lukaku to transition into a fully-fledged physical Mourinho side. Alexis Sanchez would arrive five months later. United would improve that season, finishing second in the league, but supporters at the club were voicing strong concerns over their manager's style of play and the murmurings that he was mishandling players by trying to manage them by means of the media became a constant. Despite United having their best Premier League season since he retired, Alex could see few redeeming qualities in the United side he was observing, even though he attended almost all home games. Despite his disappointment with Woodward's desperation, Alex was as personally content and as good-humoured as he had ever been. There was a clear and evident added vigour to his general mood. He was constantly joking and it seemed to all around him, especially to Cathy, that the weight he often carried on his shoulders had well and truly lifted in his retirement. The volatile man he had been in a past life as a football manager had unquestionably gone into

hibernation. Then, one Saturday morning, just before eight a.m —
and bored from sitting up in bed doing nothing — he peeled the
duvet away from his lap and swept his legs to the floor so he
could get to his feet. But as soon as his body rose, everything
went blank.

Four hours later, Mr. Joshi George would estimate to his
surgical team just before Alex was wheeled into his operating
theatre in the bowels of Salford Royal Hospital that his patient
only had a twenty percent chance of surviving the bleeding on
his brain. When Alex would wake up from his coma two days
later and immediately ask how Doncaster Rovers had gotten on
in their game against Wigan Athletic, everybody perked up. The
staff, including Mr. George, would be surprised by his patient's
initial recovery in coming out of his coma, but it soon became
clear that Alex wasn't fully out of the woods. He began to panic
as he became more and more aware of his situation and his
obsession with not losing his memory came to the fore again. He
would grab at sheets of paper and a pen and begin to scribble
notes to his loved ones, proving to himself more than them that
his memory was still intact. However, over the next three days he
was unquestionably melancholic. As he watched the sun rise
outside his ward window, he began to ask himself how many
more sunrises he would ever see again. Five days later, more and
more close family and friends would come to visit him and at one
stage there were up to fourteen people in his ward. Trying to
keep up with the conversations, Alex was overworking his brain
and fell so tired and overwhelmed that the guests were asked to
leave. Later that afternoon, while in the company of just two of
his grandsons, Jake and Harvey, Alex opened his mouth to ask
them a question and realised his voice had deserted him. He sat
more upright in his hospital bed, panicked, and tried to force
himself to speak louder. Nothing came out. In that moment, the
worst panic of the whole ordeal washed over him. He had to lie
back down as his grandsons rushed to call for assistance. That
night, the Ferguson family were as concerned as they had been

when Alex was first wheeled down for his surgery the week prior. It would take ten days for his voice to return fully following extensive work with a voice therapist. Within two weeks of that scare, he was inviting visitors to his ward again so he could reel off stories of yesteryear, as if to prove his memory to himself again. He would be monitored very closely by Mr. George's team and the staff at Salford Royal and, having shown day-to-day improvement, Alex would finally be discharged just shy of four weeks after his successful emergency brain surgery. He would later be told that Salford Royal Hospital had admitted five brain haemorrhage patients on May 5, 2018. Three of them died. Alex was one of only two survivors.

Recovery at home would be physically comfortable, but mentally challenging for a man who didn't like to sit around doing nothing. What he missed most of all was the glass of wine doctors had strongly urged him to forgo (he would have to wait until Christmas Day, 2018 until Cathy allowed him a sip), and — when the new football season kicked off in the August — visiting Old Trafford. He had agitated to return for the first home game of the campaign, but Cathy wasn't taking any chances. Six weeks later, she would give him the green light and he would return to his seat in the director's box to a thunderous round of applause from the United supporters for a home game against Wolves on the September 22—exactly twenty-one weeks after his surgery. His joy for the game hadn't waned and his passion for the club instantly returned to peak level. Which was just as well. Because ten weeks later he would be invited into a meeting that — out of the blue — would gift him control of the club he adored once more. Ed Woodward informed Alex that he was about to pull the plug on Jose Mourinho's disappointing tenure. Having hired the two best managers with the biggest CVs and spent over a billion pounds in transfer fees for multiple big-named players over the past six years, the commercial genius had realised his fantasy football approach hadn't worked. The club needed a reset. And there was no better man to talk to about a reset than Alex Ferguson. During that meeting, Mauricio Pochettino would be spoken about in length. The Argentine, who was managing Tottenham Hotspur at the time, was both Alex's and Woodward's obvious choice for a role they both agreed *had* to be made with a long-term vision. Alex professed he felt Pochettino held all the assets to become a legacy manager, somebody who could cycle and recycle through teams if backed with appropriate support and patience. However, they both realised they would have to wait until the end of the season to land their man from Spurs.

'Ole Gunnar Solskjaer,' Alex said to Woodward.

Woodward nodded. It wasn't a huge surprise. Solskjaer's name had often been mentioned around the corridors of the club in coaching terms. There existed a hope over the years that he may return in some guise. Perhaps as a first-team coach again. At no point, however, was Solskjaer's name ever considered for the manager's position over Woodward's tenure. Not until this point. But it made perfect sense. Until the end of the season, there was nobody in the game better equipped to bring the dressing-room Mourinho had well and truly divided back together again. Solskjaer was a beloved figure in the game, but especially so at Old Trafford. A lover, not a fighter. He also, in Alex's eyes, is about as smart a football man he has ever come across in all his years. He had led Molde to back-to-back titles in Norway when they had never once won the championships through their history before that, but he would blot his CV when tempted to England to help Cardiff City out of their relegation struggles. Solskjaer couldn't drag Cardiff out of their mire, and the stigma of the resulting relegation clung to him. Incidentally, Solskjaer had phoned Alex when offered that Cardiff job, to be told he didn't think he should take it.

After Alex and Woodward shook hands on their meeting, the Govanman would ring Solskjaer to offer him his dream job, albeit on a temporary basis for six months, (Solskjaer had it specifically written into his Molde contract that the only club he could leave for without notice was Manchester United). Alex also suggested during that telephone call that the Norwegian bring Mike Phelan in as his assistant—a man he felt should never have been relieved of his duties at Manchester United in the first place. An hour later, Solskjaer would ring Alex back to tell him Phelan wasn't answering his phone. Phelan was living in New South Wales, Australia at the time where he was working as the football director of A-League side Central Coast Mariners. Alex would hang up from Solskjaer and ring Phelan himself knowing he would answer as soon as *his* name popped up on the screen of his phone.

'The missed calls yiv had over the past hour?' Alex said to his former assistant manager, 'They're from Ole Gunnar Solskjaer… you're gonnae wanna answer next time he calls.'

That's all Alex said. He didn't mention the reason Solskjaer was ringing.

As soon as the Norwegian walked back through the doors of Carrington three days later, the atmosphere around the entirety of the football club lifted. The Norwegian would bring gifts to the staff at the club — most of whom he hadn't seen for years — and suddenly the players were all singing from the same hymn sheet. The team would go on the best run of results they'd experienced since Alex had last been in charge. And it was in the midst of that amazing run of results that the destiny of Manchester United would be secured. The ship was well and truly about to be turned back around.

Because Solskjaer had proven to be somewhat a shrewd piece of business, Woodward would invite him to a meeting at Old Trafford to include him in discussions about the handover to Pochettino. Having assumed Ole would turn up casually for the chat, Woodward's eyes would light up upon hearing the Norwegian ask if they could meet in a room that had a projector in it. Over the next hour and a half Solskjaer would present, in fine detail, his football philosophy to Woodward and pitched that, if implemented, would ensure Manchester United were no longer desperate to win their next league title, but primed to compete for multiple titles over multiple years. Woodward was stunned. In that presentation, Solskjaer showed the vice executive chairman what the Manchester United squad should look like in five years' time, when Jurgen Klopp and Pep Guardiola were expected to leave their current jobs. It was a plan devised to ensure United would be the club best primed to take advantage. The squad list Solskjaer produced for Woodward included the names of Harry Maguire, Aaron Wan Bissaka, Jadon Sancho and Mason Greenwood—long before any of them had ever appeared for the club (or the first team in Greenwood's case). The Norwegian would also detail how and why the squad should have a range of ages in it, as well as a different range of contract rundown dates. He would also include an intricate scouting plan that he pitched would ensure United could snap up the best teen talent from not only within the UK, but worldwide. Woodward was blown away. He would speak to Alex later that night, almost certain he had put Solskjaer up to it. But he hadn't. The pitch was all on Solskjaer. Influenced by Alex? No doubt. Put up to it by Alex? Absolutely not. During that phone call, Alex and Woodward would both agree to end their interest in appointing Pochettino and instead offer Solskjaer the role full-time. It wasn't just the presentation that helped make their decision, or the fantastic results the team were achieving, a lot of their decision centred around the Norwegian proving himself to have the most immaculate approach to man-management.

After the amazing start, Solskjaer's United would flatline as the season waned to a conclusion. But almost immediately following that campaign, the construction of the long-term football philosophy the Norwegian had impressively pitched to Woodward would begin in earnest. Over the next twenty-four months, United would snap up twenty-six teenagers—who were largely considered to be among the best teen talents in world football. What was most eyebrow-raising was the fact that they managed to snatch these players up from under the noses of their greatest rivals both home and abroad.

Solskjaer oversaw, through an intense scouting mission he set up, the incoming signings of Marc Jurado from Barcelona, Alvaro Fernandez from Real Madrid, Alejandro Garnacho from Atletico Madrid, Charlie McNeill from neighbours Manchester City (a player who scored a record-smashing 600 goals at youth level) and Ethan Ennis from Liverpool as well as Amad Diallo who was considered the most exciting teen prospect plying his trade in Italy, and Facundo Pellistri—one of the hottest prospects in South America. Willy Kambwala, Matej Kovar, Hannibal Mejbri, Joe Hugill and Shola Shoretire were among the other names snapped up. All of them were under eighteen years of age.

While Solskjaer has been waiting on those players to cook in the youth teams of Manchester United (most of whom he knows won't quite cut the mustard at Old Trafford, but some of them, he is convinced, certainly will), he set about adding to his immediate first team with buys such as Harry Maguire, Aaron Wan Bissaka and, eventually, Jadon Sancho—as well as promoting Greenwood from the academy. These were players the Norwegian had mentioned to Woodward during his five-year pitch.

He also oversaw the sales of Marouane Fellini (almost immediately), Alexis Sanchez, Romelu Lukaku, Marcos Rojo and Matteo Darmian—players he felt epitomised the mess the squad had turned into in the post-Ferguson years.

It wasn't just the playing staff that would get an immediate makeover. As part of Solskjaer's long-term plan, it was necessary to implement a specific structure at the club. It was Woodward, to his credit, along with Richard Arnold — the club's managing director — who conceived the new-look Manchester United, but it was all built with input from Alex and Solskjaer himself to suit the Norwegian's long-term vision.

John Murtough would become the club's first ever director of football, with the specific purpose of ensuring the conveyor belt would continue its cycle to assist the club in competing for multiple trophies over multiple years. Murtough had impressed in his role as the club's head of football development and was thought of as the best man to oversee the restructure. Darren Fletcher was brought in to work alongside Murtough. But whereas Murtough has the responsibility for seeing new signings into the United first team, Fletcher has been put in charge of overseeing the youth academy players' development into that first team. The former United midfielder holds the responsibility of seeing to it that as many of the teen talent named earlier in this chapter prove good enough, both mentally and physically, to perform on the stage that is Old Trafford. On top of these two major appointments, it was agreed that Ed Woodward would step down in the midst of the reshuffle. He had been disappointed that he let the juggernaut Alex had built crash and burn in the aftermath of the Govanman's retirement, but it was his involvement in the Super League that would be the catalyst for him calling time on his Manchester United career. United fans may not remember the balding, smiling commercial genius with great fondness. But aside from fudging the post-Ferguson years, Woodward did take the club to another level in terms of increasing revenues, and his input into setting up a new revolution may buy him some sympathy with those supporters in time.

Aside from the boardroom reshuffle, Solskjaer would restructure the scouting at United with the brief ringing loud and clear in the newest scouts' ears—Bring me constant list updates on the greatest young talent around the world.

However, despite the long-term attempted renaissance of Manchester United under Solskjaer, it remains to be seen whether the Norwegian has what it takes to eventually turn United into contenders for multiple titles over multiple seasons. Solskjaer may have proven to everybody at Manchester United that he has a philosophy to match the greatest managers the club has ever had, but he still hasn't proven he can instil a winning mentality. On top of that, quite how long the inconsistencies shown through the Norwegian's reign (inevitable when rebuilding) as he reaches three years in situ can last in the era of reactionary and incessant social media scrutiny remains a mystery to even Alex himself.

Solskjaer simply may not pass the test of such modern-day scrutiny, and it's increasingly likely he will not be afforded the time Alex was. The structure the Norwegian has put in place, however, certainly will be given the luxury of time. United will not be returning to desperate measures. The newly-structured board are content to be patient, and to build towards competing for multiple titles over multiple seasons, rather than rushing to win their next one.

This attempted restructure was all being put in place while Alex was still being observed as part of his recovery from his brain haemorrhage. Because of this recovery, he and Cathy didn't go on their usual holidays to France and New York in 2019. Although Alex was excited about regaining a heavy degree of control over the football club, he was stricken bored without much else to do—even if Cathy had begun to allow him the odd glass of red. He was missing his getaways, desperate to tick off more adventures he had long been dreaming of and scheming up. There was one short trip he did make during this time as part of his role as a lead committee member of the League Manager's Association in which he would share laughs and glasses of red with Messrs Guardiola, Mourinho, Klopp and Wenger before the award for the best manager of the year was announced (now named the Sir Alex Ferguson trophy). He would quite often attend Old Trafford to watch Solskjaer's rejuvenated side as they began their first full season under the Norwegian (in which they would finish third). However, football outings aside, 2019 was a bit of a flat year for Alex in a personal sense because he was finding himself at home more than he would have liked. He had no idea what was around the corner. Nobody had. By the start of spring in 2020, the population of much of the world would find themselves at home more than they would have liked.

When COVID hit, Alex felt bereft. Not only was he mystified by the handling of the pandemic globally as well as the racketing number of lives the virus was claiming, but he felt personally hard done by given that he had spent the year previous in near-isolation due of his recovery. He had been waiting on tenterhooks for 2020 to come around so he could resume normality.

He would be rocked by the passing of three people close to him over the course of the pandemic. Lyn Laffin, his long-time personal assistant from the moment he walked through the door at Manchester United, sadly slipped away. So too did Maurice Watkins—the former Manchester United solicitor who was a great personal friend of the Govanman. Debbie Morgan — the wife of Alex's former kitman and one of the closest people he met through football, Albert Morgan — also lost her life. Alex was particularly fond of the Morgan family, and Debbie's loss deeply saddened him.

Albert would say during the pandemic and not long after he lost his wife, 'I speak to him (Alex) almost every day and he is on a total lockdown at the moment. He has not been out of the house. I think his Missus has had to nail his feet down! He is in good form, he is doing his exercises every morning. He has got his dumbbells out, he is on his rowing machine, his walking machine, so yeah, he is doing well. I've been caring for my wife for the last few years of her life, so it's been so hard since she's been gone, but the gaffer has been unbelievable. There aren't the words for what he's done for me. He's been absolutely wonderful for me, for what I've gone through. He's just top dollar as a man.'

It wasn't all doom and gloom for Alex during the pandemic, however. Aside from having input as Manchester United reinvented, Jason would begin production on his film *Never Give In* in 2020 which would offer his father great respite just when he needed it the most. They'd spend countless hours deliberating and researching the production together and would grow as close as they had ever been during the process. Aware of his father's level of recall, Jason would probe him on his earliest days growing up in Govan and Alex would even surprise himself by dragging up memories he hadn't thought of in decades. The closest Jason managed to bring his father to tears during the production was when researchers managed to find sixty-year-old, long-lost footage of Alex leading men three times his age on the apprentice strike in Glasgow way back in 1960.

'Bloody hell,' Alex said. 'That's me!'

He had never seen it before and didn't even know such footage existed.

The film would go on to receive great critical acclaim, yet despite its global impact Alex is mostly proud of the time the filmmaking afforded him during lockdown. He simply hates to sit still doing nothing.

When the world began to open back up somewhat by the end of summer 2021, Alex and Cathy began to plan dates for holidays with Alex mostly keen to visit New York, and Cathy very keen to go back to France. They also spent time planning the celebrations for Alex's eightieth birthday on the last day of that year.

In the meantime, the high of both their lives has been the conveyor belt of visits from their latest offspring every weekend.

'At least three, sometimes four of them at a time stay over every Friday and Saturday night, aye,' the Govanman said. 'They take turns. I have tae say, I love it.'

Alex feels genuinely proud, humbled and hugely fortunate that he has been afforded the winter years of his life to bask in the company of his grandchildren.

All eleven of them.

The end.

COVER PHOTOGRAPHY

Paul Cooper

EDITORS

Brian Carroll
John Marrinan
Brigit Taylor

RESEARCH SOURCES

BOOKS

Managing My Life, by Sir Alex Ferguson with Hugh McIlvanney, published by Hodder (1999)

My Autobiography, by Sir Alex Ferguson, published by Hodder & Stoughton (2013)

Leading, by Sir Alex Ferguson with Michael Moritz, published by Hodder & Stoughton (2015)

Football, Bloody Hell—The biography of Alex Ferguson, by Patrick Barclay, published by Yellow Jersey Press (2010)

The Boss—The Many Sides of Alex Ferguson, by Michael Crick, published by Simon & Schuster (2002)

This is the One: The Uncut Story of a Football Genius, by Daniel Taylor, published by Aurum (2007)

BROADCAST

Sir Alex Ferguson: Never Give In. Produced by DNA Films and Passion Pictures (2021)

The Alex Ferguson Story. Produced by ITV (1998)

David Lyons read through hundreds of newspapers & magazines and watched countless hours of interviews with Sir Alex Ferguson during the writing of this biography. He would like to offer a huge thank you to all who gave their time to be interviewed for this project.

Happy 80th birthday, Sir Alex Ferguson